BAD INK

How *The New York Times* Sold Out Transgender Teens

RIKI WILCHINS

For more information contact:
Riverdale Avenue Books
5676 Riverdale Avenue
Riverdale, NY 10471
www.riverdaleavebooks.com

Design by www.formatting4U.com
Cover by: Blake Chamberlain

Digital ISBN: 9781626016811
Print ISBN: 9781626016828

First edition, July, 2024

Dedication

To Gina and Dylan: You are my life.

My thanks to Alissa Jordan and especially Alison Kim for their very careful fact checking,

to Camilla Saly for her patient editing,

and to Lori Perkins of Riverdale Avenue Books for her unwavering guidance and support.

Table of Contents

A Word about Language

This book uses "trans" and "transgender" interchangeably. "Trans" is becoming increasingly common to indicate that the category is unfinished and remains open to new identities, especially since its fastest growing segments are not those who (like me) identify as binary "transgender woman" or "transgender man" but as nonbinary, gender-fluid, genderqueer, agender, and so on.

Although a recent Washington Post/KKF poll also found that only 31% of those identifying as *transgender* or *trans* had undergone any kind of gender-affirming medical care, obviously the most virulent legislative and journalistic attacks have focused on them. [1]

In a few places, I have used "transsexual" when those under attack are specifically those who have or are seeking to medically change their sexes and/or genders. This is usually in earlier *Times* pieces before "transgender" replaced the narrower and more medicalized term.

Terms like "children," "teens," and "youth" are often used interchangeably, but in view of spurious right-wing charges that gender medical care is being pushed on those too young to receive it, I have tried to use them more precisely here. I have used "trans children" to refer to young people who are pre-pubescent; "trans teens," "trans adolescents," and "trans youth" to refer to those from about 13 to 19. And I have used "trans kids" to refer to all those from about six to the age of 18 or legal adulthood.

Social transition, which involves kids adopting clothes, hairstyles, names, and pronouns that match their gender identity rather than their birth-assigned sex, can happen from as early as age four or five. Medical affirming care like puberty blockers (i.e., "blockers") which temporarily pause the physical effects of puberty are provided primarily to adolescents—both trans *and* cisgender. Hormone therapy with either estrogen or testosterone is never provided at early ages, and offered only to trans adolescents and trans teens. Breast reduction (i.e., "top surgery") is only provided to teens approaching adulthood—again both for trans and cisgender. Finally, Gender Affirming Surgery (i.e., "bottom surgery") on one's genitals is almost never provided to minors of any age because that contravenes the accepted medical Standards of Care that are followed by any reputable doctor. Despite the claims of the anti-trans right, a survey by Komodo Health of 330 million health insurance claims over five years (2017 through 2021) found that top surgeries for trans teens number less than 300 annually, and bottom surgeries are nearly non-existent.[2] [3] [4]

I don't think it helps to continually remind the reader that I'm speaking of transgender kids, so I trust that when I refer to "children" or "kids" in discussions of blockers, hormones, or social transition, the reader will recognize that—unless specifically noted otherwise—I am referring to those who are trans-identified.

Similarly, having once introduced the topic of pediatric gender-affirming medical care, I simply refer to "care," or "affirming care" from then on because the phrase is overly long and the acronym "GAC" feels awkward. I used “cisgender” to refer to those who are not transgender, and as a way of indicating that each of us—and not just those who are trans— are performing a gender.

Finally, both the *New York Times* and the anti-trans right have tended to frame their attacks in very binary boy/girl terms. Because this book is about those attacks, there is very little about the many young people who identify beyond these binaries. I hope others will one day revisit the topic of media bias towards nonbinary, genderqueer, or genderfluid youth in more inclusive books than I have been able to write here.

Introduction

"Be truthful, but not neutral."
Christiane Amanpour[5]

"The journalist's job is truth, not objectivity."
Neil Barsky, Founder, The Marshall Project[6]

Although it has legions of haters and many failings, the *New York Times* is still the closest thing the U.S. has to a *newspaper of record*, and as such its coverage is carefully tracked by print, online, and television outlets, analyzed around the country and indeed around the world. Its editorial decisions wield outsized influence, setting the agenda for other newsrooms, Capitol Hill debates and White House discussions on the day's most important issues.

Yet when it came to transgender kids, beginning around 2015, the *Times* underwent a strange transformation, shifting from an early and long-time support of transgender rights to the nation's leading voice attacking transgender kids. And stranger still, this wasn't based on new reporting or fresh medical evidence, but on talking points being promoted by white Christian nationalist (WCN) organizations that were devoted to eradicating transgender kids in order to reignite their stalled anti-gay culture wars.

Although you may not have heard of groups like Alliance Defending Freedom or American Principles Project, Family Research Council, or the Heritage Foundation, they are among the largest and most well-funded nonprofit organizations in the world. Their views are deeply rooted in a form of evangelical Christianity that believes the founders intended the U.S. to be an officially Christian nation in which God—not "*We the people*"—is sovereign, white Protestant males are ascendent, and society and government are structured along strict, Biblical lines.

As Donald Trump's National Security Advisor Michael Flynn explained: "[W]e have to have one religion, one nation under God and one religion under God, right?"[7] [8] Or as another prominent Trump supporter, Jack Posobiec, announced from the stage of CPAC, the biggest conservative conference, "Welcome to the end of democracy. We're here to overthrow it completely. We didn't get all the way there on January 6th, but we will endeavor to get rid of it and replace it with this right here [holds up cross]… Because all glory is to God."[9] [10]

In this sense, WCN groups are at war with modernity and civil society itself, and thus have continuously fought a rear-guard action to stop nearly every social advance: Black civil rights, women's rights, gay rights, reproductive rights, and now transgender rights.

As a belief system, white Christian nationalism is perpetually aggrieved, religiously intolerant, inherently racist, and supremacist in its ambitions.

Unfortunately, it was just as the Right was executing a carefully planned, well-funded and coordinated crusade against trans youth that the *Times* also began airing regular attacks on trans youth's legitimacy *as* transgender, their right to transition, and their right to medical care.

In fact, *Times* articles would be cited by evangelical extremists across the South and West by MAGA legislators and public officials to justify bills to eliminate nearly every aspect of trans kids' lives: from school sports to bathrooms, birth certificate changes, puberty blockers and hormone therapy—even to the right to be addressed by their correctly-gendered name and pronoun at school and in public buildings.

The *Times'* coverage was so reflective of right-wing talking points that one of the more virulently anti-transition TERF groups *bragged publicly* about having hoodwinked "*The New York Times*, of all newspapers" into carrying their carefully crafted disinformation as news, thus helping prevent many transgender youth from undergoing gender transitions (TERF stands for "Trans Exclusionary Radical Feminists").[11] [12] [13]

It was one of the weirder "strange bedfellows" aspects of the anti-trans crusade that white Christian nationalist groups found common cause with mostly-white feminist TERFs, as the Southern Poverty Law Center (SPLC) has noted, even launching the Hands Across the Aisle Coalition (HATAC) specifically to coordinate their efforts.[14] [15] This led to the peculiar sight of lesbian feminists like Martina Navratilova being lauded for her bitter transphobia by a Family Research Council, a SPLC classified hate group which was also busy denouncing gay people as being pedophiles and lesbians as anti-motherhood, anti-family, and anti-God.[16] [17] [18]

From 1995 to 2005 the *Times* had been a media leader on transgender rights, and its about face roughly coincides with A. G. Sulzberger's rise through management, beginning with his being named Associate Editor for Newsroom Strategy in 2015. It then accelerated roughly about the time he was tapped to be Publisher in 2018. By 2022 the *Times* was publishing more anti-trans pieces in a single year than it had in the past seven.

This ended the only way it could, with an explosion: the community revolted, and the national LGBTQ+ media watchdog, GLAAD, led a protest of the *Times*. It was joined by nearly 100 organizations, and a thousand *Times*' contributors. Tens of thousands of subscribers and other readers also condemned the cascade of biased articles.[19]

As a veteran *Times* reader since my teens, it seems important to document how and why this has happened. Doing so also has enabled me to use the *Times* archives as a means of documenting the growth of media discourse on transgender: how we first entered it, what kinds of language has been used and how it has changed over time. I've examined the kinds of stories that were considered newsworthy, and how such stories were finally promoted from *soft news* confined to Style, Fashion, or "local color" pieces to the Opinion, U.S. and Washington desks, as trans rights began to be covered, at last, as *hard news*. Over the years, the coverage of trans coverage went from 10 or more articles annually to 10 or more articles a week—totaling, in 2017 over 700.

The New York City I lived in from 1980 until 1999 was, in many ways, the epicenter of the nascent transgender rights movement, and I had the privilege of knowing more than a few of the people and topics well that were being covered, and I also knew several of the *Times'* reporters. I recall excitedly consuming the paper's early coverage: a witness, and sometimes even a participant, in the events being documented. But by 2020, while I still checked the *Times* most days, I had stopped reading it in detail, and most days I visited its site with a sense of dread, wondering what new attacks I would read that day.

Finally, this book has provided me with a looking glass into the most pressing media problem today: how to cover the Christian nationalist groups and MAGA politicians whose media strategy is to create "alternative facts," bogus "experts," and official-sounding professional groups and pseudoscience studies, at a time when mainstream journalism still approaches every issue by interviewing "both sides" and leaving it to the reader to make sense of it.

With regard to transgender kids specifically, this has often meant media outlets quoting the American Medical Association (AMA) as "one side," and an evangelical extremist hate group committed to eradicating transgender kids as the "other side." This counts as journalistic "balance." But the latter is not interested in participating in a civil society in which everyone presents their arguments in a reasoned debate. Rather, as SPLC has documented, their goal is to manufacture disinformation in order to subvert reasoned debate.[20] They do not see their role as one voice in a democratic, pluralistic society; rather, they feel they have a mandate to replace it with a Christian nation under God in which transgender kids do not exist.

This is the fight transgender people are in. And we should not have to wage it fighting WCN groups on one hand, and the largest non-governmental news organization on the planet on the other.

As FAIR has noted, "six of the *Times*' nine front page articles about trans issues wove narratives of transition being risky, likely to be regretted, or prematurely forced onto unwitting youth" (on 9/26/22, 11/22/22, and 1/23/23),[21] and/or of trans people threatening others' rights, such as those of cisgender women and parents (on 5/29/22, 6/9/22, 7/21/22, and 1/23/23). These six articles also consumed far more space than the other three, averaging 2,826 words versus 1,636, suggesting which kinds of stories about trans people the paper believes are most worthy of deep investigation."

But I don't think we're going to get accurate and fair media coverage of trans kids until we document exactly how, where, and why things went so badly off the rails. Or as *Xtra Magazine*'s Jude Ellison Doyle puts it: "Someone has made the decision for the paper of record to publish a torrent of anti-trans propaganda, and to do so at a moment when trans people are being attacked in state legislatures. Given the urgency of the situation, it is a matter of public interest to figure out how exactly the situation at the *Times* got this dire."[22]

There have been many, many articles about this, and writers like *Assigned Media*'s Evan Urquhart and Media Matter's Ari Drennan post about it regularly on X and elsewhere.[23] [24] I certainly don't expect to settle anything here, but to my knowledge no one has ever documented it in detail—from the beginning, article by article—and I believe it is important to do so.

However, to do so in-depth would require a much longer book than this one. Otherwise it is impossible to rebut every shaded truth, unfounded inference, or anomalous example in dozens of pieces that can frequently run 5,000 or even 8,000 words. Thus for each piece, I tried to focus on the key claims and biases, as well as the main rhetorical techniques being used to stack the deck against trans kids. In some cases, where one or more articles or an author covered the same or similar ground in separate pieces, I combined them into a single chapter.

This book is divided into four parts:

1. the first wave of anti-trans articles;
2. the *Times*' pivot to attacking trans kids' transitions;
3. a review of the *Times*'s coverage of transgender from its inception to provide context and background;
4. the final awful cascade of disinformation around the 2022 Holiday Season which led directly into the revolt by contributors, readers, and LGBTQ+ groups.

Writing this book has often felt overwhelming, like fighting an octopus that kept sprouting new arms, as a seven-billion-dollar news organization kept generating new and anomalous stories of unhappy transitions to highlight, new holes it could poke in studies that reported positive results, new hypotheses for why transgender kids were probably *not* really transgender after all, and new ways to reject a broad and unanimous medical consensus.[25]

I hope this book will prove to be a resource in keeping the *Times* and other media outlets accountable for their unfair and biased coverage of transgender children and youth, especially at a historical juncture when their lives are under a nearly unimaginable and nationwide legislative assault.

Above all, I have tried to document what happened at the *Times* and to make some reasoned guesses as to why it occurred. In doing so, I'm sure there are places where I have over-interpreted the facts, mistaken synchronicity for causation, and allowed preconceptions to color my judgment.

In addition, with over 700 endnotes covering tens of thousands of words in dozens of news articles spanning nearly a decade, it is inevitable that errors have crept in. Obviously, my fact-checker and I have tried to minimize these, but I have no doubt that there are still "orphan" or missing endnotes, or some with URLs that are no longer active. All errors are of course mine and mine alone, and I apologize in advance for any imprecision.

Whatever my own shortcomings or those of this book, I sincerely hope that they will not in any way detract from the seriousness of the events it seeks to document, and it will prove useful to those who are journalists, LGBTQ+ advocates, parents or friends of trans kids, in women's or gender studies, or simply the many readers like me who still regularly wonder: "Whatever happened to the *New York Times*?"

Chapter One:
Origins of a Newsroom Crusade

"The Times *positions transgender youth and their healthcare providers next to anti-LGBTQ+ politicians, as if these are remotely comparable or honest in some kind of twisted 'both-sides' coverage that gives equal weight to people simply living their lives, and unhinged extremists..."*[26]

GLAAD, Email to *Assigned Media,* 2024

"The New York Times *has decided that the news about trans issues that's worthy of the front page is not, primarily, the massive right-wing anti-trans political push and its impact on those it targets, but whether trans people are receiving too many rights, and accessing too much medical care, too quickly."*[27]

Julie Hollar, FAIR, "NYT's Anti-Trans Bias—by the Numbers"— May 11, 2023

"Perhaps no mainstream publication did more in 2022 than the New York Times *to shift the mainstream conversation around transgender equality away from obstacles to access in housing, employment, and health care and toward the idea that the most pressing issue facing the trans community is actually too much medical care."*[28]

Ari Drennen, Media Matters "The New York *Times* Helped Fuel an anti-Trans Panic in 2022. Will 2023 Be Any Better?"—February 8, 2023

A "Very Real Debate"

In May of 2023, five years after becoming publisher of the *New York Times*, A.G. Sulzberger took to the pages of the prestigious *Columbia Journalism Review* (*CJR*) to offer a 12,000-word statement setting forth his journalistic vision. In it he responded to the *Times*' many critics, including the transgender community, whom he specifically criticized for "focusing on a small number of pieces that explore particularly sensitive questions that society is actively working through, but which some would prefer for the *Times* to treat as settled."[29]

It was true that the *Times* often did extraordinary and ground-breaking coverage of the political war on transgender people launched by white Christian nationalists, and their occasional focus pieces on transgender lives were exemplary. But the idea that this provided license to repeatedly print misleading and transphobic pieces that undermined the very rights and legitimacy that were under assault in that war was risible—as was the obvious straw man of "some" in "some would prefer…"

Other major mainstream outlets like *Reuters* or the *Washington Post*—which had had their own glaring problems with trans-denialist coverage—would run prominent articles highlighting the fact; the *Times* never did, even as the number of peer review studies showing low regrets continued to mount.[30] [31]

Sulzberger implicitly compared the "small number" of *Times* anti-trans articles to other prominent contrarian *Times*'s pieces: an essay by a Taliban leader, its bizarre *neo-Nazi next door* profile, and in the infamous op-ed by Sen. Tom Cotton (R-AR) calling for federal troops to be turned loose on largely peaceful Black Lives Matter demonstrators grieving the police murder of George Floyd.[32] Then-Opinion Editor James Bennet later admitted he never read that piece, and the ensuing employee outcry prompted an "icy" Sulzberger to call Bennet at home and fire him.[33][34]

The *CJR* piece was an illustration of Sulzberger's and upper management's inevitable line of defense when called out by critics: *We publish a lot of good fact-based reporting on trans people, so its unfair to pick out a few dozen biased articles.*[35] Also that the medical issues it was reporting on were somehow "unsettled"—although it was actually a case of the *Times'* institutional refusal to accept medical consensus and seek out political controversy where there was little or no medical one.

Sulzberger would make many of these same arguments once again in an 8,000-word interview following his *CJR* piece with the *New Yorker*'s Editor David Remnick, referring once again to "very real debates" and "an active debate" that the affirming-care medical field was "actively working through," and accuse the trans community of "asking us to pretend that debate is not happening." He would add piously, "[O]ur job is to write the stories that society is working through—stories that are less cut-and-dried…"[36]

But pediatric gender-affirming care wasn't "less cut-and-dried."

On the contrary, it was completely cut, and completely dried. Nor was the medical community working through "very real debates," because there weren't any. That ship had sailed long ago, after all 27 medical organizations responsible for providing gender affirming care to trans kids—from endocrinologists, pediatricians, surgeons, and psychologists to nurses, osteopaths, social workers, and psychiatrists—went on record declaring it safe, effective, necessary, and recommended—as have scores of peer reviewed studies.[37] [38]

For instance, as I write, the Associated Press (AP)—one of the last major wire services and about as politically neutered as you can get—has just run an unremarkable story titled, "How Common Is Transgender Treatment Regret, Detransitioning?" it notes that "a review of 27 studies involving almost 8,000 teens and adults who had transgender surgeries [found that] 1% on average expressed regret."[39] This was *so* unremarkable, it was even republished by America's own Voice of America, which is reaches 320 million people abroad in 49 languages.[40] [41] Yet the *Times* continues publishing long-form attacks on transition that are little more than scare stories about transgender desistance.[42] [43] [44]

There was a medical and academic consensus—but Sulzberger simply refused to accept it. The *why* is one of the questions this book tries to address.

He was essentially saying that parents of transgender kids couldn't trust what their pediatrician, or the American Academy of Pediatrics, or the American Psychiatric Association, or even the American Medical Association was telling them—and so the *Times* had a journalistic responsibility to step in and provide them with timely and accurate medical information. It was an interesting posture for a publisher to take, and pretty much paralleled what the Christian right had been saying.

There was simply no bar, no threshold of proof, the medical or academic community could provide that the *Times* was prepared to accept. Even when new studies came out that showed the medical consensus was right, the *Times* would ignore them, and it has yet to run anything like that AP story on the real rates of detransition.

Because that "very active debate" was a *political*—not a medical—one, just like the "very active debate" that the medical field is still working through on "dangers" posed by vaccines or abortion.[45] And for much the same reasons: these are all *faux* controversies created by Christian nationalist groups at war with a science that conflicts with their religious beliefs.

And they and their Republican legislative allies quickly weaponized the *Times'* trans denialism.

Just four days after the *Times* published it, one particularly awful anti-trans op-ed made it into a brief, arguing that pediatric care should be a felony in Idaho.[46] This was just part of a history of *Times* pieces being so aligned with right-wing talking points that they were quickly weaponized by them to restrict trans kids' rights:

- Missouri Attorney General Andrew Bailey cited a *Times* piece in declaring a state-wide "emergency" banning *all* gender affirming medical care for adolescents *and* adults.[47]
- Texas lawmakers and its Attorney General quoted *Times* articles justifying its investigating of families for child abuse who were providing affirming care, and policies mandating that schools forcibly out LGBTQ+ students to their parents.[48] [49]
- In Nebraska, *Times*'s coverage was cited to advance a bill making it a criminal offence to provide medical care to youth.[50]
- An attorney invited to testify before the Nebraska legislature in support of its anti-care ban cited the *Times'* trans-denialist coverage as the "newspaper of record."[51]
- Five red-state States' Attorneys General filed in

support of an Alabama law that would make affirming care a felony, and cited *three Times* pieces in support of their position.[52]

- Sen. Josh Hawley cited a misleading *Times'* piece on a supposed "whistleblower at Washington University's St. Louis gender clinic" in launching one of several investigations that would lead to it being shuttered.[53] [54]

These evangelical religious biases have infiltrated mainstream media through a well-planned and coordinated strategy in which palatable, non-religious messaging is backed by pseudoscience—as documented by the Southern Poverty Law Center (SPLC) in excruciating detail in its 61,000-work investigative report, Project CAPTAIN.[55]

As the Project's chapter on *manufacturing doubt* documents, WCN groups made common cause with anti-trans parents and TERF groups who provided quotes from "grassroots" voices.[56] For the veneer of academic backing, they turned to the old-guard of 1980s anti-gay "conversion therapists," as well as newer-guard, anti-trans ones. Together they published pseudoscientific "studies" and white papers, hosted panels, held conferences, and launched official-sounding professional organizations. It is virtually the same ecosystem constructed by WCN groups to manufacture doubt about issues like gay parent adoption or COVID vaccination.

And it works. The anti-trans backlash that this strategy helped spark has been wildly effective.

As early as 2014, the largest Christian nationalist group in the country—Alliance Defending Freedom (ADF)—had already solicited and paid for a series of reports from the Christian-based American College of

Pediatricians, which SPLC has classified as an anti-LGBTQ+ hate group. In language mirroring its anti-abortion stance, ACPeds' "biological integrity" project had determined that gender is set in stone "from the moment of fertilization."[57]

The report was to be used as academic justification for manufacturing a public "debate" over pediatric gender care.[58] And ADF had thoughtfully specified in advance the five points that ACPeds' "research" should find—each of which later showed up in the *Times* as story hooks for anti-trans articles:[59] [60]

- "Time to Desegregate the Sexes?" by Judith Shulevitz, October 15, 2016 which posits that cis girls are psychologically harmed by having their privacy invaded by trans girls
- "As Kids, They Thought They Were Trans. They No Longer Do" by Pamela Paul, February 2, 2024, which says that identifying as the opposite sex is a phase and should be neither affirmed nor treated medically
- "Who Gets to Compete in Women's Sports? There Are Two Almost Irreconcilable Positions," by Gillian Brassil and Jeré Longman, August. 18, 2020; and "What Lia Thomas Could Mean for Women's Elite Sports" by Michael Powell, May 29, 2022, which declares that cisgender girls are hurt when trans girls participate in girls' sports
- "They Paused Puberty, But Is There a Cost?" by Megan Twohey and Christina Jewett, November 14, 2022, and "Chest Binding Helps Smooth the Way for Transgender Teens, but There May Be Risks," by Amy Sohn, May 31, 2019, saying that

affirming medical care doesn't make trans kids happier, and may actually be harming them.

- "How Changeable Is Gender?" by Richard Friedman, August 22, 2015 claims that chromosomal or anatomical sex is definitive, and there is no such thing as "brain sex."

As this book will show, a very similar three-legged stool approach would often be used by the *Times* itself in its own articles undercutting care, leading with predetermined conclusions based on bogus data by anti-trans professionals, and illustrated with human interest quotes from anti-trans parents and their groups.

In effect, the *Times* was promoting a Christian theocratic agenda in the guise of covering Sulzberger's "very real debate." If there *was* a scientific debate to be had here, it was an extraordinary way for a reputable news organization to go about covering it.

It is hard to overstate how unique this is among mainstream news organizations. For example, talking points from anti-LGBTQ+ hate groups did *not* show up as main story hooks at outlets like *CNN* or the *Washington Post.* The fact they did at the *Times* illustrated a quiet but dramatic shift in which Christian nationalist organizations devoted to the eradication of trans kids were not just being quoted as the obligatory "other side" in its articles, but were actually driving and shaping its coverage of them.

"It's Strategy People!"

Much of this was made possible by a conscious decision among WCN and TERF groups to drop religious and transphobic hateful language for secular, mainstream-acceptable messaging. This was spelled out in an unsigned 2022 Substack post from Parents with Inconvenient Truths about Trans (PITT).

Titled, "It's Strategy People!" it pushed back on the desire of many anti-trans groups to wear their true transphobia and vitriol openly, and showed how media had already rewarded those willing to strategically conceal their real feelings beneath palatable, mainstream-friendly language. It even went so far as to compare this unpleasant necessity to the French resistance having to learn to speak German in order to fight the Nazis.[61]

> *"We are being told* [by other anti-trans groups] *that we can't use the words "transgender" or the word 'gender,' at all. [But] we have put parents' faces on two national TV networks, telling the world what's really going on. There's no way this would have happened if the producers had seen words like 'deluded' or 'mentally ill' on the banner of our website…*
>
> *"[And our approach is working. We have had stories placed in other parts of the mainstream media, like the BBC, Telegraph and Times. Already this year we have had the New York Times, of all newspapers, start to question pediatric transition…* [which] *has resulted in stopping actual kids from being socially transitioned, in actual schools. We successfully got a British detransitioner on national television. You think that language like 'mutilated' will get a detransitioned person on television?… please show me an example…*
>
> *"War is about strategy… Imagine that you are in Nazi-occupied France. You're in the resistance, and you need to blow up the railway lines, in order to stop*

the enemy from advancing. If you don't have a German speaking diplomat on your team, you don't know which railway lines to bomb..." [emphasis added.]

When an uber-TERF group like PITT brags publicly about getting the newspaper of record to carry its carefully curated disinformation and prevent "actual kids from transitioning," Elvis has definitely left the building.

"Needle Lady"

But behind the guise family-friendly messaging the vitriol was still all there.

The *Times* quoted groups such as:

- ADF which had been classified by SPLC as an anti-LGBTQ+ hate group and which asserted that gay people were pedophiles.
- 4thWaveNow, which was central in promoting the canard that being trans was spread by *social contagion.*
- Richard Green, who devoted years of his career to "conversion therapy" experiments to *cure* what he called "sissy boys," and also to "the prevention of transsexuality."
- The Society for Evidence Based Medicine (SEGM), which was among the secret working groups of WCN organizations that developed and launched the first wave of anti-t[62]ransgender bills (reported by *Mother Jones* from leaked emails).[63]
- Heley Joyce (the reception of an admiring *Times* books review) who was the featured speaker on a

podcast titled, "They're Sterilizing Gay Kids."[64 65] On another podcast she suggested that governments must "reduce or keep down the number of people who transition" because every transgender person "is basically, you know, a huge problem to a sane world," adding that trans people "[h]ave created a social movement out of an obvious crazy delusion."[66 67 68]

- Stephanie Winn, identified by the *Times* as "a licensed marriage and family therapist," who had recommended that parents help discourage their trans children by having them undergo acupuncture so "[t]hey can see how they like having needles put in them… something they are going to have to become very comfortable with if they want to pursue cross-sex hormones…"[69 70 71] She was promptly nicknamed "The Needle Lady" by many activists.

Winn also suggested parents should give their trans boys long-lasting henna chest tattoos so they could experience the scarring they would have after top-surgery, and make their trans sons use only a designated Men's Room at home, which was "intentionally kept gross and rarely cleaned [with] the toilet seat up… [and] a picture of a man using a urinal" that he would have to view every time he peed.[72] Some people might call this child abuse. Weirdly, Winn's blog was titled "You must be some kind of therapist." Indeed.

Not a New Look

In sum, it was simply impossible to square all this with Sulzberger's high-minded claims in the *Columbia*

Journalism Review of his deep commitment to "high standards of accuracy, fairness, and intellectual rigor," or to believe that this open transphobia was not coming from him.

But intolerance for sexual minorities was not a new look for the *Times*. Executive Editor A. M. Rosenthal was legendary for his virulent homophobia, promoting anti-gay stories, suppressing gay-positive ones, [73]keeping gay staffers terrified and closeted, banning the word *gay* "unless it appears in the name of an organization or in a quote," and downplaying the HIV/AIDS epidemic detonating just outside the *Times* front door and eventually within its own newsroom.[74] [75]

Just as Rosenthal's *Times* had covered homosexuals in the 1950s and 1960s as *troubling*, *posing problems*, *provoking concern*, and *causing panic,* so Sulzberger's *Times* in the 2000s covered trans kids as another *bad object* that was always a *vexing problem*, a *sensitive issue*, and causing cisgender people *wrenching tension.*[76] [77] [78] [79] [80]

Sulzberger and the *Times* defended its trans-denial pieces against the increasing outpouring of public criticism by declaring that they were "deeply reported and sensitively written."[81]

But the criticism being leveled at them was not that they were shallowly reported or insensitively written (although some were that, too). It was that they were biased and inaccurate, violating the first rule of journalism: Get Your Facts Straight. And not just the op-ed writers, but also regular *Times* reporters and even its investigative journalists who are usually held to a higher standard also struggled with the facts, because, as Stephen Colbert has noted, "Reality has a well-known liberal bias."[82] [83] [84]

As journalism, this was shocking for its ignorance. Not *factual ignorance,* where a reporter doesn't know something, or even *object ignorance,* where they were misinformed about it. It was what scholar Charles Mills (speaking of racism) termed *epistemic ignorance:* a deliberate not-knowing of freely available facts because to recognize them was politically inconvenient.[85]

The Thumb on the Scale

Each article would offer the appearance of balance, while putting its thumb heavily on the scale of one side. It was often subtle: a series of ominous implications, highly unrepresentative examples and over-stated risks.

The *Times* could be Trumpian in its ability to "flood the zone with shit" in tens of thousands of words in dozens of stories attacking trans people across a wide variety of fronts with biased pieces, each of which was virtually impossible for a reader to unpack.[86]

Among the finest examples of debunking is Science Based Medicine's magisterial dissection of Megan Twohey and Christina Jewett's 5,764-word piece, "They Paused Puberty, But Is there a Cost?" It took SBM nearly 8,000 words to do it.

Times articles used every time-worn trick in the journalistic grab bag to tilt the playing field in favor of the arguments it wished to promote. In practice, this included well-worn rhetorical techniques such as:

- Using sensationalist or pointlessly alarmist headlines
- Offering meaningless justifications for anti-trans story lines ("some people are saying…")[87]

- Repeating wild and incendiary right-wing claims without debunking them[88] [89] [90]
- Implying affirming medicine is risky or harmful when it is accepted common practice, and/or the same procedures are provided to cisgender kids[91]
- Under-quoting or ignoring transgender people as sources, while quoting trans-deniers at length[92] [93]
- Under-identifying anti-trans and evangelical ideologues or organizations[94] [95]
- Pitting established medical consensus against pseudoscience as false "balance"[96]
- Quoting fringe voices outside the mainstream as "experts"[97]
- Quoting doctors out of context to make it appear that they did not support pediatric care or were concerned about its risks when neither were true[98]
- Under-quoting positive experts and over-quoting negative ones[99]
- Cherry-picking medical problems to show that care is harmful[100]
- Nitpicking peer reviewed studies but accepting doubtful adverse ones at face value[101]
- Using the parts of studies that appear to show problems but ignore the rest of the text[102]
- Putting big, scary numbers up front and burying how few kids are actually affected and burying other relevant data.[103] [104]

It was all there, even though as the *Times'* own staffers have pointed out these flaws, and it completely violated the *Times*' own standards and ethics.[105]

The Real Story

The irony was that the *Times* was perfectly capable of producing outstanding, even groundbreaking, journalism about transgender people just as trans-denialist pieces were busily undermining them. I recently published a book on the evangelical extremists' war on trans youth, and the *Times* was not only one of my most cited sources, but often its investigative journalism provided irreplaceable facts and context.

Eventually it became obvious that what the anti-trans crusade was covering wasn't transgender people themselves, but the extremist right's fear and loathing of them, along with their cascade of QAnon-like conspiracy theories: the "destruction" of women's sports; trans women predators in Ladies Rooms; etc. The headline for all of these was what researcher Andrea James called, "Cisgender People Under Siege."[106] [107]

That was the *real* story.

It is almost impossible to imagine the *Times* today inflicting this kind of journalistic crusade against any other minority: young people seeking abortions, Black youth, gay children—even as the very community it covered howled in protest at the bias and inaccuracies, and 1,000+ of its contributors rebelled in protest.[108]

Sulzberger's high-minded pleas for a civil debate and his accusations that trans advocates were trying to "win a debate by avoiding one" were not helped by the fact that in the nearly two centuries since its founding in 1851, the *New York Times* had never had a single trans person on its masthead, had few trans journalists, and the one semi-regular trans op-ed writer it had ever hired, Jennifer Finney Boylan, had her contract terminated and the position filled just weeks later by an anti-trans culture warrior.[109] [110] [111]

Her firing was also followed shortly by the hiring of David French, a former attorney with ADF who had a long history of anti-trans activism, including a National Review column which linked to two of the three major anti-trans websites, TransgenderTrend and 4thWaveNow, and cited an *American Conservative* magazine article calling transgender a "cult" spread via "social contagion." His column was emailed by ADF to its members.[112] [113] French had also signed the notorious 2017 "Nashville Statement" declaring the sinfulness of "homosexual immorality or transgenderism."

All of this was conveniently *omitted* from the *Times'* laudatory announcement of French's hiring, as well as from his official company bio—actions which were hard to read as anything other than a clumsy attempt to cleanse the record.[114] [115]

"Heads-I-Win"

"*The* Times *has devoted an inordinate number of words to minor criticisms and controversies within a well-established treatment field at a time when these treatments were being singled out for extraordinary and unwarranted legislative attention by Republican lawmakers… and minority [views] when mainstream practitioners were in danger of their work being criminalized.*"[116]

Evan Urquhart, *Assigned Media,* "Erik Wemple Doesn't Believe the New York Times Is Biased"

Of 12 articles and 33,00 words attacking teen transitions in whole or in part from 2015 through 2022, *The Times* never once devoted a single article to the science and medicine on the issue. Only four of these articles appeared in the Health section, and just one in Science. Because the *Times* wanted to cover controversy, and there was none in the medical community, it was not covering established medical opinion or scientific opinion. It was covering the *political* debate, something it failed to acknowledge,

Why else would it devote so much ink to the 1% of American teens who medically transition, and to the 1% or so of that 1% who eventually detransition?[117] [118] Here's what that looks like graphically:

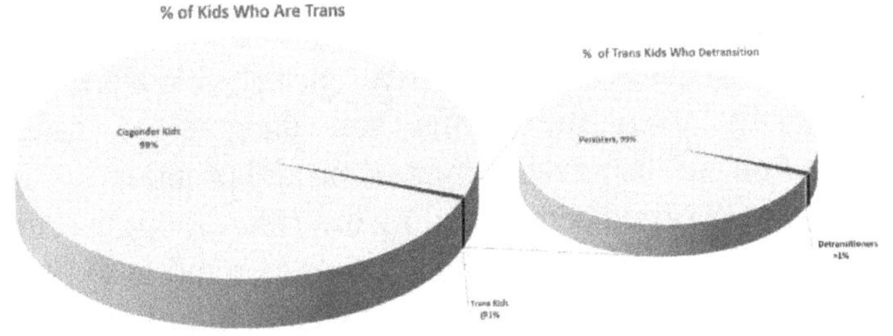

The real crisis in teen detransitions is the 100,000+ trans adolescents in 23 states who have had their hormones outlawed and are in danger of being *forcibly detransitioned* to the wrong gender every day, and up to another 50,000 in states where such laws have been introduced but not passed.[119] And then there are the tens of thousands whose parents are hostile to them being trans, or who are supportive, but have no insurance to pay for care. But the *lack* of care for a couple hundred thousand trans kids was not a topic of much interest to the *Times*.

And when the medical community and trans advocates rallied around the science and research on teen transitions, Sulzberger accused them of stifling dissent or demanding they pick a side. Even after the *Times* repeatedly complained in print about the lack of long-term follow-up studies, and then a five-year study of 317 kids was published and found that 97.5% were still trans-identified five years later—the *Times* devoted most of its coverage to poking holes in it, and virtually ignored it in future coverage.

It was a kind of *Heads-I-Win/Tails-You-Lose* situation, in which broadly accepted medical consensus could never be good enough. The *Times* continued to find some controversy, and then would cover that.

And it wasn't just medical transitions.

Front page articles warned of the dangers of temporarily pausing puberty with puberty blockers, and eventually even the harms and dangers of *social transition*—of using a different name and pronoun.

To a worried parent reading the *Times* it might seem that *anything* their transgender kid or teen did to express their gender identity would be potentially harmful.

The truth is quite different. Transition care is so overwhelmingly not-regretted that it should be celebrated and held up as a major medical success story.

This even includes surgeries—the most radical change. For instance, a review of 27 studies in the National Library of Medicine at the National Institutes of Health found a regret rate among 7,928 patients 13 or older of just 1%.[120] This appeared in March of 2021. Nonetheless, a *Times* article 18 months later still warned of the dangers of top surgery, and its subhead read, "data is sparse."[121] Another review in the American Journal of Surgery of 55 studies of GAS found the same 1%, and that this was lower than for almost any other form of non-medically-mandated care.[122]

In fact, regret rates for gender transitions are lower

than for almost any other major non-mandated medical procedure. And although Sulzberger repeatedly accused critics of demanding that the *Times choose sides*, trans advocates were not asking anyone to side with *them*—they were asking the *Times* to side with the kids: to believe in transgender teens, and to believe in the medical consensus and the science—just as it does in nearly every other area of medical care but this one.

No One Reads Newspapers Anymore

When he took over as publisher in 1963, A.G.'s father, Arthur Ochs (A.O.) Sulzberger Jr. shocked the editorial staff by announcing among his top priorities forward would be "diversity"—by which he meant finally covering *homosexuals* and AIDS.[123] [124] [125]

It was quite a different statement that A. G. Sulzberger would make upon becoming publisher, reportedly telling staff that among his top priorities would be shedding the *Times*'s reputation as a "liberal rag" to court conservative readers.[126]

A.O. needed to appeal to an emerging demographic of NYC gays and liberals being lost to more progressive outlets, but A.G. wanted to go backwards and appeal to an emerging market of MAGA Republicans and illiberal-bros lost to outlets like Brietbart, nimbler competitors like Buzzfeed, and apps like TikTok.[127]

A. O. labored in the immense moral shadow cast by AIDS —which the *Times* at first ignored and then tragically downplayed, consigning coverage to the back pages. Conversely, when Legionnaire's Disease struck in 1976, the *Times* repeatedly put it on its front page, helping focus media and government attention.[128]

A. G. seemed to labor in the absence of any moral shadow at all, except perhaps the imperative to avoid being The Sulzberger Who Lost the *Times,* as revenue increasingly flowed not from print advertisers but from customers, and media's job had shifted from challenging and informing to engaging and entertaining.[129]

A. G. had led the team which produced a 97-page study, "The Innovation Report," that was by turns scathing, prescient, and inspirational about the dangers bearing down on a print-oriented *Times* ("It took seven years to begin tagging stories 'September 11'"), "Reporters should submit five possible tweets when they file stories [with a] social strategy…", and "Our Twitter account is run by the newsroom and our Facebook by the business side.")

'Digital-oriented competitors were beating the *Times* to the punch, often by aggregating, repackaging, and promoting their own coverage faster and better than it did. It was followed by A.G.'s 2017 plan for a subscription-based digital-first *Times* that could double online revenues to $1 billion in just three years, called "Our Path Forward.'"[130] [131] [132] [133] [134]

And it worked, at least financially.

At a time when the *Times* had lost well over half (56%) of its print subscribers, by 2023 it was bringing in $1 billion from digital ones.[135] [136]

Sulzberger's plan would dismiss ProPublica, whose motto was "Investigative Journalism in the Public Interest," as "that bastion of old-school journalism values." Among his plan's main goals was tearing down the traditional firewall between the journalism and business sides so that coverage could better reflect the *Times*' economic interests.

It was all in pursuit of that Holy Grail of the digital age: user engagement—which is why Facebook's algorithm prioritizes conspiracy and outrage posts, and TikTok's uses your viewing history to present content that is increasingly disturbing.[137] [138] Among other strategies, the *paper of record* was going to play this game too.

As one expert explained to the AP, "The art of trolling is getting the other person enraged [because] we now know that getting someone enraged really fuels engagement and gives you followers, and so you will get paid. So now it's sort of a business."[139]

Amping user engagement helped to ensure that The Family Business wouldn't be reduced to needing a rescue by some benevolent internet billionaire, like Bezos buying the *Washington Post* after four generations in the Graham family, or being acquired by some bean-counters who would milk it for its last dollars by halving the newsroom staff, as Gatehouse Media had done to the once-proud Gannett News.[140]

But no one buys print anymore, and no one reads newspapers. The *Times* is no longer *the newspaper of record*; it's Facebook with more news.

It's a digital lifestyle destination, stuffed with personal blogs (Cooking, Personal Tech, Modern Love, Mother Lode, etc.), a popular podcast (The Daily), endless product reviews ("Most Comfortable Bras," "This Adorable Butter Warmer Isn't Just for Butter," and "The Best Vibrators"[141] [142]); personal advice columns that would feel right at home in your supermarket checkout line ("Better Ways to Clean Your Ears" and "My 75-Year-Old Husband Wants Sex Every Day. What Do I Do?"[143] [144]) and games like Sodoku, Vertex, Tiles, Wordle, Spelling Bee, and the traditional Crossword and Mini Crossword. (To identify the best vibrators, the Wirecutter blog's crew crowed about putting in "150 hours of research and testing…" The mind boggles…)

A Little Street Cred

"I believe they're using trans people as a political pawn to maintain a centrist reputation to keep from being seen as too liberal of a paper."[145]

S. Leigh Thompson, Trans consultant hired by *Times*, in The Daily Beast

In principle, it should be easy to squeeze good right-wing news into all this.

But the problem is, the white Christian nationalism that passes for "conservative" discourse today is so detached from reality that it is virtually *unplatformable*—obsessed with bogus conspiracies about "replacement theory," DC pedophile rings, immigrant drug runners, non-existent election fraud, and, of course, drag queens.[146] [147]

So despite A.G.'s yearnings to monetize their bigotries, whenever the *Times* dipped its toe into the MAGA-fied right—as with Cotton's notorious op-ed—a predictable firestorm ensued.[148] [149] [150]

But the *Times can* platform MAGA-fied evangelical right voices as the "other side" of a "very active debate" on the legitimacy of transgender kids, and particularly their medical care, because, while the right is pushing 1,000+ bills in state houses across the country that test the limits of how many ways a vindictive majority can wreck its vengeance on a small minority of children, most of the progressive civil rights community is still ambivalent and sitting on its hands, wrestling with the idea of teen transitions.

Sulzberger *can* painlessly buy himself and the *Times* a little journalistic street cred with the right, and milk the Perpetual Outrage Machine for subscriptions, while not harming any of the core investments in things he really cares about: women's equality, abortion, or gay rights, and he can still position the paper as a bold teller of inconvenient truths that others dare not speak.[151]

The enablers here are liberals, many of whom are supportive of trans rights, but remain ambivalent about teen transitions.

In examining statements by 18 of the largest civil society, civil rights, and women's rights groups, I found nearly 100% made statements in support of abortion rights and gay marriage. But that figure plummeted to less than half (44%) for trans kids' care.[152] [153] And the volume dropped too: from about 70 statements supporting abortion rights or gay marriage to a meagre 10 for care—a decline of 84%.[154] [155] [156]

In other words, the *Times* can go full Joe Rogan on trans kids with impunity. And as The Social Talks' Jakob Moscow would ask, "Why shouldn't the *New York Times* harvest some of that fear and loathing for itself?"[157]

Like Twitter or Facebook, the *Times* tracked metrics and rewarded writers for content that engaged readers and resulted in subscriptions.[158] If it wasn't *journalism in the public interest*, at least it would be engagement-bait with an intellectual polish. This wasn't Infowars or HuffPo, after all. It jumped headfirst into the new culture war that WCN groups had launched over transgender bodies—and the *Times* could monetize it.

The strategy is entirely cynical and bloodless. Just like Bezos or Musk, or especially Zuckerberg—whose own internal research showed clearly how Instagram was harming young girls but who didn't care—Sulzberger would prove to be another internet titan whose only morality was market share and user engagement.[159]

Not Your Friends

And it all works, at least financially.

Print ads that had been the mainstay, accounting for fully 70% of revenue in 2000, had been sinking like a stone, down two-thirds to just 28% in 2015.

In its place, digital advertising—just 1% of revenue in 2005—jumped to 12% by 2015. And once the *Times* embraced the paywall, digital subscription revenue— zero in 2000, 2005 and 2010—also jumped to 12% by 2015. Print ads may have been dying, but digital was beginning to make up the difference.[160] Today, 1.5 million subscriptions now amount to $200 million a year.

A man for his times, Sulzberger is a pioneer at paywall journalism and digital content when most legacy newspapers considered it a dead end, and were instead chasing eyeballs online to sell to advertisers.

Sulzberger turns the so-called "failing New York *Times*" around, becoming among the only legacy outlets that is hiring large numbers of journalists as others are cutting to the bone, selling themselves, or closing their doors in an industry that had shed a quarter million jobs since 1990.

In the midst of this carnage, the *Times*' "Last Man Standing" strategy enabled it to "skim the top tier of local and regional newspaper audiences as those outlets declined."[161] [162] [163] [164] [165]

This *Times* would still produce amazing coverage, and its reach and depth would still be unexcelled. But it would seem morally rudderless with no guiding vision, and devoid of underlying morality—an exceptional news service that often enthusiastically took part in right-wing culture wars.[166]

During the heyday of "yellow journalism" when the newspapers of the day competed to push sensationalist coverage to boost their readership, the *Times*'s legendary publisher Adolph S. Ochs published a statement on April 1896 declaring that the *Times* would chart a lonely and different course: covering the news of the day "without fear or favor."

For many years it would be embraced as a kind of company credo, displayed on the wall in the lobby of the *Times*'s entrance.[167]

Despite the high-minded appearance of journalistic integrity and ethics, in place of *Without Fear or Favor,* Sulzberger had, himself, minted a new motto. It would appear on no wall or entrance, but it was there all the same:

We are not your friends. We're a business. And we sell what we can to whom we can.

Part One:
The Crusade Begins (2015-2021)

2015	2016	2017	2018	2019	2020	2021
Books						
Opinion	Opinion			Style		
Opinion	Opinion			Well	Sports	Books

Chapter Two:
Being Trans Is a Perversion

Title:	**"Galileo's Middle Finger,' by Alice Dreger"**[168]
Originally:	"Truth Be Told"
Date:	**April 17, 2015**
Byline:	**David Dobbs**
Section:	**Book Review**
Words:	**1,283**

It would all start with a single article in 2015 that was just… *off.*

It was the first of five such articles and all the rest would be in Opinion—which proved to be Sulzberger's preferred venue for shoveling red-meat to the digital MAGA readership he hoped to attract, because it could be written off as someone's *personal belief,* and thus didn't require the same fact-checking as hard news or investigative stories.

The piece wasn't openly transphobic—although that would come later—nor did it quote white Christian nationalist hate groups as experts—although that would come later, too. But it did endorse shockingly transphobic views without ever mentioning or quoting a single transgender person.

It was almost exactly 20 years earlier to the day that

writer Carey Goldberg called me in 1995 to do a profile after the founding of GenderPAC. I was warned "This won't be political" and mostly it wasn't. But just carrying a profile of an openly transsexual woman in a business suit and short hair, not making any effort to "pass" as cisgender, and talking about civil rights rather than her body was in its own way quietly political.

And Goldberg followed it with the first hard news piece about trans rights on the National Page, *above* the fold, when GenderPAC held the first National Gender Lobby Day on Capitol Hill. The *Times'* Editorial Board was the first major outlet to endorse this new, emerging movement for transgender people's rights.[169] [170]

In the intervening years the *Times*' coverage—like its coverage of other marginalized groups—had huge flaws, but most of them were those of the casual kind of casual bias that often infects journalism that deals with an unfamiliar and perhaps even unsettling minority.

But all that changed with David Dobbs adulatory April 2015 of Alice Dreger's book, "Galileo's Middle Finger."

Dreger was a curious figure: an early and important academic backer of the intersex rights movement which also took off in the mid-1990s as Bo Laurent (*aka* Cheryl Chase) founded the Intersex society of North America.[171] However, many ISNA activists became incensed over Dreger's attempts to reframe being intersex as a disorder (intersex is also referred to Differences of Sexual Development (DSD)).[172]

Alas, when it came to transsexual women, Dreger went down a rabbit hole of transphobic pseudoscience. About half of Dobb's review was devoted to Dreger's support for a particularly nasty pseudoscience theory proposed by Canadian sexologist Ray Blanchard and popularized by psychologist J. Michael Bailey which held that transsexuality in women resulted from a new and heretofore unknown form of sexual perversion, and then celebrated Dreger's survival of the predictable outrage from the transgender community.[173]

As if we didn't already have enough theories pathologizing transsexual woman as really being effeminate boys or hyper-feminine homosexuals looking for sex with straight men, this one added that we were really hetero men acting out a deep erotic fetish over our feminized bodies. As theorist Julia Serano has pointed out, trans women have historically been sexualized by researchers, theorists, and doctors.[174] And because these groups were inevitably obsessed with transsexual *women*, such theories always said almost nothing about trans men.

Dobb's frame for this part of his piece was Dreger being attacked by "people in power… self-appointed guardians of the nonpowerful… a motivated group of activists with a playbook of ugly tactics with a scientific finding they don't like, often dominating public discussion in a way that replaces a factual story with a false one."[175]

In other words the All-Powerful Trans Horde.

This was the first of many, many *Times* pieces to invoke a dark and shadowy cabal which was both tiny and highly marginalized yet somehow still managed to "cancel" the careers of well-respected and established authors and academics—most of whom inexplicably went on to enormous success with prime coverage in major outlets like the *New York Times*.[176]

Dreger herself has been the subject of no less than two glowing *Times'* pieces, a lengthy *Washington Post* article, her own long-form piece in *The Stranger* and pieces in the *Atlantic*, as well as publishing a new novel and appearing on *Oprah.*[177] [178] We should all be so *cancelled.*

Dobbs closed by asking plaintively, "But how do we discern the charlatan… without persecuting the innocent?… It's incredibly difficult… Clearly we need people like Dreger…"

But clearly we *don't* need transgender people—because even though we are the topic of discussion, Dobbs apparently didn't bother interviewing a single one of us. Nor, for that matter, a single intersex person.

Strangely enough, Dobbs' book review was followed just two months later by a statement from the *Times*' that May, entitled, "The Quest for Transgender Equality." It was accompanied by a "Transgender Today" feature, called "Transgender Lives: Your Stories "—to which over 300 trans people lent their personal stories and photographs.[179]

It was a singular achievement, and one that quickly became a relic of a bygone *Times* that was already fading from view, even though no one knew it. Today it is almost impossible to imagine hundreds of trans people trusting the *New York Times* with their stories, just as it is almost impossible to imagine it hosting such a section once Sulzberger took over as Publisher barely three years later.

But the Editorial Board—a group of selected editors and writers who present the *Times* own viewpoint and generally speak for the Publisher—again endorsed the idea of full social participation, acceptance, and civil rights for transgender Americans:

> *"Being transgender today remains unreasonably and unnecessarily hard. But it is far from hopeless. More Americans who have wrestled with gender identity are transitioning openly, propelling a civil*

> *rights movement that has struggled even as gays and lesbians have reached irreversible momentum in their fight for equality. Those coming out now are doing so with trepidation, realizing that while pockets of tolerance are expanding, discriminatory policies and hostile, uninformed attitudes remain widespread... They deserve to come out in a nation where stories of compassion and support vastly outnumber those that end with a suicide note. The tide is shifting, but far too slowly, while lives, careers and dreams hang in the balance."*[180]

The op-ed was published only days before Caitlyn Jenner's April coming out in *Vogue*, and, as *The Advocate* would note, over the next half-year the *Times* would mention Jenner and her transition no less than 50 times.[181]

But then, A. O. Sulzberger was still Publisher, and his son A. G. just a Deputy Publisher, and the *Times* had barely begun its long, slow shift into his digital-first plan to court a conservative readership.

It would be the last time for a decade that the Editorial Board would have much that was good or kind to say about transgender Americans—or for that matter many of its writers, as the *Times* then published four openly and clearly transphobic op-eds in quick succession.

Dobbs was the first example of what would become a kind of trademark of the new *Times*, treating trans people as objects to be talked *about,* rather than as people to be heard *from*. A Media Matters and GLAAD analysis titled, "Seen But Not Heard," examined a full year of *Times* articles just as the flood of anti-trans bills attacking trans people was reaching its peak along with the *Times'* coverage of them. Yet it the *Times* failed to quote trans people in fully *two-thirds* of these. This was a journalistic treatment that it is nearly impossible to imagine the *Times* visiting on any other minority.[182]

Transgender people were increasingly being treated like Banquo's ghost in such articles: unwelcome guests who are neither seen nor heard from, but serve as spectral presence that reminds everyone that something is terribly amiss.

The next op-ed directly attacked the legitimacy of transsexual women, and the one after that kicked off the *Times*' decade-long crusade to undermine trans kids' affirming care. In a complete turnaround, Sulzberger and his reinvented *Times* were about to play a leading role in why "being transgender today remains unreasonably and unnecessarily hard."

Chapter Three: Transsexual Women Aren't *Real Women*

Title:	**"What Makes a Woman?"**[183]
Date:	**June 6, 2015**
Byline:	**Elinor Burkett**
Section:	**Opinion**
Words:	**2,207**

Pitting one group against an emerging minority by claiming the latter was stealing something from the former is a familiar right-wing tactic.

Evangelical extremists used it to defeat gay anti-discrimination laws in the 1990s by claiming they conferred "special rights" at the expense of heterosexuals. And of course racists have long made the same argument about affirmative action, claiming that it steals jobs and opportunities that should have gone to whites.[184]

At first glance, Elinor Burkett was not an obvious choice to make this argument. She was then perhaps best known for charging, Kanye-like, onto the 2009 Oscars stage to interrupt director Roger Ross Williams accepting his award for "Music by Prudence," his documentary of Zimbabwean singer-songwriter Prudence Mabhena and her all-disabled band.[185] [186] [187] Burkett—who later reportedly claimed that, "The movie was my idea...

Roger had never even heard of Zimbabwe…"—apparently had herself removed from the movie's credits over creative differences.[188]

But neither this, nor the fact that Williams was the first Black director ever to win an Oscar stopped her from charging up to interrupt him just 10 seconds into his giddy acceptance speech to publicly accuse him of sexism: "Isn't it always the way that the man doesn't let the woman talk? Isn't that just the classic thing?"[189] [190]

Burkett's piece was a compendium of well-chewed TERF arguments dating back to the 1980s, and such an open, straightforward attack on the legitimacy of trans women that in retrospect it should have been understood as a warning shot fired across the community's bow: an institutional shift was beginning.

What triggered Burkett's outrage was Caitlyn Jenner's *uber*-glam coming out cover story in that month's *Vanity Fair*. An accurate headline would have been, "Why Jenner Can Never Be a Woman," encapsulating its main argument: womanhood is biological and trans women and girls seeking acceptance *as* women and girls and especially their misguided allies on campuses and in women's groups were "undermining," "erasing," and "silencing" Real Women and stealing their "right to define ourselves, our discourse, and our bodies."

Whew—it was a lot. Cisgender Women Under Siege! Simply because of a one-off cover on a completely atypical, Republican. transsexual woman.

Just for purposes of scale and comparison, the adult U.S. population of cisgender women is approximately 128,000,000. The total population of transgender women supposedly "threatening" and "silencing" them was about 500,000. That's about .04%, or less than one-half of one percent.[191] [192] Yet these trans women apparently wielded power over cisgender women not seen since Emperor Palpatine powered up the Imperial Death Star.

The title of Anna March's reply in *Salon* the following day, "Memo to Crotchety Old Feminists…" said it all.[193] You could almost *hear* the eye-rolling of millions of young women as they muttered to themselves *sotto voce*, "Okay, Boomer…"

March compared Burkett's hierarchical feminist gate-keeping and rank-pulling to the same tactics being used against the lesbian "Lavender Menace" supposedly threatening 1960s feminism, who were also told they would never be Real Women— in their case because as lesbians, they didn't want to be heterosexual housewives and mothers.

As for Burkett's fury at having to endure inclusive language like "pregnant people," March advised her to "stop talking about inclusive language as something that erases you and your vagina… There simply isn't anyone erased by using a word that includes everyone."

But the Language Genie was out of its bottle for good, and the *Times* would devote half a dozen more pieces, including one on its front page, to the vast dangers of trans-inclusive words.

Perhaps in a sign of how unusual and troubling this behavior was from the *New York Times*, *Salon* published a second piece *the same day* by Katie McDonough criticizing Burkett and the *Times* for their lack of *nuance, patience,* and *empathy.*"[194]

Even *Cosmopolitan* jumped into the act: "Would it have been more feminist for Caitlyn Jenner to be on the cover of Vanity Fair in a pantsuit? Perhaps. The same thing could be said about Madonna, Kerry Washington, Tina Fey, Cher, Scarlett Johansson, Jennifer Aniston, and a whole host of other women who have been on the *VF* cover in various states of cleavaged and aggressively sexy poses…"[195]

When a rag like *Cosmo*—synonymous with sensationalized, hyper-sexualized headlines like "*What Your Va-jay-jay is Dying To Tell You,*" and "*An Orgasm Almost Killed Her—We Are Not Kidding,*" and "*Touch His Secret Erotic Spot (It Doesn't Rhyme With "Shmenis")*"—publishes a 2,400 lecture on the joys of feminism and inclusion, you know you're in trouble.[196]

But Burkett's piece also drew surprising support from some quarters, particularly among other white, urban, educated, upper-class, second-wave feminists who felt left behind by younger trans-positive feminists and deeply resented their acceptance of transgender women *as* women, but feared saying so in polite company.

Ironically, prominent among these was Bette Midler, who had honed her signature campy delivery and risque' side patter, "They had me booked at Fire Island, but they couldn't find room in the bushes." playing to packed rooms of gay men at Manhattan's well-know sex club, the Continental Baths.[197]

Midler would enthusiastically tweet in all caps: "REQUIRED READING!!" FOR WOMEN!!" and also, "They don't call us 'women' anymore; they call us 'birthing people' or 'menstruators,' and even 'people with vaginas'! Don't let them erase you!"[198] [199] Midler would later defend the exclusionary and transphobic things she had said by tweeting that there wasn't "anything exclusionary or transphobic in what I said…"[200]

These first two articles had attacked only trans adults; in fact, they really attacked only transsexual women. But the next article directly targeted trans kids. It was subtle, but it was the first of a flood of pieces playing to the right's virulent hostility towards transgender kids.

Chapter Four:
Stop Giving Trans Kids Affirming Care

Title: "How Changeable Is Gender?"[201]
Date: Aug. 22, 2015
Byline: Richard A. Friedman
Section: Opinion
Words: 1,999

"The idea that we had to be fair to Republicans-vs.-Democrats instead of being fair to the public and the facts, was a great gift to professional political liars. They were able to insert fake issues into mainstream news [and] see their falsehoods repeated by 'objective' journalists... Old-fashioned journalism has been no match for right-wing propaganda. It's been a slaughter."[202]

Mark Jacob, Former Editor of *Chicago Tribune* and *Chicago Sun-Times* in *PressThink*

Making Society Less Tolerant

"How Changeable Is Gender?" is the *Times* maiden voyage into misrepresenting pediatric medical care, and it's an unmitigated disaster. It may have been a measure of the *Times*' own lack of confidence in it, that it was published in Opinion—as if the research and data it cited were a matter of private belief—rather than in the Science or Health sections.

As SPLC noted, it was around this time that websites central to the attacks on trans kids' care were launching—TransgenderTrend and 4thWaveNow among them—which have played leading roles in promoting fear-mongering and conspiratorial claims about transition.[203]

It was also a time when the 19 anti-trans bills were being introduced in state legislatures, which would soon grow into hundreds of bills annually.[204] [205]

It was the first in a long line of *Times* articles attacking care which appeared to be closely synchronized with claims by the Christian right and anti-trans parent groups who were permanently enraged by the idea of teen transitions.

Richard Friedman was a Cornell Medical College professor of clinical psychiatry who had no apparent expertise in or publications about transgender people generally, or trans kids specifically. He did have a renowned background as an early proponent for normalizing homosexuality—which makes his hostility to transgender people and their medical care all the more puzzling and sad.[206] [207] [208]

His op-ed opens with a commendable discourse on gender existing on a spectrum and a plea for more tolerance towards transgender people.

Having dispensed with the pleasantries, Friedman settles down to his real topic which is the same recycled biological essentialism as Burkett: gender = biology, and anatomy and can't be changed. Yet just three years later, the *Times'* own Science Desk published "Anatomy Does Not Determine Gender, Experts Say" which would *directly contradict* everything Friedman was asserting, Specifically, it would declare that:

> *"Defining gender as a condition determined strictly by a person's genitals is based on a notion that doctors and scientists abandoned long ago as oversimplified and often medically meaningless... The idea that a person's sex is determined by their anatomy at birth is not true, and we've known that it's not true for decades."*[209]

To prove his assertion, Friedman cites a single obscure 2014 study by a Viennese neuroscientist with no apparent expertise in transsexuality which found minor morphological differences in the subcortical connectivity of 23 transsexual women.[210] [211]

Intellectual Malpractice

Based on this, Friedman makes the striking declaration that "transgender people have a brain that is structurally different than the brain of a nontransgender male or female — someplace in between men and women." For a Cornell medical doctor this is so medically obtuse as to qualify as intellectual malpractice.

Having now established that transsexuality is linked to irrevocable differences in brain biology, Friedman argues that there's no point in providing medical care to change someone's gender when it is unalterable and cannot be changed.

He starts with adults, trotting out the well-worn TERF canard that gender dysphoria with one's body is the result of social intolerance, asking rhetorically, "How many transgender individuals would feel the need to physically change gender, if they truly felt accepted with whatever gender role they choose?" The answer is: none.

Dysphoria is a discomfort with one's body, not with a lack of social acceptance (painful as that might be).

A reverse way to frame Friedman's question might be, "How many Cornell doctors would feel the need to undermine trans medical care, if they truly accepted of the fact that trans people actually existed?"—but I digress.

To provide the appearance of "balance," Friedman describes what seems to be a highly positive meta-analysis of 28 studies encompassing nearly 2,000 participants, which found that transsexuals overwhelmingly *improved* after receiving medical care. Alas, he dismisses it a few sentences later because some of the 28 studies were "suboptimal." This, from a man who paragraphs earlier had diagnosed the entire population of transsexuals based on a single study of two dozen Viennese women.[212]

Friedman makes no attempt to review any of the 28 studies that might not be "suboptimal." As SPLC documented in Project CAPTAIN, this pattern of having a high-to-impossible threshold of evidence for studies which find that treatment is beneficial and a low-to-no threshold for studies which find treatment isn't helpful is one common hallmark of anti-trans pseudoscientists, and it was a pattern that would feature prominently in almost every *Times* article that cited facts around affirming care.[213]

Three-Card Monte

Having dismissed this one seemingly positive survey of 28 subjects, Friedman then introduces what he *thinks* is a "negative" study—one cited so often by anti-trans ideologues it's been nicknamed— "The Swedish Study"— which supposedly found that affirming care doesn't work.

However all it did was compare suicide rates for transgender people after care with suicide rates among the average Swedish population.[214 215]

As Zack Ford noted on the news site *Think Progress*, Friedman is playing Three-Card Monte with his facts. He never mentions that suicide rates were *only* higher for those who received their care *before* 1989, and ignores that those in the study afterwards had rates comparable to the rest of the Swedish public.[216] In other words, if a Swede transitioned in the 60s, 70, or 80s, perhaps their life was problematic; on the other hand, if you transitioned from the 90s on you were probably no more or less miserable than any one else in Sweden.[217 218 219]

Nonetheless, based on this, Friedman concludes that gender-affirming care isn't all it's cracked up to be, concluding that gender transitions don't make trans people any happier.

This is flatly untrue.

We know it is untrue because Cornell, Friedman's own institution, has thoughtfully provided an analysis of 72 outcome studies, along with links to 51 of them on its online portal called, "What We Know."[220 221] It is the first example of the *Times* twisting the data in order to support an argument based on prejudice rather than facts, that refutes both the science and medical consensus.

In addition, the U.S.'s first pediatric gender clinic (GeMS) had been open at Boston's Children's Hospital since 2007, and it —along with dozens of clinics that followed in its wake —have compiled almost a decade's worth of extensive clinical experience with thousands of adolescents. Those studies show that affirming care has been highly effective at improving suicidality among kids.

Having shown adult affirming care for adults is

ineffective, Friedman turns his attention to children, citing Richard Green's notorious "sissy boy" studies from the 1970s and 80s which sought to prevent homosexuality in "effeminate" homosexual boys, as well as a Dutch study that included all kinds of gender-diverse kids.[222] As one might expect, both of these found that most of the kids identified with their birth genders as they aged, proving that gender identity in cisgender (and, by extrapolation, transgender) kids is likely fixed at a very young age.

It never occurs to Friedman that his "*gender identity in kids isn't stable*" argument also means that we can never know if cisgender kids really *are* cisgender.

As Diane Ehrensaft of UCSF's Adolescent Gender Center's told *Vox*, "When kids whose gender matches the sex on their birth certificates say, 'I know my gender,' nobody questions that… But if a kid says, 'I know my gender,' but it's not the sex on their birth certificate, people ask, 'Oh, how could you possibly know that?'"[223]

A Very Different Story

Friedman also declared that since up to 80% of trans kids *desist* and detransition to their natural state of blissful cisgender-ness, just as with adults, affirming care is not a good idea, and even if it was, the evidence is "simply poor," there are "no randomized clinical trials," and there is "an absence of good treatment-outcome data."

Randomized clinical trials (RCTs) in which one group gets a therapy or medicine and the other is denied it are considered unethical with clinical practices that already have long track records of effectiveness. This appears to be the reason the FDA has actually discouraged their use to test pediatric affirming care.[224] [225] [226]

Luckily, Friedman's claims have been repeatedly tested in open court, and trial judges who review the actual data tell a very different story. For instance, a Florida State judge found that while trans-denialists "stridently assert that the evidence supporting treatments is 'low' or 'very low quality'… the evidence purportedly showing these treatments are ineffective or unsafe is far weaker—not just of 'low' or 'very low' quality, [but it is actually] nonexistent."[227]

Similarly, a federal judge in Georgia said that: "[L]ess than 15% of medical treatments are supported by 'high-quality evidence.' In other words, 85% of evidence that guides clinical care, across all of medicine, would be classified as 'low-quality' under the scale used by Defendants…"[228]

In place of actual treatment, Friedman recommends so-called "watchful waiting," which involves keeping trans kids closeted and denying them any social affirmation of their correct gender identity. A more accurate name for "watchful waiting" would be "passive denial."

The words "watchful" and "waiting" are supposed to imply that parents are actively conducting something like due diligence prior to reaching a decision. But this is a head-fake.

As the term "waiting and watching" is used, young people are forced to suffer through the wrong puberty, which is why it is embraced by Christian nationalist, TERF, and trans-denial groups like PITT, TransgenderTrend, and 4thWaveNow—and denounced by major medical associations like the American Academy of Pediatrics (AAP), the AMA, and 17 other medical organizations…

…including Friedman's own—the American Psychiatric Association—which found that "'watchful waiting" lacks scientific support and "can cause adolescents immense harm."[229] [230]

Friedman also embraces "conversion therapy" to cure trans kids, declaring that while "there is abundant evidence" that it hurts *gay* kids, there is none that it hurts trans kids."

Yet just two months later, the U.S. Substance Abuse and Mental Health Services Administration (SAMHSA) declared precisely the opposite in a report entitled, *Ending Conversion Therapy: Supporting and Affirming LGBTQ Youth.* "Interventions aimed at a fixed outcome… including those aimed at changing gender identity or gender expression are coercive, can be harmful, and should not be part of behavioral health treatment."[231]

That same year, the American Academy of Pediatrics (AAP) condemned "reparative" or "conversion" therapies as "unfair and deceptive," and in 2018 they issued an additional statement, explicitly declaring that such therapies "have been proven to be not only unsuccessful but deleterious, and are considered outside the mainstream of traditional medical practice."[232] [233] [234]

It's subtle, but Friedman just moved the goalposts to accommodate his own biases, which were that on one hand, the evidence for affirming care isn't strong enough, so we shouldn't be giving it to trans kids; but on the other hand, there's no evidence *against* "conversion" therapy for trans kids, so why not try it on them?

Friedman's op-ed is really announcing the *Times'* willingness to engage in repeated goalpost-moving, and, in pursuit of its trans-skepticism, a *black-is-white/up-is-down* reporting style that flies in the face of the research, medical consensus, and clinical research. That has come to characterize all of the *Times'* trans-denial pieces on pediatric care for the next decade.

Friedman closes with what might seem at first like a

commonsense rhetorical question: What could be wrong with holding off care and treating transgender youth with "a little skepticism."

But forcing kids to watch their bodies undergo the wrong puberty is not *a little skepticism*; it's a lot. At the very least it is a major family medical decision with enormous consequences for kids as teens and, later, as adults when, like me, they have to endure the pain, cost and trauma of trying to unwind what were once easily preventable physical changes. Moreover, studies have repeatedly found that parental rejection is among the strongest predictors of transgender suicidality.[235]

Friedman's "simple question" also betrays a deeper priority which remains unspoken but nevertheless informs all of the coming trans-denialist writing: *Better a hundred transgender kids have their medical care delayed or denied and suffer through the wrong puberty, than one cisgender kid make a mistake and has to detransition.*

Because of this, across nearly a decade of trans-denialist stories, the *Times* does not conduct even a minimal analysis of the costs of the skepticism which it is promoting, and how it will affect trans kids. They are not its concern.

The Default Frame

Despite all the right-wing hysteria, pediatric affirming care is a pretty standard part of medicine. Until the Christian right decided to make it a political issue, thousands of trans kids were receiving hormones and blockers in all 50 states without comment or controversy. Moreover, both have been provided to cisgender kids since the 1980s (more on this later), and so the science around their modest side-effects is well-known and settled. The only objections to it are religious or political.

Yet Friedman's trans-skepticism has become the *Times'* default frame for all journalists about teen transitions. To do so, it has taken a posture of institutional distrust towards medical consensus, accumulated clinical experience, the self-report of thousands of trans kids and affirming families and tens of thousands of trans adults, as well as the growing number of quality academic studies. I am unable to think of any other area of medicine where the *Times* has been so aggressive about promoting its own doubts over the nearly-universal judgment of the medical community. But as Upton Sinclair warned, "It's difficult to get a man to understand something when his income depends on his not understanding it."[236]

Sulzberger and the *Times* are now willing to go after transgender kids; indeed to mount a decade-long journalistic crusade against them. Friedman's op-ed was its first step.

Chapter Five: Trans Women Are Invading the Women's Room

Title:	**"A Bathroom of One's Own?"[237]**
Date:	**May 18, 2016**
Byline:	**Peter H. Schuck**
Section:	**Opinion**
Words:	**789**

Title:	**"Is It Time to Desegregate the Sexes?"[238]**
Date:	**October 15, 2016**
Byline:	**Julie Shulevitz**
Section:	**Opinion**
Words:	**2,574**

A Site of Earlier Victories

"Protecting the dignity of transgender Americans is a noble cause [including] their equal access to housing, jobs, services and other social opportunities," announces Peter Schuck in his opening. He means everything—housing, jobs, services—except of course bathrooms, which those cisgender people that we're now so equal to would have to share with us.

Public restrooms have been white Christian nationalists' preferred site for social panics for 125 years, beginning it in its crusade to stop Black civil rights, then women's rights, then gay rights, and now transgender rights.

During Jim Crow, the white evangelical right launched a social panic across the South with vile racist portrayals of Black men as predators on white women trying to relieve themselves in what would now be in close proximity, and of Black women as carriers of disease that would be spread via shared sinks and toilets.[239] [240]

Christian nationalists then updated this In the 1960s to attack the emerging *homophile rights* movement with a moral panic over homosexuals lurking around every men's room, waiting to seduce young men into lives of depravity.[241]

And in the 1970s, when bipartisan Congressional majorities easily passed the Equal Rights Amendment, Christian nationalists returned to the public bathroom as Phyllis Schlafly and her Eagle Forum launched a new social panic, claiming, in part, that the ERA was a Trojan horse *unisex bathroom bill* that would force vulnerable women and girls to relieve themselves right next to male predators.[242]

Leveraging the anti-segregation language of Jim Crow, she claimed the ERA would "integrate public toilets." One flier made the connection even more explicit: "Do you want the sexes fully integrated like the races?"[243]

It was a racist dog whistle no Southern legislator could miss and few could afford to overlook, and in 1982 the ERA would fail by just three states—all in the South.[244]

And now, for the 2000s, WCN groups have returned to the site of all their earlier victories to launch yet another social panic over transgender women invading the public women's room.

A distinguished Yale law professor, Schuck is far from a neutral party: he is listed on the website of the ultra-right Federalist Society which was well-known for supporting virulently anti-trans candidates for the bench, and to which a newly-elected Trump was about to outsource his reshaping of the federal judiciary and the Supreme Court in just a few months.[245] [246]

"Safe As Your Own Bedroom"

Schuck's outrage was supposedly triggered by an Obama directive noting that it expected public schools to allow trans students to use bathrooms consistent with their gender identity, hotly claiming that the administration had embarked on a "bathroom war."[247]

He left out that the administration had *already* been applying the law this way for several years —a fact of which Schuck, as a Yale law professor, could hardly have been unaware.[248]

Schuck makes the bizarre claim that "most people consider [public] bathrooms almost as safe and intimate as their bedrooms"—which makes me wonder when was the last time he used bathrooms at LaGuardia Airport, Yankee Stadium, or in NYC's Penn Station during rush hour.

It does not occur to him that trans people have *never* had the luxury of considering public restrooms as "safe and intimate spaces," because 59% of trans adults and 39% of trans kids avoid them out of fear of harassment, bullying, and assault. But our safety is not on Schuck's mind: "How uncomfortable are [cisgender] people with the prospect of those with different anatomies sharing [our] bathrooms?"

Then, as inevitably as the sun rises in the east, Schuck trots out the unicorn-like specter of the male sexual predator who declares himself trans so he can attack women in public restrooms.

This canard is especially appalling in light of the fact that studies find that 27% of transgender boys and nonbinary youth assigned female at birth, 18% of transgender girls, and 18% of nonbinary students assigned male at birth report having been *sexually assaulted* in "safe and intimate" restrooms and locker-rooms.[249 250 251]

And these terrible rates are even higher in conservative jurisdictions where local laws force them to use the wrong facilities.

Schuck proposes that transgender kids settle for "alternative bathroom arrangements that might strike a better compromise among legitimate conflicting viewpoints,"—by which he means *stay out of the women's room.* Ironically, his op-ed appeared just six months before North Carolina's Gov. McCrory would lose his office after the country rallied against his state's trans bathroom ban, HB 2.[252]

On to the Locker-Room

Julie Shulevitz extended Schuck's argument to transgender girls in locker-rooms.

As Jack Mirkinson would point out in *The Nation*, Shulevitz is actually updating Anne Roiphe's legendarily homophobic 1997 *Times* piece, *The Trouble at Sarah Lawrence*, which turned out to be lesbians. "Might it be possible, without reversing the sexual revolution or infringing on anyone's civil rights, to suggest an effort to control the visibility of homosexual activity, so that the campus can again attract some of the students who are now frightened off?"[253] [254]

Loose translation: *Can the lesbians please cool their jets and stop scaring the straight girls?* Similarly, Shulevitz's asked whether it might be possible to address the "problem" of transgender girls if they would just cool *their* jets and stop scaring the cisgender girls.[255] In what was a major departure from Roiphe's piece, Shulevitz turned to white Christian nationalists as the authoritative voices for her article. Her op-ed is even titled, "Is It Time to Desegregate the Sexes? Here is the unmistakable echo that transgender girls' presence amounts to Phyllis Schlafly's old battle cry about the dangers of '"unisex bathrooms.'"

Shulevitz opens by pitting what she calls a "girl-born-a-girl" against a "born with a boy's body" girl, encapsulating her whole argument: that transgender tolerance is a zero-sum game in which it is only possible if cis girls lose something. She repeatedly invites readers to consider the feelings of the *girl-girl* who doesn't want to strip naked before the *boy-girl*. But, like Schuck, she never considers the feelings of the latter, who is being publicly humiliated. Such a young trans person is the centerpiece of a lawsuit brought by Alliance Defending Freedom, which is suing a school on behalf of evangelical parents, who claim the girl's mere presence in the locker-room violates their religious beliefs.

In fact, ADF had emailed school superintendents across the nation in December of 2014, encouraging them to defy the Obama guidelines on transgender bathroom and locker- room use, and offering *pro bono* legal representation if they were sued for doing so.[256] [257]

Shulevitz blandly identifies ADF, in passing, as "a Christian legal advocacy organization with mostly evangelical clients," but it has been classified as a hate group by the Southern Poverty Law Center, and since this is the first of many times they will be quoted as an authoritative source on transgender kids, it's worth pausing to unpack their status.[258]

Founded in 1993, ADF was envisioned as a "well-funded, well-trained army of religious rights attorneys" dedicated to imposing an evangelical agenda on the U.S. by leveraging the U.S. legal system.[259] As its training program declared, ADF "seeks to recover the robust Christendomic theology of the 3rd, 4th, and 5th centuries [and its] catholic, universal orthodoxy…"[260] [261] ADF has built a business model out of seeking out white evangelical corporations, schools, families, and individuals who will claim that their religious beliefs are violated by LGBTQ+ people exercising their civil rights, and then attempt to redraw the law in favor of the former. They have met with notable success.

Since ADF's goal is making the U.S. a white evangelical nation ruled by scriptural principles, it is deeply committed to eradicating all rights for gay and transgender people and has litigated or filed in almost every important anti-LGBTQ+ case.[262]

Abroad, ADF has fought to preserve the death penalty law for "aggravated homosexuality," and to preserve laws in 20+ EU countries that until recently required trans people to undergo compulsory sterilization before they could legally change gender.[263] [264] [265]

In ADF's Biblically-ordained society, there will be little tolerance for other people's faiths, races, gender identities, sexual orientations, or for any reproductive right of any kind.[266] It is one of the great ironies of white Christian nationalists that they are so successful at leveraging the very civil and legal rights that they hope to deny to everyone else after they prevail.

As the crusade unfolds, the *Times* has habitually quoted Christian nationalist groups like ADF, using the most anodyne language possible. A Media Matters and GLAAD analysis found that the *Times* consistently "obscures the anti-trans background of sources [and has] erased histories of extremist rhetoric or actions."[267]

It is easy to miss how radical this is: as an authoritative source on transgender kids, the *New York Times* is citing a group which has linked being LGBTQ+ to pedophilia, and whose leaders have called the "homosexual agenda" a "conspiracy comparable to Nazi propaganda." They then virtually turned an entire op-ed department into a platform for its views.[268] [269]

Another Rubicon is quietly being crossed: Christan nationalist hate groups dedicated to eliminating all rights for transgender kids have been henceforth considered legitimate sources of expertise on them, in the *Times*.

A Tilted Playing Field

Although Shulevitz presents locker-rooms as a nationwide issue, beyond two cases brought by ADF she presents no further context or data, even though it appears likely that both arose from ADF's plaintiff-shopping for anti-trans lawsuits it could bring on religious grounds. It will not be the last time the *Times* will cherry-pick legal disputes instigated by ADF to suggest some larger, pervasive, and urgent national trend.

Shulevitz approvingly cites the well-known TERF

group Women's Liberation Front (WoLF)—without disclosing that it has twice received significant grants from ADF, as well as libertarian Harvard Law professor Jeannie Suk Gersen, then midway through her own dismaying transphobic series of articles in the *New Yorker*.

About the only pro-transgender voice Shulevitz offers is her own—certainly not my own first choice—because apparently she didn't interview any transgender kids, or their parents, or LGBTQ+ advocates, or pediatricians, or teachers, or school administrators.

In fact, she does not appear to have even spoken with the ACLU, which is most often opposing counsel in the flood of lawsuits ADF has filed on behalf of white evangelical wedding cake bakers, white evangelical photographers, white evangelical website designers, white evangelical school athletes, and now white evangelical parents bent on defending the sanctity of their local school locker-rooms.[270 271 272 273 274]

According to news reports, on more than one occasion ADF has even stood up Christian-oriented companies as little more than Potemkin façades, simply so it can bring lawsuits asserting their right to discriminate against LGBTQ+ people.[275]

Yet Shulevitz accepts every statement by ADF and its evangelical plaintiffs at face value. This includes their claim that the mere presence of a trans girl violates their religious beliefs, declaring piously that we cannot dismiss this intolerance as "mere intolerance."

When pressed on this by the ACLU's Chase Strangio on Twitter (now X), Shulevitz at first doubled-down on her declaration that ADF was simply defending "religious freedom," before deleting her posts and then ghosting him.[276]

But a federal appellate court in a similar ADF lawsuit would conclude what Shulevitz was unable to: namely, that in school locker-rooms—where everyone regularly undresses in front of one another—even the most modest kids have no real expectation of privacy and even if they did, personal prejudice towards a trans girl—whether religiously-based or not—is not a license to discriminate.[277]

"The Imagination of Bigots"

Finally, as surely as the sun rises in the east, Shulevitz, like Schuck, trots out the unicorn-like specter of the male predator who declares himself transgender so he can attack cisgender girls in locker-rooms and restrooms.

In the 73 years since Christine Jorgensen began using women's rooms after her highly public 1952 transition, there have been exactly *zero* actual reported cases of this fabled creature being spotted in the wild. We know this because the *Times'* own Editorial Board had *just pointed out* six months earlier that it "exists only in the imagination of bigots."[278] [279]

Alas, they are bigots to whom the *Times* is entirely willing to turn over its op-ed pages.

As Media Matters has documented, the *Times* coverage would recycle this vile canard over and over, often followed by weak counter-statements like, "…but transgender advocates dismiss this as unfounded," as if it had now covered "both sides" of the issue so readers could make up their own minds.[280] [281] [282] [283] [284]

Notably, the *Times* did not do this with other claims by Christian nationalist groups such as that gay people are pedophiles, the 2020 election was stolen, abortion was murder, Democrats want immigrant voters to replace white people, or vaccines cause autism.

But when it came to transgender people, the *Times* would suddenly morph into Fox News: "*We report. You decide!*"

Pieces like Burkett's could be written off as one woman venting her spleen, and Friedman's and Schuck's as medical and legal discussion, even if they were right-wing ideologues.

But Shulevitz's piece is something different: it runs in the Opinion pages but it is the first to be presented more like news coverage of current events. It is also the first to turn to white Christian nationalists as its main sources of "expertise," and then to unequivocally take their side. Most importantly, it is also the first piece to unambiguously train the *Times'* immense journalistic firepower directly at the lives of transgender kids.

It will not be last.

Chapter Six: Chest Binders Are *Dangerous*

Title:	**"Chest Binding Helps Smooth the Way for Transgender Teens, But There May Be Risks."[285]**
Date:	**May 31, 2019**
Byline:	**Amy Sohn**
Section:	**Well**
Words:	**1,350**

Amy Sohn's was the fourth piece attacking various aspects of trans teens' transition, its subhead adding ominously: "People who use binders report symptoms like back and chest pain, overheating and shortness of breath." Reading this it might first appear to readers that Sohn had accidentally overlooked the vast dangers posed by raw or chafed skin, but she would get to those, too.

Unlike the last two anti-kid pieces, this was not only presented as straight news, but it was not published in Opinion, but in the Well Section as factual health reporting. It was not.

Transgender teens face any number of major health risks, often made worse for those who are low-income, of color, undocumented, disabled, or rejected by hostile families.

While such risks can and do include severe depression, suicide, contaminated street hormones, sexual assault, school bullying, family rejection, excessive policing, over-commitment to foster care programs and over-incarceration in juvenile probation systems, chest binding is not among them.

This is just the first in what would become a long-running series of articles sensationalizing and politicizing teen transition, and their hallmark would be dark warnings of impending harm for what were common, safe, and well-known practices.[286]

Noting that teens who bind often go to hormones, Sohn warned ominously that hormones can harm teens' "future fertility," which is not true (more on this later).[287]

To pump up the drama, she then quoted a terrified mom worried that her son "is causing irreparable damage." This is from a *binder*, folks: an athletic bra on steroids (pun intended).

Cosmo had recently run an article stripped of all this *Times*-ian scaremongering titled, "A Complete Beginner's Guide to Chest Binding," featuring such crucial medical advice as "12. Oh My God, Wash Your Binder."[288] Even BuzzFeed was able to run a binder piece without all the medical alarmism.[289]

But Sohn's piece was well-timed to appeal to a MAGA readership, coming out just a month after the Heritage Foundation hosted one of the first public presentations by the evangelical right on banning teen affirming care, and also just as the number of anti-care bills introduced in state legislatures would be about to explode.[290] [291]

In another strange bit of timing, Sohn's piece also ran almost exactly one year after a *Magazine* article devoted nearly 6,000 words to the memory of six gay journalists who worked at the *Times* in the 1980s when Rosenthal's homophobia still ruled the newsroom and its coverage of gay men and AIDs was terrible—but apparently the credits didn't transfer.[292]

Of Raw Skin & Chafing

Sohn provided only a single unambiguous quote on how binders reduce gender dysphoria—the very reason that trans boys use them in the first place—and she does not appear to have interviewed a single LGBTQ+ organization, pediatrician, or medical assocation.

Instead, she noted that "some worry" that binding causes "self-hate"—a favorite accusation by TERFs who believe that trans males ought to learn to enjoy having women's breasts. To validate this absurd accusation, Sohn turned not to psychologists or pediatricians, but to Rethink Identity Medicine Ethics, which she identified as "examining standards of care for gender-variant children."

It does not.

ReIME is devoted to eradicating both transgender medical care and transgender kids. It promotes "conversion therapy," believes that affirming care is both unnecessary and dangerous; claims trans teen suicide rates are inflated; denies that teens are competent to consent to blockers or hormones; and encourages professionals to avoid providing them under any conditions. [293]

In addition, one of ReIME's co-founders has reportedly blamed trans men for causing "lesbian erasure," while the other,—Jane Wheeler, whom Sohn quotes — reportedly planned a panel on how trans rights was "utilizing gay children as fodder for scientific experimentation."[294] [295]

Sohn also quotes 4thWaveNow, which she calls "a community of parents and others concerned about the medicalization of gender atypical youth." In fact, SPLC identifies 4thWaveNow as a "pseudoscience website" that considers affirming care "a vast conspiracy [that pushes] gender ideology" on kids.[296] Typical posts include comparing care to Nazi eugenics experiments and also to "alien mind control." (I am not making this up).[297]

4thWaveNow has published a detailed denunciation of binding entitled, "Breast Binders and the Helpful Strangers Pushing Them on your 'Son,'" which implies that trans boys were being assaulted by unnamed outsiders.[298] Even a casual review of 4thWaveNow's website and materials, replete with its childish putdowns and self-satisfied sarcasm, would have revealed it was being a risibly bad choice for a source.

Despite this, 4thWaveNow and ReIME are the *only* advocacy organizations Sohn quoted. She also briefly quoted two physicians who provide care as a gesture at "balance."

To recap, on one side we have rabidly anti-trans groups devoted to stamping out affirming care and preventing kids from being transgender, while on the other side we have doctors that have actually treated trans kids and are trying to stick close to the science.

"Binding or Suicide"

Looking back, Sulzberger appears to have reached a decision not only to focus on kids' transitions, but to cater to the prejudices of right-wing readers by treating them as controversial, unproven, and unsafe. Maybe he sincerely believes it; maybe it's for subscriptions. Either way, the specter of this tiny subpopulation of already-embattled kids just trying to live their own lives being repeatedly torpedoed by the world's largest and most powerful private news publisher is, in its own way, quietly despicable.

Weirdly for a piece almost entirely devoted to the attack on binding, since it was published in Well, a helpful breakout nearby included upbeat links to "Common-sense binding guidelines," a teen's How-To video, and online binding vendors. Please make up your mind.

Sohn only presented a single transgender teen in the entire piece, and then it was a young man whose dysphoria was so fierce that he intentionally bought a binder too small and developed skin problems—supporting the thrust of the story line that binding is dangerous. Even so, the *Times* buried him below the fold.

As one physician told Sohn at the end: "[I]t's strange to me that someone would think of a binder as being a form of self-harm when there are so many other garments used by gender-typical people to change their appearance that are also extremely uncomfortable…" (I'm looking at YOU, high heels).

Only in the final sentence, almost as an afterthought, did Sohn mention the elephant in the room: that if transmasculine teens *were* given blockers and hormones they wouldn't develop breast tissue in the first place, and thus would never need to bind. It's such an obvious point, but would derail Sohn's focus on the harms of binding, and in any case it would have challenged the *Times'* institutional skepticism about all things transition-related.

To its credit, the Reader Center at the *Times* (which is far from a monolithic institution) seemed to realize this, and posted a request for letters with the headline, "Do You

Use Chest Binders? Tell Us About Your Experience." The collection of impassioned and often tormented letters that resulted two weeks later was poignantly titled, "It's Binding or Suicide."[299]

Read one from 24-year-old Vincent Burke: "The first time I put a binder on I cried out of pure happiness. I was flat for the first time since puberty. Putting a shirt on over it was like actually seeing myself, and a tiny sliver of confidence poked out of the writhing mass of self-loathing that gender dysphoria created."

Another from 17-year-old Raphael Sanchez read: "Binding is not fun. It's not a trend. We are well aware of the risks. But for many transmasculine people, it's binding or suicide."

Chapter Seven: Trans-Denialists Are Doing Great!

Title: **"Those People We Tried to Cancel? They're All Hanging Out Together."[300]**
Date: **November 2, 2019**
Byline: **John McDermott**
Section: **Style**
Words: **2,599**

One of the more bizarre pieces published in the anti-trans crusade appeared in Style, which was then under former Gawker bad-boy editor Choire Sicha.

Of the 13 people featured by writer John McDermott, all but three had been "cancelled" for writing or vlogging transphobic hit-pieces, so the "we" in the headline was misleading. An honest headline would have read, "Those Writers You Transgender People *Cancelled*? They're Having a Blast."

It was an in-your-face celebration of the thriving careers of a *who's-who* of anti-trans writers, in what *Xtra* writer Katelyn Burns called the "transphobic journalist grift economy that has popped up over the last six years mostly on Substack." These are content creators who have produced transphobic and trans-denial writing, and then harvested the resulting outrage to build careers, followings, and bank accounts.[301]

It was hard not to read the piece as a giant "fuck you" to the trans community, which was beginning to make those same criticisms of the *Times* for the same kind of writing.[302] It would not be the last time the *Times* editorial staff showed itself capable of stooping low to get a little *payback* at the expense of the transgender community when it was feeling aggrieved.

The accompanying illustration showed a vulnerable, feminine, young white woman, oblivious to the giant black-hooded goblin stalking her from behind, as if these writers and podcasters, who had made unprovoked attacks on transgender kids, were the *real* victims.

As usual, everyone McDermott profiled was severely under-identified, and there was literally not a single trans voice anywhere. It was another closed loop: cisgender people interviewing other cisgender people to get their feelings about transgender people.

Dance of Defiance

McDermott opens with Alice Drager (again), who had been interviewed by writer Katie Herzog for her infamous piece in *The Stranger,* entitled, "The Detransitioners: They Were Transgender, Until They Weren't"—which says it all.[303] [304]

Detransition is another favorite of illiberal cis writers because while they and their audiences *can't* imagine being transgender, they *can* imagine transitioning and having it be all a terrible mistake. Ironically, exactly what transfixes and horrifies them—having one's body forced to become the wrong sex—is exactly what the transgender youth they are attacking are trying so desperately to avoid.

Herzog had quoted the author of the same vile theory

that Dreger defended: that transsexual women are really straight men in the grip of a weird sexual perversion, and also quoted Canadian sexologist James Cantor, who has suggested adding "P" for pedophiles to LGBT, and whose attacks on affirming care are cited by ADF.

Herzog had also cited the discredited theory of Rapid Onset Gender Dysphoria (RODG): that youth are coming out because they are victims of peer pressure that creates a *social contagion*[305] [306] [307] [308] [309]—even though it is an order of magnitude more likely that many trans kids do *not* transition because of peer pressure, family rejection, and social hostility.

For all this Herzog was roundly criticized online, and now reports feeling shunned and "cancelled." In his sympathetic interview, McDermott did not mention that Herzog went on to create a Substack blog and podcast with professional trans-denier Jesse Singal that has covered such fun topics as denying the science behind transgender care, and testing ways to get ChatGPT to say the N-word.[310] [311]

With Singal himself, another poor unfortunate who has been "cancelled" by the Horde, McDermott neglected to mention his *Atlantic* cover story on trans issues; his long-form piece in *The Cut*; his book review in the *NYT*; his three-year editing gig for *New York Magazine*'s website; his podcast; his Substack column; or his book deal with Farrar, Strauss, and Giroux. As a community, we are really doing a shit job at this *cancelling* thing.

McDermott also sympathetically profiled Bridget Phetasy, whose articles have railed against "biological men competing as women;" the transgender people's attempt to 'indoctrinate children into *gender ideology* and "trans them;" the "dehumanizing" effects of trans-inclusive words" and so on.[312] Not to mention her podcast featuring trans-denier Helen Joyce, "They're Sterilizing Gay Kids!"[313] [314]

Their cries of being "cancelled," which are pretty much like Sulzberger's own claims of being attacked, are really just resentment at the fact that the digital age has provided the transgender community—for decades a sitting duck for attacks by academia, psychiatry, feminism, and the media—with tools of pushback that are highly public and highly scalable. It's not so much that these people are being "cancelled," as their outrage at losing the privilege of attacking trans people at will in a consequence-free environment.

McDermott offered up almost a dozen more like Singal, Phetasy, and Herzog, nearly all as odious, and cheerily quoted from each in turn, cheering their newfound successes and celebrating their warm support for their fellow cancel-ees. Claps on the back all 'round. They were certainly doing a lot better than the community they were attacking.

The whole piece was best summed up by Singal, who, without a shred of irony, observed that, "I have lost Twitter friends, but I haven't lost real-life friends."

But I *have* lost friends. And many of my friends have lost friends: to suicide, drug use, early death, addiction, or violence. And even among those who aren't in my circle, I carry the names of scores of dead transgender people whose murder vigils I've organized or attended, or whose parents I've tried unsuccessfully to console.

For McDermott and his writers, the stakes are whether anti-trans writing might cost them some followers. It never occurs to them that the stakes are very different for those whose lives they're trolling for clicks and amusement. They're appealing primarily to white, educated cisgender heterosexual with little or no personal experience of being on the wrong end of the stick.

As The New Republic pointed out, as McDermott was publishing his celebration of anti-trans writers and podcasters the Trump administration was eliminating federal recognition of trans people; the DOJ was asking the Supreme Court to withdraw their civil rights; trans servicemembers had been banned from the military (again); the Bureau of Prisons had eliminated protections for trans people behind its bars; and Health and Human Services had proposed new rules to enable it to begin denying child-welfare, HIV/AIDS prevention, and anti-trafficking services to transgender Americans.[315] TNR doesn't mention it, but that year the right's attack on access to pediatric care was taking off in earnest, and the murders of transgender women, mostly young and Black, were also hitting a new high.[316]

Yet at the end, McDermott observed—again without a shred of irony—that "cancellation presents a question about power, who has it" and who doesn't. As if it was the trans community and the Horde that held the real power here.

Chapter Eight:
Trans Girls Are Destroying School Sports

Title:	**"Who Should Compete in Women's Sports: There Are Two Almost Irreconcilable Positions"**
Originally:	"Who Gets to Compete in Women's Sports"
Date:	**August 18, 2020**
Byline:	**Gillian R. Brassil and Jeré Longman**
Section:	**Sports**
Words:	**2,304**

Title:	**"What Lia Thomas Could Mean for Women's Elite Sports"[317]**
Originally:	"Much Debate but Little Dialogue on Transgender Female Athletes"
Date:	**May 29, 2022**
Byline:	**Michael Powell**
Section:	**Front Page (print) / U.S. (digital)**
Words:	**2,951**

"[Billie Jean] King, arguably the main face of gender equality in all of sports, said… 'I've spent most of my life working for equality for all. Sport has given me an incredible platform because sports are a microcosm of society and can be used as a catalyst for social change. Everyone should be treated equally.'"[318]

Julie Kliegman, "Idaho Banned Trans Athletes From Women's Sports. She's Fighting Back," *Sports Illustrated*

"This season left Thomas feeling both liberated and besieged... Thomas has been threatened and called so many names online that she turned off some direct messaging... Every day this season felt like a challenge to her humanity."[319]

Robert Sanchez, "'I Am Lia': The Trans Swimmer Dividing America Tells Her Story," *Sports Illustrated*

The Cage Match

NYU professor Jay Rosen is famous for his epigrammatic advice for how media should cover Presidential elections: *Not the odds, but the stakes.* In other words, not the horse-race, but the consequences for democracy.[320] A similar injunction to the *Times* might have been, *Not the conflict, but the context.*

But Brassil and Longman go for conflict from the start. The original headline—"Who Gets to Compete…"—implied that trans and cis girls were competing for limited slots, medals, or scholarships, while its subhead—"two irreconcilable positions"— implied that they were engaged in a colorful cage-match, pitting them against one another.

This is nonsense: the real problems of girls' sports are the lack of funding, decent facilities, equipment, and media attention—not to mention the ugly tide of coaches found to have molested their own athletes.

But the hook here is *Trannie* Cage Match, and first up is runner Lindsay Hecox, who they describe as competing in her "declared gender." Simiarly, in Powell's sports piece 10 months later, swimmer Lia Thomas is described as competing in her "chosen gender identity." Translation: cis girls *are* girls; trans girls *decide* to be girls.

As FAIR points out, this is particularly noxious for Powell, who contrasts Thomas' "chosen" womanhood against cisgender girls who have "fought hard" for their rights as women—as if they were there because they had earned it, while Thomas just walked by on a whim.[321]

This kind of language is the transphobic equivalent of the old anti-gay slurs "chosen lifestyle" and "lifestyle choice," which was used by the evangelical right to imply that homosexuality was freely chosen and thus could be just as freely given up.

However, with trans girls this framing is especially loaded, inviting the longstanding TERF canard that a flood of males will temporarily "chose" to be girls in order to invade women's sports and take over the medal stands—even though this has never happened in the history of sport, or in the history of the known world.

Sure enough, *uber*-TERF Martina Navratilova, who has been leading the charge on this front, shows up right on cue to make precisely this accusation, declaring that "any male could "decide to be female," take hormones, and become a super-athlete before "going back to making babies."

For good measure, Navratilova adds gratuitously that if she ever had had to compete against a transgender woman, she would have had "no shot"… except that Navratilova *had* competed against a transgender woman—Renée Richards in the Finals of the 1977 U.S. Open Doubles, crushing her handily in straight sets: 6-1, 7-6. But Powell apparently doesn't have internet access, and so cannot fact-check Navratilova's obvious falsehood.

Brassil/Longman also profile the author of one of the nation's first anti-trans sports bills: Idaho Falls' own Rep. Barbara Ehardt, whom they identify as deeply "concerned" about transgender girls who she believes will dominate sports and drive out cisgender girls so that all "the progress women have made over the last 50 years is for naught, and we will be forced to be spectators in our own sports."

Unfortunately, at least in Idaho, they will be spectators looking down on empty stadiums, because before Ehardt's bill was even introduced, she helpfully admitted to an Associated Press reporter that she was unaware of a *single one of* Idaho's 125,000 teen athletes who was transgender.[322]

This even included runner Lindsay Hecox, who told ESPN when she heard of Ehardt's bill, "'I said to myself, this applies exactly to me. 'How many other trans women athletes are in the state of Idaho?'"'[323]

There were none. But like Powell, Brassil/Longman also lack internet access, and so never read the AP's story.

.025%: Not One in the Past Decade

In between the fearmongering, Brassil/Longman do point out in passing that of 200,000 athletes in women's college sports, only about 50 are transgender—that's 0.025% or one-quarter of one percent—and only one has won an NCAA championship, and even that was a regional, *not* national, meet.

This includes Idaho's Hecox, whose biological advantages as a trans woman were so overwhelming that she failed to make the Boise State's Women's Track team when she went off to college the following year, explaining disarmingly that, "I literally just love the sport and don't care if I'm in last place or first place [but there were] too many good female athletes."[324] [325]

For all the apocalyptic vibe of these *Times* articles, most trans girls are just looking to enjoy their sports. Or as one exasperated mother of high school field hockey player put it: "[A]ll my daughter really wants to do is sing 'Pitch Perfect' on the bus to out-of-town games, and throw up after she does too many burpees."[326]

Well below the fold Brassil/Longman also noted in passing that, "[T]here has been no large-scale dominance of transgender athletes in women's sports." But this crucial bit of context is just one sentence, buried 1,000 words down, *after* all the fearmongering, when it should have been in the first paragraph.

Where the Consensus Was

Trans kids in sports only became an issue because the American Principles Project (APP) had been conducting field research in 2019 to find an issue that could reignite the stalled anti-gay culture wars. After North Carolina's bathroom debacle and Gov. McCrory losing office, Republicans were gun-shy, and none wanted to touch LGBTQ+ issues. As APP's president Schilling later explained, they had had no particular issue with trans kids in sports, and the animus had surprised them. It was just that their field research showed that it was "where the consensus was."[327]

In fact, trans women and girls had been competing in NCAA sports without any problem or complaint for almost a decade.[328] I know this, and both Brassil/Longman and Powell knew it, because it was the *Times* that broke the story in a remarkable investigative piece by Jeremy Peters in November, 2019.[329] [330] So there was no big, irrevocable conflict arising naturally over who should compete —

despite Navratilova's fearmongering—none had or were about to dominate women's sports. On the contrary, it was a non-existent problem until APP and ADF found that it would motivate the base and enable white evangelical Republicans like Erhardt to run on LGBTQ+ issues again.

Brassil/Longman also introduced Connecticut runner Andrea Miller, but omitted mentioning that ADF hand-picked her as the poster girl for its anti-sports lawsuit because she was the *only trans-female athlete* in the country having any success. As Shannon Minter of the National Center for Lesbian Rights noted, "[Miller] was their Exhibit A. And there was no Exhibit B—absolutely none."[331] It didn't hurt that Miler was also Black.

Nonetheless, Brassil/Longman mentioned the problem of "safety" *three times*, suggesting that trans girls lining up to run are in danger of somehow harming their cisgender competitors. This is a track meet, people.

In ADF's lawsuit against Miller, one of the three plaintiffs complained publicly that, "No matter how hard you work, you don't have a fair shot at victory." Which—like Navratilova's—would have been a great argument except that she immediately went on to beat Miller handily in two races over the next nine days.[332] Another ADF plaintiff complained that, "All the biological females know who is going to win before we even start. It's sad to see that all our training just goes to waste."

Again, it would have been a great argument except that *she,* too, went on to beat Miller two days later.[333]

Brassil/Longman get lost in the biology, arguing about the testosterone ranges acceptable for various governing bodies: "5 nanomoles per liter," "10 nanomoles per liter," and ".12 to 1.79 nanomoles per liter compared with 7.7 to 29.4 nanomoles."

None of this has *any* bearing on the real topic, which is the evangelical right's Biblical objection to transgender women. This explains why their attacks were so remarkable in their sheer pettiness and spitefulness—pushing to ban trans women from chess, darts, sailing, roller derby (?), and even seeking to disqualify a 13-year-old who won an obscure regional Irish Dance competition.[334] [335] [336] [337] [338] If you're willing to disqualify a 13-year-old in Irish Dance, what difference will all Brassil/Longman's discussion of *10, .12, 1.79, 7.7,* or *29.4 nanomoles* make?

A Record Unheard of in Any Sport

At six feet tall, her height already put in the top 99th percentile of women, and she was obviously stronger and certainly faster than any woman she raced, posting record times in the 400, 800, and 1500-meter freestyles, and then in the 500, 1000, and 1650-yard events.[339] In one World Championship, she finished a full 14 seconds ahead of the cisgender woman who finished second.[340] After she went undefeated for *13 straight years*— a record unheard of in any individual sport, men's *or* women's—there was the inevitable grumbling that she was so dominant that racing her was unfair and everyone knew the winner before the race had started.

Panicked to maintain the integrity of their sport, the international swimming body, FINA, banned her and others like her from women's competition permanently.

Oh wait… that was cisgender athlete Katie Ledecky.[341]

And FINA didn't ban her: they celebrated her incredible 13-year dominance of swimming and promoted it publicly. Because *biological advantages* only count when *transgender* women have them.

The Panic Over Lia Thomas

Powell's piece opens with a lead, though it could have come straight from ADF's talking points: "The women on the Princeton University swim team spoke of collective frustration edging into anger… [and] parents and grandparents, sisters and brothers of swimmers… talked about the thousand of hours the young women put in… [only to have] 'a biological male taking over women's sports…'"

As with the Brassil/Longman coverage of runners Lindsay Hecox and Andrea Miller, Lia Thomas is quoted only briefly, and then from public statements, since it appears she, too, was not interviewed. This reduces these athletes to little more than coat racks on which to hang anti-trans scare stories. As FAIR pointed out in regard to a similarly awful sports story in the *Washington Post*, trans women in these stories never *confront* problems or challenges: they appear only as problems and challenges which cis girls must overcome.[342] [343] [344]

Powell tags all the bases in a show of balance, but also puts his thumb heavily on the scale. He quotes just three people who are unambiguously supportive of trans girls' participation, while quoting three times as many who are opposed, including three athletes, two physiologists, one biologist, one law professor, one philosophy professor, and one angry mother—10 in all.

Thomas is no doubt an outstanding swimmer, but for all Powell's *sturm und drang* over her supposed "advantages," he never mentions that even her big NCAA win was well behind a record time, and there were *27 other records* set by *cisgender women* at the same NCAA event, none of them hers— including an unbelievable 18 records broken by swimmer Kate Douglass. In other words, despite the very dramatic headline, Thomas's participation probably would have meant very little to women's sports.

Not the conflict, but the context.

Trans sports stories in the *Times* always seem to exist in two registers, as if they're written by two writers who aren't entirely on speaking terms.

On the one hand, trans women were bigger, stronger, faster, biologically dominant, and cisgender girls have no chance against them. On the other hand, and always well towards the bottom, trans women were a fraction of 1% of athletes, none of them have ever dominated anything, only two had done well against top NCAA's Division 1 athletes, and none had ever made the Olympics.[345]

Although it's at the very end of his piece, to his credit, Powell closes on a note that finally humanizes Thomas the person: *"Ms. Thomas lost by a broad margin. She slipped out of the pool, picked up a towel, sidestepped embracing swimmers and walked out, a solitary figure. 'In fairness to Lia,' he said, 'the emotional toll.' He added: 'I look at her and see the pressure she's under. And I think: She's a 22-year-old kid.'"*

Chapter Nine:
Trans Kids Are a Social Craze

Title:	**"Trans Rights and Gender Identity"**[346]
Originally:	"Gender Identity"
Date:	**September 7, 2021**
Byline:	**Jesse Singal**
Section:	**Books**
Words:	**1,638**

The Clicks, Not the Crazy

If the *Times* wanted one reportedly professional trans-troll to hire another, to write about a third, it couldn't have done much better than having Book Review editor Pamela Paul bring Jesse Singal in to review Helen Joyce's ode to unabashed transphobia, "Trans: When Ideology Meets Reality." It was a trifecta.

This was same Singal who TransLash noted was among the first mainstream journos to spread the lie that kids were *catching* transgender through a *social contagion*, and who seemed to relish provocative attacks on the community, while harvesting the outrage.[347]

It was also the same Singal who had such white-bro *fun* on his podcast trying to get ChapGPT to say the N-word. In a moral breakthrough for illiberal white bros everywhere, Singal declared that the only way to end racism was to "recognize that race is mostly made up… [and stop] seeing people as 'Black' or 'Asian' or Latino'."[348]

Singal was already the writer of a noxious 2018 trans denial *Atlantic* cover story titled, "When Children Say They're Trans." The cover art screamed pure clickbait: "Your Child Says She's Trans. She Wants Hormones and Surgery. She's 13."[349] This same *Atlantic* editor, Jeffery Goldberg, had interviewed Sulzberger, milking the outrage of publishing this, right during Pride Week, and he went on to publish scores of *trans-ploitation* pieces.[350]

As *Jezebel*'s Esther Wang reported, Goldberg had recruited veteran UK culture warrior Helen Lewis, known for working both sides of the street: declaring her sincere "belief that trans women are women and trans men are men…" in the *New Statesman,* before complaining in the *Times of London* that trans acceptance had gone so overboard that a women could no longer "challenge someone with a beard exposing their penis in a women's changing room."[351] [352] [353] [354]

Wang explained, hiring people with retrograde ideas in the name of diversity of opinion was not new for the *Atlantic*. In 2018, the magazine announced it had brought on the rightwing ideologue Kevin Williamson who was known for comparing Black children to primates and for writing in the *National Review* about Laverne Cox's lovely *TIME* cover story, '[W]hether he has had his genitals amputated, Cox is not a woman, but an effigy of a woman… [who has] amputated healthy organs in the service of a delusional tendency…'"[355]

This op-ed was reprinted in the *Chicago Sun-Times,* which would eventually retract it under fire and apologize—mumbling the now-standard line about "presenting a range of views… initially struck us as provocative…" Translation: A *junior editor thought it would be good for traffic, but now everyone is pissed off at us, and since we've already milked it for all the clicks, it's coming down.*

As if this wasn't enough, Goldberg fired Williamson a month later after Media Matters noted that he had suggested that, "Women who have abortions should be hanged."[356] Apparently this crossed a line invisible to everyone but Goldberg, who had initially defended his hiring of Williamson as part of his deep and abiding commitment to "my mission to… achieve gender equality and racial diversity… [so] that we are ideologically diverse… [which] opens us up to new audiences."[357 358]

Bingo—we have a winner: when you promote misogynist and transphobic bigotry you tap into new markets. Sulzberger's marketing plan exactly.

However, Goldberg's deep commitment to "diversity in all forms" did not include transgender people, because, like the *Times*, the *Atlantic* had never had a transgender person on its masthead since its founding in 1857. Between them it was an unbroken string of three and half centuries and counting.[359]

The *Times* also got burned dipping its toes into the MAGA waters, trying to get the clicks but not the crazy, announcing the hiring of Quinn Norton as a lead editorial writer to great fanfare… only to fire her before the day was out after the Twitterati noted she had used both anti-gay and racial slurs, and befriended a writer at *The Daily Stormer*, a particularly odious neo-Nazi/white supremacist website.[360]

Even more humiliating was the experience of the

once-venerable BBC, which published 4,000 words of overheated click-bait entitled, "The Lesbians Who Feel Pressured to Have Sex and Relationships with Trans Women" about cisgender lesbians who claimed they were being attacked for being transphobic over refusing to sleep with transgender women.[361]

It was based entirely on a single online anti-trans hate group, "Get the L Out," which simply polled its own Twitter followers. After the inevitable outcry, an internal review would find that it violated even the BBC's own low standards for reporting.

That would have been bad enough, but apparently, swinging for the fences, the piece also folded in noted UK transphobe and porn star Lily Cade, then being investigated for multiple claims of sexual assault. Cade posted an exuberantly unhinged 15,000-word rant online, claiming that transgender women were self-mutilating men "with a mental illness… vile, weak, disgusting, whiny, fake-victim masturbators, predators… rapists… evil pedophiles… a pedophile cult…" Adding, unnecessarily, that "I'd execute every last one of them."[362]

Shocked at its oversight, the BBC issued a full retraction, apologizing profusely to its readers generally, and to the transgender community specifically. Just kidding. As with the *Atlantic* and *Chicago Sun-Times,* and nearly every other outlet caught with its hand in the transphobic cookie jar, the BBC simply doubled-down, editing Cade out, while declaring that the piece remained "an important piece of journalism that raises issues that should be discussed."[363] [364]

Pedophile cults, executing trans women, penises in the changing room, people of color as primates, hanging women who need abortions, and the Jewish billionaires behind the transgender movement (more on this in a moment)—this is what mainstream media had brought itself to, trying to milk the clicks, but not the crazy.

And as it sought to move further right in search of new eyeballs beyond the long shadows cast by TikTok, Twitter, Buzzfeed, and Facebook, it was experiencing the same content-moderation issues. Except that social media's content problems came from random users posting erotic, racist, or violent content, while mainstream media's were entirely of its own making because of the journalists with whom it was now choosing to get into bed.[365]

"No One Has Ever Gone Broke…"

Although Singal's *Atlantic* piece was supposedly about transgender kids, nearly everyone in it had detransitioned, and, thus, was actually cisgender. As Alex Barasch noted in *Slate*, the piece was "without a single happy, well-adjusted trans teen among its host of central characters for the first 9,000-plus words… a trend that can be seen throughout Singal's history of biased reporting on trans lives."[366] [367] Singal was also known for a strangely sympathetic 11,000-word profile in *The Cut* of yet another Canadian sexologist, Ken Zucker, whose clinic had been closed amid allegations of inflicting "conversion" therapy on trans kids.[368] [369] [370]

As researcher/activist Andrea James has noted, "No one has ever gone broke publishing anti-trans hit pieces." Singal's book review of *Trans: When Ideology Meets Biology* by one of UK's more prominent TERFs, Helen Joyce, was no exception. [371] [372]

When Ideology Meets Biology identifies transgender as a *social contagion*, calls trans women *males*, declares that most trans children "grow out of it," and recommends *watchful waiting* and "reparative" therapy to cure them in *lieu* of affirming care, which she calls "a fast track to sexual dysfunction and sterility" being pushed on manipulated and damaged children. And that is just the introduction—literally.

Singal gives a great deal of attention to attacking the straw man of *gender ideology*—a phrase cultivated by the Catholic Church to promote its paranoid view of a global gender conspiracy that is advancing homosexual, women's', and now transgender rights in order to eradicate all differences between men and women, thus eliminating the basis for the heteronuclear family and Ending Life on Earth As We Know It.

Joyce cleverly expands this *gender-identity ideology* to be specifically anti-trans, and Singal runs with it, attacking what he sees as the many harms inflicted on cisgender women by transgender women, and along the way—as surely as the sun rises—he trots out the unicorn-like specter of males who pose as trans so they can attack cisgender women in restrooms.

Singal complains that gender non-conforming kids "are told from a young age that if their sex or its associated gender roles make them uncomfortable, that's because, despite their body, they have a 'boy brain' or a 'girl brain' and that's who they really are on the inside… [S]o their only real choice is to transition or to suffer forever… despite evidence suggesting that gender dysphoria… [often] dissipates over time…"

Not a word of this sentence is true.

Andrea Long Chu, writing in *New York m*agazine years later in "The Moral Case for Letting Trans Kids Change their Bodies," would credit this piece for "providing a template for the coverage that would follow it. First, it took what was threatening to become a social issue, hence a question of rights, and turned it back into a medical issue, hence a question of evidence. It then quietly suggested that since the evidence was debatable, so were the rights. This tactic has been successful: The political center has moved significantly on trans issues."[373]

When the Mask Slips

Joyce had been a writer for the British weekly the *Economist*, which had its own awful history of transphobic coverage, but she can sound quite reasonable when she chooses. However, like nearly all TERFs, she can also be rabidly transphobic and prone to wild conspiracy theories when the mask of reasonability slips off. For instance, on Megyn Kelly's Sirius Radio show, Joyce apparently suggested that the Assistant Secretary for Health, a transgender woman named Rachel Levine, should kill herself, mangling the Biblical injunction that "better that you tie a millstone around your neck and cast yourself into the sea than that you harm children like this."[374]

You'd be better off dropped in the middle of the lake with a millstone around your neck. Doom to the world for giving these God-believing children a hard time!"

As *Assigned Media*'s Evan Urquhart has pointed out, this passage is often used by far-right extremists to threaten violence against transgender people in a way that is socially acceptable.[375]

It was also Joyce who was in Bridget Phetasy's podcast, "They're Sterilizing Gay Kids," and among those trans-denialists whose successes McDermott's article had celebrated. On the podcast, Joyce declared that being transgender was "an obvious crazy delusion," and that when "you decide that men can be women [then]… gay rights organizations become horrific, rape-y, disgusting organizations trying to push heterosexual men on lesbians and sterilize gay kids." She added that transgender women were "crossdressing men who get a sexual kick out of going into women's changing rooms."[376]

As reported by the ACLU's Gillian Bransetter, on another podcast Joyce also wove anti-Semitic conspiracy theories into her transphobia, blaming the increasing social acceptance of the transgender movement on three Jewish billionaires.[377] This canard is a central tenet of Christian nationalism, as the Anti-Defamation League notes. Supporters of the Great Replacement Theory believe that being gay and transgender is "promoted by Jewish elites to decrease white birth rates," and because of supposed "Jewish plans to 'replace' the white population with Black and Brown people."[378] It was why white Christian nationalists paramilitary groups marching in 2017 in the Charlottesville, VA rally that turned deadly were chanting, "Jews will not replace us!"[379]

We are obviously not in Kansas anymore, and just a few feet shy of QAnon, Pizzagate, and tinfoil hats because the CIA is reading our thoughts. It is simply impossible to imagine the *Times* quoting someone who is so spectacularly unhinged on any topic other than transgender children, and, as such, it provides a litmus test for just how far down Sulzberger is wiling to go to monetize right-wing transphobia.

Part Two:
A Plain Old-Fashioned Crusade:
The Attack on Care

2015	2016	2017	2018	2019	2020	2021	2022
							U.S.
							Health
							Opinion
							Opinion
							Opinion
							Opinion
							Opinion
							Magazine
							Health
							Science
							Americas
							Opinion
							U.S.
Books							Health
Opinion	Opinion			Style			Health
Opinion	Opinion			Well	Sports	Books	U.S.

"In the past eight months [of 2022] the Times *has now published more than 15,000 words' worth of front-page stories asking whether care and support for young trans people might be going too far or too fast. ...That cumulative figure of 15,000 words doesn't include the 11,000 or so words the* New York Times Magazine *devoted to a laboriously even-handed story about disagreements over*

the standards of care for trans youth; or the 3,000 words of the front-page story from its designated anti-wokeness-beat reporter, Michael Powell, on whether trans women athletes are unfairly ruining the competition for other women; or the 1,200 words of the front-page story on how trans interests are banning the word "woman" from abortion-rights discourse... [or] 2,000 or so words in the story from the roundup box about intimidation and violence against trans people. The Times *published that one on page A25. Page A1 is where questions go. This is pretty obviously—and yet not obviously enough—a plain old-fashioned newspaper crusade.*

"Month after month, story after story, the Times *is pouring its attention and resources into the message that there is something seriously concerning about the way young people who identify as trans are receiving care..."*[380]

> Tom Scocca, "The Worst Thing We Read this Week: Why Is the *New York Times* So Obsessed With Trans Kids?", *Popula*

"Perhaps no mainstream publication did more in 2022 than the New York Times *to shift the mainstream conversation around transgender equality away from obstacles to access in housing, employment, and health care and toward the idea that the most pressing issue facing the trans community is actually too much medical care."*[381]

> Ari Drennan, "The New York *Times* Helped Fuel an Anti-Trans Panic in 2022. Will 2023 be any better?", Media Matters

The Full Weight of Its Authority

The *Times*'s anti-trans coverage had been slowly circling trans teens: Friedman in 2015, Schuck and Shulevitz in 2016, and Brassil/Longman and Powell in 2020 and 2022. They have been picking one issue after another: binding, bathrooms, locker-rooms, sports. But in all of these, only Friedman's had directly attacked providing medical care to transgender children or teens, and then only at the very end of is *Biology-Is-Destiny* op-ed. Otherwise, the *Times* had left family medical decisions, as they did with procedures like teen abortion or breast surgery, where they belonged: between parents, kids, and their physicians.

But that was about to end. Seven years after Friedman, as Sulzberger was putting his imprint on the *Times*, its coverage pivoted again, putting the full weight of its immense journalistic authority on *manufacturing doubt* about affirming care, and undercutting public and political support for it, just as WCN groups and their Republican sock puppets in state legislatures were busily turning *their* attention to making it illegal. It was a deadly combination.

As noted earlier, the *Times* provided excellent ammunition for these attacks, and began showing up regularly in statements by Republican legislators and in legal briefs filed by Christian nationalist legal groups like ADF in support of banning affirming care.

Roughly 1,700 anti-trans bills have been introduced since 2015, with most targeting trans kids, and about one-third (468) of them specifically target some aspect of their access to medical care and/or transition.[382] [383] But just as the *Times* was proving ammunition for state bans on care, it was also undercovering or actively ignoring them in print.

It didn't bother to cover bans enacted in Mississippi and Tennessee until a month afterwards, and ignored similar bans in Arkansas, Kentucky, West Virginina, and Wyoming until the day they were signed into law, or even weeks afterwards.[384]

So while a single trans woman swimmer, a couple hundred trans boys getting top surgery yearly, and trans-inclusive language were all front-page news, thousands of trans kids losing their access to their medical care across six states barely warranted a mention. It was as perfect an illustration of Sulzberger's news priorities as possible.

The *Times* would devote only one substantive article on the nationwide legislative assault: Megan K. Stack's exemplary "When Parents Hear That Their Child 'Is Not Normal and Should Not Exist'")[385] [386] But three negative articles on various facets of teen transitions would also be published by the Health desk's Azeen Ghoryashi alone, from January to September of 2022, including one on the front page.[387]

In fact, from her perch on the Health desk "covering the intersection of sex, gender, and science," Ghorayshi would become a kind of *go-to* writer for anti-care articles, publishing no less than five trans-skeptical pieces in the space of just 15 months: May 4, 2022 (detransitions), June 10 (the rise in trans teens), July 28 (UK halts care), September 26 (teens having top surgery), and August 23, 2023 (on a small number of detransitions at a St. Louis gender clinic which the *Times* then appeared to take a victory lap for helping shut down the following month).[388]

I spoke with parents of trans kids who were leading state-wide activists in Georgia and Texas who felt so burned by *Times'* reporters that they would no longer speak with them, and advised any parent within earshot to do likewise. Missouri's LGBTQ+ advocacy organization, PROMO, even went so far as to put out a state-wide "Community Alert," warming families not to speak with Ghorayshi and asking for help in tracking her efforts because of the "immense harm" her writing had done.[389]

But it was Emily Bazelon's horrific, "The Battle over Gender Therapy" in June, 2022 that distilled every bit of damage the *Times* could do to kids' affirming care into 8,000 words, becoming, in the process, one of the *Times* most-quoted pieces by the evangelical and Republican right.

It was a kind of backhanded vindication of Sulzberger's vision of remaking the *liberal rag* into a digital destination for the right, and while folks at groups ADF and APP might not be exchanging their Fox or Newsmax logins for *Times* subscriptions, at least they were now quoting from it in their attacks on trans kids.

Teen medical care was qualitatively different from anything that the *Times* or the extremist right had gone after before: sports, bathroom use, and name changes were things trans kids *did,* but attacking care attacked something they *were.* Teens could drop sports teams, use different bathrooms, and suffer through misgendering—but they had no alternative to the enormous humiliation and dysphoric pain of watching helplessly as their bodies were forced to undergo the wrong puberty.

Yet the meta-narrative the *Times* began promoting was that the major problem facing these youth—who are already underserved and marginalized, and whose care was under active assault —was *too many kids getting too much care too quickly:* exactly the same line being pushed by the Christian nationalist right.

The name for this is "concern trolling": pretending to

care about trans kids, while actually working to defeat their expressed needs because it would "help" them (*"we're only doing this for your own good"*). As if transgender kids needed to be protected from unintentionally harming themselves with their own gender identities, much as one might protect an infant child from hurting themselves from touching a hot stove.

It's a political strategy that trans anthropologist Mikey Elster calls "insidious concern," in which assaults *on* trans people are framed as compassion *for* them.[390] All the while actually *ignoring* the real and pressing life problems trans teens were actually struggling with—as this chart shows.[391]

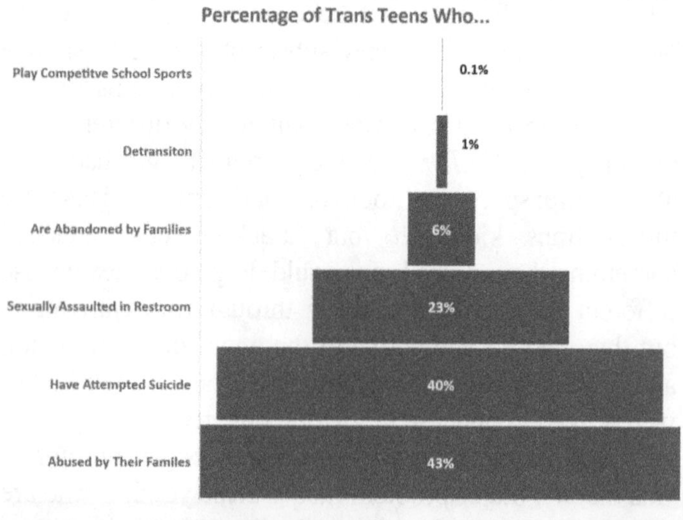

Even when the *Times* did cover these problems—and it did—it was usually in brief, one-off articles far from its front page, which still deployed its usual journalistic tricks, such as one on transgender suicides that cited a nationally-recognized expert who had authored dozens of studies during decades of research, and then cited Republicans declaring that the problem was exaggerated—as if that constituted *balance* and there were no real facts to be reported.[392] [393] [394]

The *Times* coverage was so lopsided that the satirical outlet, *The Onion*, finally encapsulated its concern-trolling in the perfect take-down piece, appropriately titled: "It Is Journalism's Sacred Duty To Endanger The Lives of As Many Trans People As Possible.[395] In their satirical story, they profile the fictional.

'Quentin' [who] is a 14-year-old assigned female at birth, who now identifies as male against the wishes of his parents. His transition was supported by one of his unmarried teachers, who is not a virgin. He stole his parents' car and drove to the hospital, where a doctor immediately began performing top surgery on him. Afterward, driving home drunk from the hospital, Quentin became suicidally depressed, and he wonders now, homeless and ridden with gonorrhea, if transitioning was a mistake..."

Chapter Ten:
Kids Who Think They're Trans Probably Aren't

Title:	**"Doctors Debate Whether Teens Need Therapy Before Hormones"**[396]
Originally:	"A Teen Trans Divide"
Date:	**January 13, 2022**
Byline:	**Azeen Ghorayshi**
Section:	**Health**
Words:	**2,043**

That Was Over Quickly

Psychologist Laura Edwards-Leeper had a promising start, working with Norman Spack when he opened the first pediatric clinic in Boston. But in the years that followed, she had become so rigid about enforcing strict medical gatekeeping on kids seeking medical care that she was well outside the mainstream of her profession, and was all but booed off the stage at conferences by other clinicians and by affirming parents.[397]

In the process, as Transgender Map notes, Edwards-Leeper has since become a preferred voice for the detransitionist right. Singal quotes her in his *Atlantic* piece ("When Children Say They're Trans"), and *60 Minutes* used her for its hit-piece on detransitions.

In an appalling *Washington Post* op-ed co-authored by Erica Anderson, titled "The Mental Health Establishment Is Failing Trans Kids," they start with the horror story of a depressed and traumatized 13-year-old who'd been sexually assaulted and introduced to drugs and violent porn.[398] This teen at first identifies as a trans boy, but with therapy eventually returned to identifying as a girl. It is an example so rare and anomalous that it cooks the books from the beginning.[399]

Both authors are *shocked! shocked!* that the therapist advising the teen's parents advised them to try affirming their child's gender—not to take blockers or hormones or get top surgery, but just to try their preferred pronouns or clothing—because it might lead to "hormonal and eventually surgical treatments."

This is totally untrue, and social transition is not a kind of *gateway drug* that gets kids hooked on the harder stuff. If it were, all the pressures inflicted on trans kids to socially conform to their birth sex would have "hooked" them on being cisgender long ago.

No matter: decrying the "rising number of detrains-itioners," they accuse the medical establishment and trans advocates of "silencing" detransitioners and "sabotaging" debate.

These efforts by the All-Powerful Trans Horde have been so successful at silencing Edwards-Leeper herself that she been reduced to appearing in the aforementioned *60 Minutes* and *Washington Post,* as well as little-known outlets like CNN, the *Atlantic*, *Quillette*, Reuters, and now the *New York Times*—where Ghorayshi gave her the lions' share of quotes. A more accurate title here would have been, "Laura Edwards-Leeper Debates Therapy."

In other contexts Leeper-Edwards uses phrases about

medical care such as: "co-opted;" "hijacked;" "off the rails;" "borders on malfeasance;" "sloppy"" "dangerous;" "substandard;" "disastrously overwhelmed" and "rushed towards the medical model."[400 401] She is not exactly a neutral Voice of Reason here.

Moreover, Ghorayshi announced in her evidence-free opening paragraphs that trans youth may be "in emotional distress or more vulnerable to peer influence," adding that "drug regimens [can] bring long-term risks such as irreversible fertility loss," "impeded bone development," and possible "detransition."

Well, *that* debate was over quickly.

After all this scaremongering, as "other side," Ghorayshi offered tepidly, the usual observations about better improved mental health and well-being. Only towards the end of the piece did she finally provide a single, unambiguous quote on what the science has already told us about delaying care: "Forcing trans and gender diverse youth to go through an incongruent puberty can cause long-term trauma and physical harm." Finally! But she quickly crushes this in her next paragraph by offering the *social contagion* lie that teens are driven to transition by TikTok and YouTube. It might have been helpful to actually interview some trans kids about this disproved claim, but although Edwards-Leeper and Anderson get four quotes between them, there are none anywhere from trans teens themselves.

More Due-Diligence-y

Ghorayshi's premise is that even *social transitions* are a huge step with major implications, so doctors should impose high standards of medical gatekeeping to prevent mistakes by impressionable teens. While this might sound reasonable, it is completely untrue.

First, let me point out once again that if social transitions were enough to override their gender identities, then having forced trans kids to live as cisgender would have already done so.

Second, in a magisterial meta-study, Florence Ashley, et al. compared the strong medical gatekeeping model against the simple *informed consent* mode, which takes teens at their word.[402] Looking at dozens of studies, they found *no difference* in regret rates between the two—which hovered at 1% or less for both.[403] In one prominent example, Ashley pointed to a long-term study of a dozen gender clinics, using the informed consent model which followed its young patients for an average of seven years. There were only 14 cases of regret among nearly 2,000 young people—a regret rate of 0.7%.[404] And although Ghorayshi doesn't mention it anywhere, this study not an outlier, but it is typical of youth follow-up studies.[405]

The three main problems Ashely cites with scaremongering about strict, long-term gatekeeping before offering care are actually obvious. First, the data for both the strong medical gatekeeping and informed consent models is the same: the teen's own self-report statements.

Second, there is no standardized test that can determine if a kid is really transgender or not, and even if there were, it would rely on those same self-report statements.

Third, when doctors *do* engage in medical gatekeeping to try to determine if a young person is really trans, they compare them against a lot of very binary and stereotypic ideas about manhood and womanhood: do they play with dolls and dress up in skirts, or play sports and dress in blue jeans, etc.

So although gatekeeping by doctors may feel more professional and *due-diligence-y*, it provides no new data and accomplishes little. This is especially true for simple social transitions, which amount to merely letting kids use their preferred name, pronouns, and clothing.

Just six months later Ghorayshi wrote about England's National Health Service (NHS) and its tragic termination of all affirming care for 5,000 teens every year following a single complaint by one detransitioner named Keira Bell. The headline described it as a "revamp," which was later changed to "overhaul," but it's was really a termination, leaving stranded the low-income kids who depend on Britain's National Health Service for medicine.[406]

While Ghorayshi cited several concerned UK physicians and Bell herself, she did not offer a single unambiguous quote about the safety and efficacy of care, nor one about the tens of thousands of kids successfully treated by NHS prior to Bell.[407] It was another debate that was over before it had begun.

While Ghorayshi did quote a parent complaining that their trans child was on a two-and-a-half-year waiting list for their first NHS appointment, she did not quote the parents of 20-year-old Alice Littman or 16-year-old Finn Hall, both of whom took their own lives the following May and November respectively, and whose families blamed NHS's long wait lists and withdrawal of care as among the causes of their untimely deaths.[408] [409]

Chapter Eleven:
97.5% of Trans Kids Persist (But, But, But…)

Title:	**"Few Transgender Children Change Their Minds After 5 Years, Study Finds"[410]**
Date:	**May 4, 2022**
Byline:	**Azeen Ghorayshi**
Section:	**Health**
Words:	**1,354**

The Encouraging Data That Wasn't

Early in this Ghorayshi piece was another of those *Times*' nonsense setups for journalistic *context:* "As tension mounts in courtrooms and statehouses across the country about the appropriate health care for transgender children…"

Where to start? First, there is no "tension;" what there *is,* is a planned, well-funded, and concerted attack by Christian national groups and their Republican allies. Second, they are not concerned about "health care;" they are determined to *eradicate* it.

Third, for that reason there is literally *no* level of medical care one could give trans kids that the right would consider "appropriate."

Fourth, Ghorayshi choses to foreground the "tension"

in courthouses and statehouses created by the Christian right but this is *nothing* next to the "tension" of families leaving behind homes, careers and pensions as they flee states determined to criminalize their kids' medical care.

Finally, the vast majority of those receiving medical care are teens, not "children"—a term favored by the right because it implies hormones might be being given to toddlers. And the "tension" in courtrooms and statehouses is nothing compared with the fear and apprehension among trans teens who know they may be forced to medically detransition.

Ghorayshi's nominal focus is a groundbreaking study from the Trans Youth Project that tracked 317 kids ages 3-to-12 who had socially transitioned at mean age of 6.5. This is well-below the threshold where trans-denialists say that kids *can't possibly know* their genders —unless they're cisgender of course. The study found that after five years, just eight (2.5%) of 317 kids had detransitioned, and about 190 of them (60%) had gone on to blockers or hormones.

What this means is that:

a) Kids who say they're trans overwhelmingly *are* trans;
b) Detransition rates are just about as small as studies, doctors, and trans advocates had been saying;
c) Since 40% did *not* go on blockers or hormones, doctors aren't rushing to push medication on every kid who says they're trans; and
d) Even five years later, social transition had not acted as a *gateway drug* locking kids into medicalization.

By any metric I can think of, this is really good news. A solid long-term follow-up study, it also contradicted a lot of their earlier coverage, so the *Times* started looking for reasons it was irrelevant, beginning with the subhead "But the study, which began in 2013, may not fully reflect what's happening today, when many more children are identifying as trans."

Of course it's out of date already.

So let's do the math: A five-year retrospective study that *Times would* accept as more reflective of 2022—assuming it would take at least 18 months to analyze the data, write it up, get it reviewed, and then published in peer review journals—would have to start in 2015. This one started in 2013; so it was off by just two years. If it had started later it wouldn't have been able to follow kids for a full five years.

Ghorayshi also protested that trans kids today are very different from earlier cohorts, for whom care has worked very well and detransition rates remained extremely low. As evidence, among other things she pointed out that more kids coming out as trans today and a higher percentage are boys than before. This might have been relevant, had she ever explained how that made them so different or why it implied that more of them were likely to detransition than earlier generations.

Finally, Ghorayshi complained that "two-thirds of the participants were white." This makes little sense given that the last census found that 59% of U.S. population was non-Hispanic white and so the study is only off by 7%—actually pretty good for research of this kind.[411]

In any case, Ghorayshi's complaint that too many of the respondents were white, educated, and middleclass was not exactly an earth-shattering shortcoming given that

—thanks to effects of structural racism—educated, middleclass and/or white families are still those most likely to: a) participate in research studies; b) be in the same location for follow-up five years later; and, c) have the money or insurance to pay for medical care in the first place so that they are available to be recruited for studies. It's like saying a long-term study of teen cisgender girls getting breast implants for their high school a graduation present has too many educated, white, middle-class girls in it.

Moving the Goalposts

What is happening here is that having repeatedly pointed to the absence of sufficient long-term follow-up studies, the *Times* was now being force to move the goalposts in order to poke holes in solid new research which inconveniently contradicted Sulzberger's stance of institutional trans-skepticism.

The complaints of an overly-white sample are especially rich coming from Ghorayshi, who, not five months earlier in her "Doctors Debate…" piece and also her piece on England's' NHS, had pointed with apparent admiration to countries that had restricted care like Finland, the Netherlands, and the UK without ever complaining that their experience was probably irrelevant for trans kids here because 98% of these countries' population was white, highly-educated, and lived under a constitutional monarchy.[412]

However there is one good reason why even good studies like these don't generalize to all transgender kids, but the *Times* never mentions it: they are limited to those whose families were affirming. Yet a poll by the Trevor

Project of 2,200 parents found that only half (54%) say they would support a trans child[413] (Other polls have found similarly high rates of parental rejection).

Finally, Ghorayshi noted that the study's cohort "has a high rate of mental health concerns," quoting Edwards-Leeper: "That's really the group I'm most concerned about these days [and] this study tells us nothing about those kids."

Fair enough. Yet Edwards-Leeper has also claimed that social transition is a huge step which often leads to "hormonal and eventually surgical treatments." But even after five years, for 40% of these kids, that is untrue.

In addition, in "Doctors Debate…" Edwards-Leeper accused doctors of "blindly affirming" adolescent patients. In other contexts, she and Erica Anderson used the inflammatory terms "hijacked;" "off the rails;" "bordering on malfeasance;" "sloppy;" "dangerous;" and "rushing kids towards the medical model"—which seem impossible to square with the fact that only 60% of this cohort moved on to medical care.

And this is not an outlier. That Komodo Health survey of 300 million insurance records found that approximately 120,000 kids were diagnosed as trans over the five years from 2017 to 2021. Yet only approximately 20,000 of these went on to receive blockers (4,780) or hormones (14,726)—or about 1*7%* in total.[414] That means that the remaining *83%* diagnosed as being transgender did not get blockers or hormones prescribed.[415]

This is even *more* conservative than the 40% in the Trans Youth Project study who did not go on to medication. But using either number, it's impossible to fit these numbers with the wild accusation that pill-happy doctors are pushing blockers and hormones on kids like candy from a Pez dispenser the moment they turn up in the office.

Two Different Standards

Actually, there is enormous social pressure on trans kids to not be trans. Ghorayshi hypothesized that the study's results may only result from the kids feeling "pressured to continue on the transition path they started..." — ominously quoting a doctor warning that "'kids get on this trajectory of development and they can't get off and... the medical interventions may be irreversible and they may come to regret it.'"

At this point, it's more than a bit like she was taking dictation from WCN's talking heads and presenting their ideas as journalism. Taken altogether, Ghorayshi was now asking for a study which had:

a) Better sampling for income;
b) Better sampling for education;
c) A different sex ratio (more boys);
d) Better control for mental health issues;
e) 7% more kids of color;
f) Begun recently but achieved long-term follow-up; and,
g) Implemented a protocol to ensure that the trans kids who continued identifying as trans weren't pressured into doing so.

Yet just two years later the *Times* would review a study of young people taking multiple psychiatric drugs in which all were drawn from a single state which it would generalize to the entire country, saying nothing about the huge demographic differences among the populations of states like Alabama, California, Maine, and Texas.[416] Nor did the article offer any Ghorayshi-like alternative hypotheses for its findings because of the sample's sex ratio, education, or income level.

The *Times* did something similar with another recent study which involved long-term Chronic Fatigue Syndrome whose sample had only *17 participants*. Not only did it fail to question the demographics or generate a hypothesis to poke holes in its finding, but it generalized the results to another illness, declaring that the results "may have implications for patients with long Covid."[417] In fact, in reviewing a dozen *Times* articles from the past two years about new studies I was unable to find a single one in which the subhead immediately undercut the findings, or so many arguments were advanced about deficiencies in its design and sample. In other words, in general, *Times* accepts *as science* peer reviewed studies published in reputable journals.

And it doesn't take a rocket scientist to see that two very different standards are being employed here.

To her credit, Ghorayshi did provide a solid overview of the study, its meaning and context, and mentioned a number of positive observations. She also thoughtfully took the time to clear up the myth, beloved of TERF and WCN groups, that most kids "desist," or detransition, as Richard Friedman cited in his 2015 op-ed.

This claim originated with Richard Green's "sissy boy" studies dating from the 1960s, and was also promoted by Canadian sexologist/psychologist Kenneth Zucker.[418] Green sought to "cure" a wide variety of boys whose parents were uncomfortable with what they considered "effeminate" behavior—throwing gay boys, trans girls, and other gender diverse children together indiscriminately.[419]

Unfortunately, this kind of scientific debunking, which should be meat-and-potatoes from the Health desk, was presented by Ghorayshi as almost an afterthought.

Yet even after being debunked, the *Times* resurrected it just two years later in another piece, this time citing some older Dutch studies which: a) like Green, combined apples and oranges, and b) assumed any child who had stopped coming had desisted—in one study 80 out of 127 kids, which is a bit like a dentist assuming a child who stops coming no longer gets cavities.[420] [421]

Chapter Twelve: Trans-Inclusive Language Erases *Real Women*

Title:	**“A Vanishing Word in Abortion Debate: ‘Women’”[422]**
Date:	**June 8, 2022**
Byline:	**Michael Powell**
Section:	**Front Page (print) / U.S. Abortion Landscape (digital)**
Words:	**1,589**

Title:	**“The Far Right and Far Left Agree on One Thing: Women Don’t Count”[423]**
Date:	**July 3, 2022**
Byline:	**Pamela Paul**
Section:	**Opinion**
Words:	**1,570**

Title:	**“In Argentina, One of the World’s First Bans on Gender-Neutral Language”[424]**
Originally:	“Adiós, Amigues: A War Over Words in Argentina”
Date:	**July 20, 2022**
Byline:	**Anna Lankes**
Section:	**Front Page (print) / Americas (online)**
Words:	**1,496**

Back in 2015, responding to Burkett, Salon's Anna March had made the commonsense observation that no one is erased when we use words that include everyone. Yet Burkett's claims that trans-inclusive words were "undermining," "erasing," and "silencing" the Real Women in the house by stealing their "right to define ourselves, our discourse, and our bodies," the idea became endlessly popular among white evangelicals and their TERF partners. Powell, Pamela Paul, and Anna Lankes ran with this *faux* outrage in three articles running to nearly 5,000 in a single *six week* period[425]—including one on the front page. It was Cisgender People Under Siege again.

Powell's studiously vacuous piece attacked the increasing use of "pregnant people" and "birthing people" mainly among civil rights, medical, and feminist organizations to ensure they did not exclude trans men and nonbinary parents when speaking about reproductive rights.

In perhaps an unconscious illustration of just how little resonance this "problem" had among young feminists, Powell turned to an 83-year-old first-wave feminist known for her attacks on the concept of "gender" to frame his piece.

He quoted a number of women who are incensed by inclusiveness, but did not ask if any of them was similarly outraged over phrases like "all mankind," "salesmen," "hi, guys," "straw man," "whipping boy," or Neil Armstrong's famous "one small step for man…"

In any case, *women* aren't "vanishing" from abortion discourse, as more trans men and nonbinary people come forward, they're simply no longer the only ones bearing children, and the importance of language that does not exclude anyone is particularly important when speaking about medical care.

Paul's piece weeks later perfectly encapsulated the *Times* tendency to use false equivalencies when dealing with transgender people. On one hand, the right is trying to strip women and others of their fundamental right to their bodies by making abortion a crime that will cause untold injury to women, including those who have been raped or incested or who are in medical emergencies.

But on the other hand, the left and trans people are trying to get people to use language that excludes them?

It is an interesting concept of equivalent harms. Or, as Press Watch's Dan Froomkin noted at the time, Paul "devotes only 52 words out of 1,300 to the right's decades-long campaign to strip women of their reproductive rights," with most of the remainder to the scourge of the left's use of inclusive language.[426]

Brimming with aggrievement, Paul hotly declared that, "Women didn't fight this long and this hard only to be told we couldn't call ourselves women anymore. This isn't just a semantic issue; it's also a question of moral harm, an affront to our very sense of ourselves… Women as a biological category don't exist."

Paul then circled back to her favorite villains, the All-Powerful Trans Horde who are "brutally" attacking any woman who dares to refuse to toe their linguistic line. She set up a column she would post shortly accusing the Horde of attacking author J. K. Rowling. And then she set up another a column she also posted shortly thereafter claiming that trans people were trying to reimpose outdated gender stereotypes that "we ditched… in the 70s." I don't know what 70s Paul lived through, but they were obviously very different from my own.

Powell returned to the meme of inclusive language with the breaking story that Buenos Aires had just become one of the first cities in Argentina to ban inclusive words in its public schools. Somehow, although this was the third article on the topic in 42 days, this ran as front-page news, making it difficult to see the article as anything other than right-wing click-bait.

Its original headline was a pun, later removed: "Adiós, Amigues." *Amigos* would be the proper formal word for "friends" and is masculine, while *amigues* is a new term intended to be gender-neutral and inclusive of women, nonbinary, and trans people.

In Spanish, as in English, masculine words are used to refer to everyone, but are more problematic because nouns and adjectives are all gendered. Power noted that other inclusive forms being adopted have been *todxs* in place of the masculine *todos* for "everyone," and *bienvenid@s* instead of *bienvenidos* for "welcome." That's gripping stuff.

The *Times* would eventually return again to the topic of language in two back-to-back pieces on April 3, 2024. The first was from right-wing Ross Douthat attacking a new Scottish law against verbally abusing minorities (using the N-word, etc.) as abridging free speech."[427] This is a favorite claim of the right: that any kind of restriction on the right to be as verbally abusive as one pleases towards minorities is state censorship, or—in Douthat's telling—a "sort of authoritarianism."[428]

That same day, academics Alex Byrne and Carole Hooven published "The Problem with Saying 'Sex Assigned at Birth,'" condemning the use of the two phrases "assigned female at birth" and "assigned male at birth."[429] AFAB and AMAB are widely used to distinguish trans people's gender from their natal sex, but the Hoovens' op-ed such terms inflict a multitude of harms, including being "confusing," "shaming," "repressive," "misleading," "patronizing," "needless," and "biased."[430]

So at 4,500 words across three articles, including two on the front-page, one wishes the *Times* would devote a fraction of this attention to the real violence done by the Christian right's anti-trans messaging which the *Times* continues to repeatedly platform without debunking, clarification, or comment, using words such as "mutilation," "disfigurement," "castrate," "sterilize," and "groomers."[431] [432] [433] [434] [435] [436] [437] [438] [439] [440] [441] [442] [443]

Chapter Thirteen:
Too Many Trans Kids Are Getting Too Many Surgeries

Title:	**"Report Reveals Sharp Rise in Transgender Young People in the U.S"**[444]
Originally:	"Number of Youths Who Identify As Transgender Doubles in U.S."
Date:	**June 10, 2022**
Byline:	**Azeen Ghorayshi**
Section:	**Front Page (print) / Science (online)**
Words:	**1,809**

Title:	**"More Trans Teens Choosing 'Top Surgery'"**[445]
Originally:	"Breast Removal Surgery on Rise for Trans Teens"
Date:	**September 26, 2022**
Byline:	**Azeen Ghorayshi**
Section:	**Front Page (print) / Health (digital)**
Words:	**3,265**

One Is Too Many

Ghorayshi's next two articles, just three months apart, were both front page trend pieces: one on the increasing number of youth identifying as trans, and the other on the rise of young trans men getting top surgeries. The first originally had a horrendous headline using the term "breast removal"—which is WCN language—rather than "breast reduction," which is both more accurate and the common term for the procedure.

Ghorayshi's first piece notes correctly that the number of young people identifying as trans has doubled. This is technically true: It has *mushroomed, spiraled, exploded* (pick dramatic adverb here) from 0.7% of adolescents all the way up to… 1.4%. It's a *social contagion* burning like wildfire through our nation's youth, but it can't even break one-and-a-half percent.

From here on, *Times* writers will repeatedly question the science behind affirming care. But whatever its supposed shortcomings, this assertion is twice better than the non-science behind this social contagion/Rapid Onset Gender Dysphoria theory, which originated in a single discredited paper based on reports of trans-skeptical or -hostile parents—not their kids—active on the three major trans-denial websites: 4thWaveNow, TransgenderTrend and Youth Trans Critical Professionals.[446] [447] [448]

The paper was initially withdrawn from publication for reassessment, and the theory has since been dismissed as a "fictitious phenomenon."[449]

Moreover, a comprehensive 2022 study published in the prestigious journal *Pediatrics* tested the idea of a Rapid Onset Gender Dysphoria spreading quickly among teens through social contagion by examining trans-identification among 100,000 kids across 16 states during the three years at issue, when the RODG paper was published and seized upon by the right. The study not only found no evidence for RODG, but it found that rates of trans-identification during the years at issue had actually *declined.*[450] [451] [452] Unfortunately, as with other studies that had inconvenient findings, this has yet to be reported in the *New York Times.*

Nonetheless, this flimsy idea, backed by little more than speculation, will become a standard talking point in nearly every future anti-trans article published by the *Times*.

Ghorayshi points that this rise has made trans kids "political dynamite, driven in part by the rise in minors seeking medical treatments." It's hard to imagine a more biased framing. First, it blames kids for the Christian nationalists' cynical use of them to drive their culture war. Even Trump pointed out to a MAGA crowd's wild response to anti-trans attack lines, "Five years ago, you didn't know what the hell it was."[453]

Second, it implies that if trans kids would just stop getting all that pesky medical treatment, then "Republican legislators across the country [wouldn't be] seeking to prohibit care…"

But we know their assaults on care are independent of trans teens' own actions. Republican legislators have repeatedly passed state laws banning affirming care, and when they couldn't find any local kids who had detransitioned they had to truck some in from out of state. They've also banned trans girls from school sports in their states, even when—like Idaho's Rep. Barbara Ehardt—they admitted they knew of none who were actually competing.

As always, the big, scary numbers come first—*Trans Teens Have Doubled*!—followed by the actual facts below the fold. In this case, that only 0.6% of the U.S. population is trans, and only about half of that is youth.[454] So this is a front-page story about 0.3% of the population. On top of that, only a very tiny fraction of this tiny fraction actually get any sort of affirming treatment.

Below are two graphs based on Komodo Health's review of 330 million insurance records. The top graph shows the number of trans kids who received puberty blockers yearly, and the bottom graph the number receiving hormones (estrogen or testosterone).

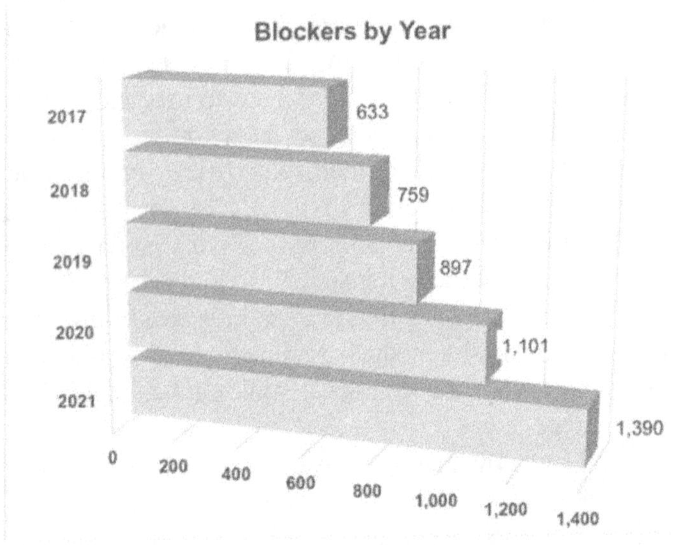

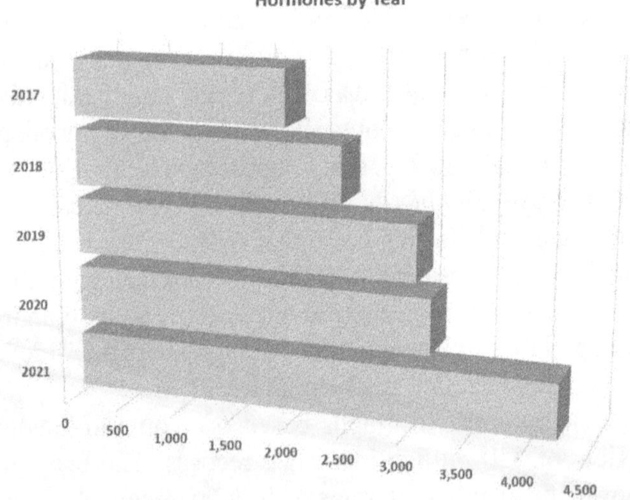

It's hard to look numbers this small and square it with the meta-narrative the *Times* has developed from multiple angles across multiple articles: *too many kids are getting too much care pushed on them too quickly.* Looking at these numbers it's also hard to understand what so many of them are doing on the front page of the *New York Times,* other than appealing to the prejudices of right-wing readers.

Missing the Big Story

But because Ghorayshi and the Times are focused solely on the tiny number of trans kids, they miss the two really big stories here. First, although the number of trans kids *is* growing, the number of LGBTQ+ kids has grown even quicker: from just 4.5% in Gen X to 22% in Gen Z. Those identifying as bisexual alone jumped from just 2% to 15%, respectively.[455]

This means, among Gen Z-ers, the largest generation in America, about one-fifth identify as LGBTQ+, with over *two-thirds* of these identifying as bisexual. It's an astonishing demographic shift.[456]

Second, and equally striking, is the movement towards nonbinary identity. As *Assigned Media* would point out, few have attempted to understand this increase. Yet studies show that from almost nothing just a decade ago, today 1-2 million young people identify as nonbinary."[457] [458] [459]

It is actually this huge jump in nonbinary identification that is really driving the *doubling* of those youth identifying as trans.

But Ghorayahi doesn't seem to have interviewed many of the kids she's writing about, or even done much digging beyond the CDC study she's writing about—which did *not even code* for nonbinary kids, yet this is quickly becoming the dominant sub-identity under the broad Transgender umbrella.[460]

Taken together, such findings are consistent with a younger generation that is increasingly rejecting simplistic binaries like gay/straight and women/man, and carving out more diverse personal identities for themselves.

We Have Too Many Top Surgeries

In her top surgery article Ghorayshi goes to great lengths to call transgender boys anything and everything… *except* "transgender boys"—which she only uses twice, and then only in direct reference to two whom she specifically profiles.

Instead, she refers variously to these boys as "young people" (once), "minors" (five times), "transgender adolescents" (six times), "teenagers"/"transgender teenagers" (10 times), and "adolescents"/"transgender adolescents" (18 times).

This is not only incredibly disrespectful, but as a rhetorical device, it subtly supports her narrative that many of those getting top surgery aren't really boys at all and are thus likely to regret the care they are getting. Which is Ghorayshi's real topic in a piece that is only nominally about top surgery. She suggests that because a small number of these "patients come to regret their surgeries," doctors should "slow down before offering irreversible procedures." But she also reports that when these boys *do* go for surgery "many report long waiting lists."

Again looking at Komodo Health's survey, the numbers have barely moved and are still miniscule: about

260 per year on average. (Komodo was only able to get three years of top surgery data, but they were three of the most recent years). Here's what this looks like:

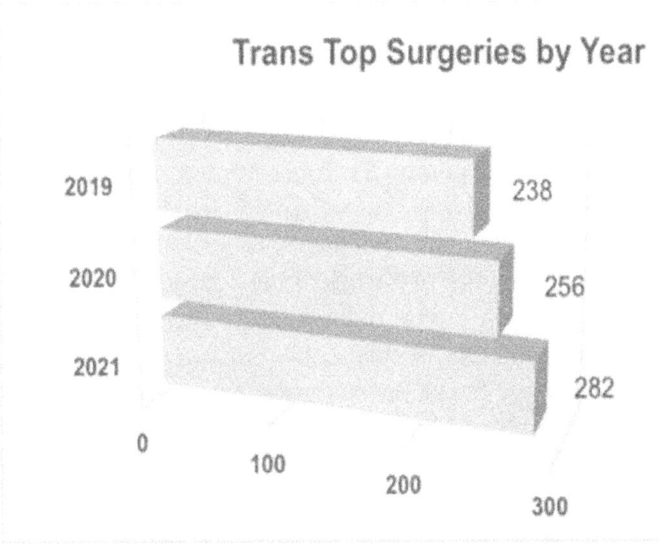

This hardly looks like a rising tide of kids going for top surgeries, as the heading implies. Indeed, Ghorayshi noted that the *Times'* own survey of the U.S. found just 11 pediatric clinics doing just 203 top surgeries among them—so even *less* than the Komodo numbers. Nonetheless she quoted a doctor making the hyperbolic assertion that the "volume has exploded."

Ghorayshi introduced detransitioners as a problem, but then quoted a doctor who said that "there are very few things in the world that have a zero percent regret rate [like] chest surgery." In fact, trans regret rates are markedly less than those of cisgender teens and adults getting breast augmentations, which is as high as 47%.[461]

Ghorayshi declares that as teens, trans boys can't consent to top surgery, but then she also notes that nearly 8,000 cisgender teens have top surgeries (4,700 of them reductions, and at least 3,200 of them breast enlargement), but presumably all of them *can* consent to theirs.[462 463]

So trans boys' breast reductions are just 6% those of cisgender teens, and just 3% of the 7,900 total cisgender top surgeries Ghorayshi mentions. If this is an "explosion," it's one of the most minute detonations in history.

To get a sense of what these proportions look like, in the chart below the two vertical bars grouped on the left are trans boys' breast reductions *vs.* cisgender breast reductions; and the two vertical bars grouped on the right are trans boys' breast reductions *vs.* all cisgender breast surgeries combined (reductions *and* augmentations).[464 465]

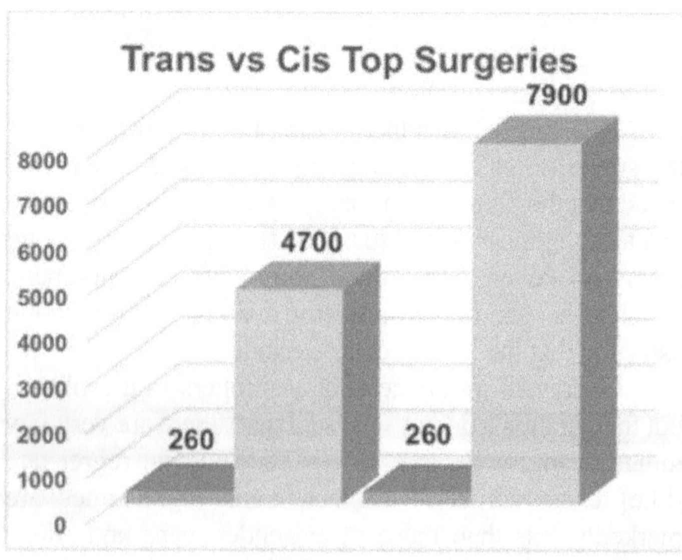

But Sulzberger's focus is on the bodies of transgender teens—even if it's only a couple hundred each year. Ghorayshi had nothing to say about the nearly 8,000 cisgender teens: not what *their* regret rates are (hint: they're higher); if *their* numbers have also increased greatly (they have); if we have enough data on *their* long-term outcomes (we don't); if a lot of *them* come to regret their procedures (they do); and if many of *them* try to reverse their surgeries (they do). Again, *not the conflict but the context.*

Totally Different Stories

To recap:

- Only a handful of trans boys are getting top surgery, and less than a dozen clinics offer it—but yet too many of them are getting it too easily.
- Doctors should slow down and stop providing trans boys so many top surgeries—but those who seek top surgery face long wait lines.
- There are only 200 surgeries a year—but the surgery is "exploding."
- Regret among trans boys is a real problem—but almost all of them are happy with their result.
- The 200 or so trans teens are too young to consent to their top surgery—but the nearly 8,000 cisgender teens who also get top surgeries aren't.

This puts on full display the logical inconsistencies of WCN talking points, and the perils of publishing articles that try to both pander to them while simultaneously reporting the facts. As with the coverage of trans girls in sports, it is bouncing back and forth between two different articles that are nominally on the same subject but aren't completely on speaking terms with one another.

The great irony is that the *Times* is still too good a news organization not to at least mention the real facts, even if it does so only in passing, and buries them after the jump, below a lot of evidence-free accusations.

About halfway through, Ghorayshi pivoted from the story of Michael, a young trans man who had a very positive result, to Jamie, who didn't. Jamie also had been sexually assaulted in school, starting testosterone shortly after, and then had top surgery after turning 18. A few years after she decided she had made a mistake, and detransitioned. Jamie is introduced as a cautionary tale for minors, except that since she waited until she was 18, she *didn't* have top surgery as a minor.

Ghorayshi also gratuitously introduced Grace Lidinsky-Smith, who transitioned as an adult at age 23 and then detransitioned later. So it turns out this cautionary tale is *not* about a minor and thus irrelevant to the topic at hand.

She didn't bother to mention that Lidinsky-Smith is president of Gender Care Consumer Advocacy Network, an organization which promotes blanket bans on both youth *and* adult care, state monitoring of all affirming care, and malpractice lawsuits against care providers. GCCAN also claimed that top surgery is marketed "like cigarette companies used to market tobacco to children."[466] [467] [468] [469]

Lidinsky-Smith was also featured on *60 Minutes*, where Lesley Stahl briefly interviewed a single, unnamed happy trans teen before devoting the bulk of the segment to detransition and regret. She also did not disclose Lidinsky-Smith's leadership of GCCAN.[470] [471] [472]

Ghorayshi quoted, unconscionably, Republican charges of "disfigurement" and "mutilation"—language it is simply unimaginable for the *Times* to use about any other common and recommended procedure, and right after they had published three articles—including one on the front page—on the harms caused by trans-inclusive language.

Ghorayshi ended with a brief story about 14-year-old William, who was pleased with his surgery. That's two positive and two negative stories, so a 50% Apparent Regret Rate for procedure, with a 1% Real Regret Rate. And here two positive stories are from actual transgender minors, and her two negative ones from women who were not minors but ages 18 and 23.

In other words, since only about 200 kids a year are getting the procedure, and on average two of these (1%) actually regret it, the most obvious conclusion is that even for a front-page story which was presumably extensively researched, Ghorayshi was still unable to locate a single minor to say they regretted surgery and had detransitioned.

Chapter Fourteen:
Blockers & Hormones Are Dangerous

Title: **"The Battle Over Gender Therapy"**[473]
Date: **June 15, 2022**
Byline: **Emily Bazelon**
Section: **Magazine**
Words: **11,690**

" 'The Battle Over Gender Therapy' ... laundered far-right views for a broader audience, making hostility to trans people's basic rights more acceptable...centering 'tricky questions' about potential regret... in what can only be read as 'dodged a bullet' stories."[474]

Julie Hollar, "NYT Centers Trans Healthcare Story on Doctors—Not Trans People," *FAIR*

"I propose an ethical relation that calls upon adults to stop questioning the being of transchildren and affirm instead that there are transchildren, that transchildhood is a happy and desired form—not a new form of life and experience but one richly, beautifully historical and multiple."

Jules Gill-Peterson, "Histories of the Transgender Child"[475]

"It's Tuesday"

Again—where to begin?

Perhaps with the headline, which is totally misleading. There is no "battle" *over* affirming care: there is a cynical right-wing campaign to *end* it.

Or perhaps with the large, opening picture—a full-color page in the print edition—of a close-up with a flower-wreathed wrist and the hand resting on a skirted thigh. But not just *any* hand resting on *any* thigh: *this* hand has chipped, bitten, distinctly unfeminine fingernails. And *this* thigh has noticeable dark, stubbly, hair. It's a cheap-shot—the visual equivalent of screaming out: "Not a '*Real Girl*'"

Or perhaps with her opening frame: that medicine is being "engulfed by two intersecting forces: a significant rise in the number of teenagers openly identifying as transgender and seeking gender care, and a right-wing backlash against allowing them to medically transition." It's another false equivalence. The kids are just trying to make some private medical decisions in peace. The only "engulfing" here is being done by Christian nationalists after they discovered the issue could drive votes. Or, as the head of American Principles Project—in the wake of the right's devastating loss over HB 2—said, "We knew we needed to find an issue that candidates were comfortable talking about. And we threw everything at the wall…" adding, "What we're doing is trying to show Republicans how to win on [trans] issues."[476] [477] Or, as the head of the Christian right group Frontline Policy Action crowed about attacking trans kids, "This is a WINNING issue"[478]

Bazelon devoted a lot to portraying pediatric care as controversial, rare, harmful, and unproven. As writer Samantha Hancox-Li explained in her *LiberalCurrents* article, "The Actual Ubiquity of Gender Affirming Care," "[the *Times' uber*-narrative in such pieces is] our children are in danger and we need to protect them. There is a crisis in America, it's bad and it's spreading… [G]ender-affirming care is exclusive to trans people: niche, experimental, untested, demanding.[479]

"[But] this is exactly backwards: gender affirming care is universal, pervasive, well-studied, and simple.

"When a trans kid wants to grow out her hair and change her name, it's national news. When a cis kid wants to do the same thing, it's Tuesday. When trans kids want hormone replacement therapy, we call it 'gender confirming treatment' and publish article after fretting article about how strange and dangerous its is; when cis kids receive medically identical prescriptions, it's Tuesday—we don't even have a name for it because what's normal is invisible."[480]

Bazelon's article, being the first long-form investigative news piece on kids' care, did more and deeper damage to their lives than any of the *Times*' previous pieces, and would be cited approvingly by 15 states attorneys general in their amicus brief in support of keeping pediatric care be a felony; by Missouri's Attorney General in his order halting all care for children *and adults*; and by Texas's Attorney General in his order reclassifying affirming care as "child abuse" in order to authorize the removal of trans kids from their families for placement into foster care.[481] [482] [483]

Running nearly 12,000 words, Bazelon's article came less than one week after Ghorayshi' s front page story about the "sharp rise" in trans youth, and remains easily the single longest *Times* piece on kids' medical care. Taken together, these are probably as close to an institutional position statement as we're likely to get. The piece is what debaters call "Gish Gallop"—a rhetorical strategy of generating so many allegations that it is nearly impossible to fact-check and debunk each one before another takes its place.[484] So I'll just settle for highlighting a few of its main deficiencies, along with some of its more major contradictions.

"No Legitimate Debate"

Bazelon staged her debate around WPATH or the World Professional Association for Transgender Health, which adjusted the Standards of Care (SOC) for youth affirming medicine and published the new version—SOC-8.[485] All standards, including these, go through revisions, which is a normal part of medicine. Bazelon sees disagreements over medical standards and adjustments to them as evidence of the great "battle" going on.

As GLAAD put it, this forced her to "repeatedly and inaccurately treat the widely-held consensus in the medical and science communities as a 'side' to be debated…"[486] To create the "other side" of this debate, as Kit O'Connell explains in "There Is No Legitimate 'Debate' Over Gender-Affirming Healthcare:" Bazelon ended up "elevating a handful of outliers and their discredited theories about trans people to a prominence they do not enjoy among the medical community."[487]

WPATH has plenty of trans-denialist clinicians. As an open membership association, it has perpetually been dogged by an *old guard* of anti-gay "conversion" therapists who have reinvented themselves as anti-trans "conversion" therapists, and who remain as deeply committed to keeping being trans a pathology to be prevented in kids, as they once were to keeping homosexuality a pathology to be prevented in kids.[488]

As a result, in the past, WPATH's Standards of Care for pediatric treatment have often displayed little editorial consistency, in some places with affirming science-based paragraphs followed by trans-denialist ones, sometimes in the same chapter. As with abortion or vaccines, this is what a medical "debate" looks like when it really is a religious and political one.[489] It is only recently that the Standards have finally come down unambiguously on the side of affirming trans kids and the safety of pediatric care.

The Dog That Doesn't Bark

Bazelon makes so many claims that it inevitably creates a number of major contradictions. One of the biggest is that if blockers and hormones had all the dangerous side effects she proposes, the *Times* should also be warning parents of the thousands of cisgender children who have been receiving the same medications, but it doesn't—because apparently they're only dangerous when trans kids take them.

Another has to do with the fact that she and Ghorayshi keep pointing to the increased number of kids coming out as trans as *prima facie* evidence that they must be different from previous generations, and therefore more of them are really cisgender and are going to detransition. But if that were true, then clinics should be seeing *double* the number of miserable cisgender kids flooding their waiting rooms, and studies should be reporting *double* the regret rates.

But neither of these is true. It's the dog that doesn't bark.

The absence of this wave of detransitioners which

Bazelon's and Ghorayshi's many hypotheses predicted is why the *Times* is always offering up fringe medical voices and backing them with anecdotal horror stories and evidence-free assertions that *something is very wrong.*

As researcher Erin Reed points out, there actually *is* a flood of miserable teens who are detransitioning, but the *Times* has yet to cover them.[490] Since about 14,000 trans kids get care each year and 38% of states (19) have banned their medication, that means over 5,000 kids each year are now either being forcibly detransitioned because they can't get medication or are in danger of losing it.[491] In addition, neither the *Times* nor any other major outlet has mentioned the plight of the many trans and nonbinary adolescents in foster care and juvenile probation systems in those 19 states who overwhelmingly skew Black and brown and/or low-income, and who are at the mercy of child welfare systems that are withdrawing their medications and forcing their bodies to once again begin undergoing the wrong puberty.

As queer writer Lydia Polgreen would put it in—of all places—a *Times* op-ed: "A single mistaken transition is a tragedy. A million children denied care? That's just a statistic."[492] Because detransitions only count if it's a cisgender child.

They're Different, So More Must Not Be Trans

After briefly acknowledging the incredibly low regret rates among both trans adults and trans kids, Bazelon offered up five main ways that the latter are different from the previous generation of trans kids who grew up to be today's unregretful trans adults. They are that:

a) More identify as trans;
b) More identify as boys;
c) More come out at older ages;
d) More find community through social media; and,
e) They have higher rates of various mental disorders.

This is her entire case. She provides no data and presents no studies for any of these, nor does she ever explain why these particular demographic differences are likely to have clinical significance. It is argument-by-implication.

Just for purposes of comparison, after Christine Jorgensen's transition in Denmark and then her extraordinarily public coming out in 1952, there was a long pause before a second cohort came through in the late 1970s and early 1980s, of which I was a part. Our demographics were also different from hers: we had a thriving gay community for support, were treated at local hospital-based clinics here in the U.S., we had these new personal computers and cellphones, and so on. It is the nature of *every* cohort to be somewhat different than the one before, but that doesn't mean it has any clinical significance for treatment such that we were less likely to benefit from affirming care or more of us were likely to "desist" or detransition.

Barely a month before Ghorayshi published her article, an article was published in the *Times* on the Trans Youth Project's long-term follow-up study of 317 trans kids, 97.5% of whom—despite all these major differences—still identified as trans five years later. Those included children as young as six, whom one would imagine would be less likely to be stable in their identities than teens. But Bazelon never even mentions it. The only possible explanation, other than gross journalistic negligence, is that she doesn't read the *New York Times*.

Just for purposes of comparison, there are more and younger teens than previous generations also going on birth control, coming out as gay, and having abortions—all of whom find community through social media.

For purposes of comparison, the number of teens undergoing breast implants, nose jobs, labiaplasties, and liposuctions has also "exploded" or "spiraled" or "mushroomed" as well, into the hundreds of thousands annually, as has the number of providers offering them care. But the *Times* hasn't suggested that this is evidence that something is wrong, or that these doctors should impose lengthy and comprehensive psychiatric assessments on them.[493] [494] [495]

Like Ghorayshi, Bazelon devoted particular attention to today's teens' "higher rates of autism, depression, anxiety, and attention-deficit disorder." They appear to be implying that being neurodivergent makes teens less likely to know their own gender identities—unless they're cisgender, of course, in which case they are to be believed without question.

On the other hand, they may be implying that neurodivergent teens are uniquely vulnerable to manipulation and peer pressure about their gender identities—unless they're cisgender, of course, in which case they are to be believed without question.

All this is another red-herring: since almost *all* teenagers today—and particularly the queer ones—have higher rates of depression, anxiety, and ADD than previous generations. According to NIMH, 32% of youth have an anxiety disorder, and 16% have depression (which has also *doubled* in the past years). According to the CDC, about 12% of young people have ADHD.[496] [497] [498] And non-trans queer kids who are gay, lesbian, and bisexual also have higher rates of mental health issues.[499] *Again: not the conflict but the context.*

As with Ghorayshi, Bazelon waves around slightly higher rates of autism among trans-identified kids as a kind of automatic red-flag that means that kids coming out as trans need strict psychiatric gatekeeping. Yet it's entirely possible that slightly more trans teens are autistic, because it makes them less susceptible to the social cues and pressures that push most of us into conforming to traditional gender norms.[500] In any case, this reflexive prejudice towards neurodivergent trans teens is now contributing to discrimination against them: one-in-three reports having their gender identity questioned by skeptical health professionals.[501]

When Teens Say They're Trans, Don't Believe Them

Having suggested that more of today's trans teens are probably not trans after all, Bazelon provided a flood of Ghorayshi-like hypotheses for why this might be, including that they are:

a) Trying "to trade a cisgender, heterosexual, white identity… [for] being marginalized and deserving of protection;"[502]
b) Trying to shed aspects of themselves they dislike;"
c) Dealing with unspecified past trauma;
d) Too ashamed to admit they want to detransition;
e) Succumbing to peer pressure;
f) Feeling "confined by gender stereotypes;"
g) Gay boys or lesbian girls who mistakenly thought themselves trans;
h) Under the secret spell of the Evil Sloth-Demon Morg.

Okay, that last one was made-up. But so are hers, since almost all are presented without data or studies. As with her laundry list of reasons that today's cohort is definitively different, Bazelon is just spit-balling. The notion that there is social pressure to come out as trans is especially bizarre, since nearly half (43%) of trans youth have been bullied, and almost a third (29%) have attempted suicide—so all the obvious and documented social pressures run in the opposite direction.[503]

It's interesting to compare Bazelon with Roiphe, who also generated a slew of hypotheses for why Sarah Lawrence's straight co-eds might be pushed into lesbian adventures, including that they were lonesome, unable to hook up with men, felt pressured by all the visible lesbianism, began to question their sexual orientation, feared being attacked as reactionary, were afraid of being thought cowardly, and were simply feeling pressured into it—everything except the idea that they might have discovered an unexpected attraction to another woman's body.[504] In other words, this appears to be a stock journalistic frame that the *Times* uses for dealing with the emergence of pesky sexual minorities.

The Many Risks of Affirming Care

Almost no aspect of pediatric care has the same kind of army of dedicated and extremist professionals and groups devoted to stopping it—except abortion.

As with affirming care, Christian nationalist groups have created an extensive network of pseudoscience clinicians and studies to manufacture doubt about *risks* and *complications* associated with safe, effective medical abortions, including severe hemorrhaging, cardiac arrest, endo-toxic shock, organ injury, convulsion, cervical laceration, uterine rupture, infections and even death—not to mention depression, eating disorders, substance abuse, and suicidal ideation afterwards.[505] Those "very real debates" among medical professionals which Sulzberger wrote about with regard to pediatric care also seem be happening around the true risks of abortion, which would seem to be another issue that society "is still working through."

Bazelon provided her own Parade of Horribles that supposedly resulted from affirming care, including abdominal pain, convulsions, difficulty breathing, fainting, fever, irregular heartbeat, muscle tremors, nausea and vomiting, unusual bleeding, seizures and finally loss of consciousness. Oops, sorry—that's the Mayo Clinic's list of side-effects for aspirin.[506]

For puberty blocker and hormones, Bazelon cites rare side-effects that may include lower bone density in adulthood relative to others, and/or diminished fertility.[507] Fortunately, as complications go, these are pretty mild and manageable.

Bone density issues can be headed off through regular bone scans (recommended as part of care) and for fertility issues—assuming trans men want their eggs, or trans women their sperm (I certainly didn't), they are either largely reversable or can be addressed through Fertility Preservation (FP) options.[508]

Bazelon quoted one surgeon who was concerned that puberty blockers might impact trans girls' later ability to orgasm. It's worth noting that in its endless search for contrarian voices and hypothetical risks, the *Times* has quietly moved on from the weak justification of "some people say," to the even weaker, "one doctor says." (Only a year later, a study published in the *Journal of Sexual Medicine* would find no such problem among 37 adult trans women who had taken blockers.[509])

Bazelon prominently quoted a single surgeon who was worried that some trans girls who get on blockers or hormones too early might end up with too little penile skin for full depth if they later opt for vaginal reconstruction. This is the very definition of journalistic *concern trolling:* is there a sentient being *anywhere* in our home galaxy who believes that the *newspaper of record* really cares if some *trannie girl* might need additional skin grafted if she one day has Gender Affirmation Surgery because the length of her phallus skin is insufficient to provide a full vaginal sheath?

Bazelon also quoted yet another doctor complaining that cisgender girls who get care and then detransition will be left *hairy,* with *large clits* and *deep voices*. As scaremongering goes this is pretty despicable, and clearly intended to terrorize parents of transgender boys into fearing that they are *ruining* the bodies of their "daughters." It does not occur to Bazelon that becoming a *hairy girl with a deep voice* is precisely the physical outcome that all those transgender girls whose care she is so eager to withhold are trying desperately to avoid.

"Some of the People" All of the Time

Bazelon wove large swaths of her narrative from threads of random anecdotes, specifically the *Times'* favorite justification in such stories: "Some People Are Saying." The word "some" occurs 27 times in various contexts here. Below is a sample:

Some Teens...

- Say social influences affected their gender;
- Say coming out as trans is different today;
- May in early generations have grown up gay or lesbian;
- May be too ashamed to stop their care;
- Only had cursory medical assessments;
- Want overly-fast access to care.

Some Doctors...

- Rush kids into care without mental-health evaluations;
- Want to shut down the complaints about under-evaluation;
- Are giving care too quickly;
- Are oversimplifying treatment;
- Are emphasizing suicide risk to strengthen the case for care.

In other words, Bazelon's writing is not exactly bristling over with factoids and numbers. This is just lazy journalism when you want to provide a debate, but you couldn't find enough facts to justify one. There's nothing wrong in principle with building an article around anecdotes, but one would hope that based on a foundation this thin, Bazelon would be a little more circumspect about promoting voices well outside the medical mainstream. She's also encouraging parents to disbelieve their teens, and scaremongering medical care—not to mention completely ignoring a groundbreaking study published just one month previously published in her own newspaper.

In the absence of the words of trans kids themselves, among the voices Bazelon chose to quote was the UK

TERF group Genspect. Founder Stella O'Malley has written that, "Transsexuals who boast that medicalization 'worked' for them are essentially high-function addicts… reliant on being affirmed in [their] delusion."[510]

In other words, many of the voices Bazelon quoted on the topic of bettering care and improving kids' outcomes had no interest in either—their only interest was in ending care and eradicating transgender kids. So this *faux* debate hasn't been between two groups with different ideas about care: it has been between one group trying to stay close to the science and help young people, and another trying to "flood the zone" with disinformation and lies in order to stop any young person from transitioning or getting any affirming care. And that is hugely unequal and misleading to readers.

In a since-deleted tweet, Bazelon defended using Genspect as a source by explaining that ignoring them "would deny that reality, which would be a disservice to readers who want to understand the full landscape."[511] The word "reality" is doing a lot of heavy lifting here, similar to the Trump administration's use of the phrase "alternative facts." It is another contradiction of the *Times* coverage that TERF groups must be heard from, but not trans teens themselves.

Another Dog That Doesn't Bark

Bazelon generates such a blizzard of claims that she also creates major contradictions for herself. One of the biggest is that if blockers and hormones had all the dangerous physical side effects she proposes that they do, the *Times* would be publishing pieces warning parents of the tens of thousands of cisgender children who have also been receiving puberty blockers and hormones to treat precocious (i.e., early) puberty and contrasexual puberty since the 1980s.[512] [513] [514]

But it isn't because apparently they're only dangerous when trans kids take them. The use of blockers and hormones to treat contraseuxal puberty—to prevent feminization in cis boys and masculinization in girls—is especially on point here, since these are *exactly* the same reasons they are given to trans boys and girls.[515] [516]

Another major contradiction emerges from Bazelon and Ghorayshi, who point to the increased number of trans kids as *prima facie* evidence that more of them are really likely to be cisgender, and thus are more likely to regret getting care and to eventually detransition.

But if this were true, then clinics should be seeing *double* the number of miserable cisgender kids flooding their waiting rooms to detransition, and studies would be reporting *double* the rate of regret.

But neither of these is true. It's yet another dog that never barks.

In fact it is this absence of the predicted wave of detransitioners which Bazelon's and Ghorayshi's many hypotheses predict that necessitates the *Times* having to write articles around fringe medical voices, anecdotal stories, and evidence-free implications that *something is very wrong.* If something were as wrong as they assert, they could write about it. But in its absence, they're force to build stories out of conjecture, supposition, and dark warnings of what is probably going to happen (but somehow still hasn't). .

In fact, in a remarkable piece less than a year later, "How a Few Stories of Regret Fuel the Push to Restrict Gender Transition Care" by Maggie Astor, the *Times* itself documented how all those predicted detransitioning youth remain so rare, that the Right has been reduced to recruiting a class of more-or-less *professional detransitioners* whom it moves around the country like chess pieces so they can testify in states where legislatures have been unable to drum up any of their own.[517] Just one of these, a Californian, has testified before *nine* state legislatures: Florida, Idaho, Kansas, Missouri, New Hampshire, Ohio, South Dakota, Tennessee and Utah.

Denying Care to a Large Majority

Bazelon presents a variety of extreme views from all sides: anti-care crazies like the aforementioned Genspect, anti-affirming care crazies who accuse providers of "chemical castration," anti-gay crazy clinicians who believe every gay or trans kid should be "cured," pro-care crazies who are "terrifying" parents with the admonition of "*better a live son than a dead daughter*,'" and finally the trans activist crazies, who are giving pretty much all of the above shit.

Having now relegated everyone to the outskirts of reason, Bazelon can present the idea of more psychiatric assessment and stricter medical gatekeeping as The Moderate Middle, which is therefore Probably the Right Thing since it is better than all the rest, none of its proponents are crazies, and it makes all the crazies equally unhappy.

She is wrong.

This may seem counter-intuitive, since it *feels* like taking more time for therapy, assessment, and unpacking any complicating factors is a good thing. And since this is the central question of Bazelon's 11,000 words on the "battle," I'd like to revisit that earlier Florence Ashely meta-analysis in a little more depth.

One of the main points Ashley makes is that the stricter and more in-depth psychiatric assessment and diagnosis that is needed to figure out who is really trans relies on four main tools: 1) The eight-item DSM-V diagnosis; 2) Detailed gender histories; 3) Standardized surveys; and, 4) Analyzing after-care regret rates.[518] [519] [520]

The problem is that all of these depend on the same input data to produce their diagnoses: teens' self-reported statements. And at least the first three involve standards that are grounded in stereotyped ideas of very binary femininity and masculinity ("Ever since I was four, I wanted to dress up in skirts, have long hair, and play with makeup…" and so on).

As for #4, Bazelon and Ghorayshi use "regret" as a synonym for "mistake" and "detransition." But this is not true.

Studies find that at least *half* of all cases of detransition are either caused or strongly influenced by family rejection and social stigma, *not* because someone regrets transitioning, and about half of these will later "retransition" as adults, once they are no longer so vulnerable to the animus of peers and families.[521]

Moreover, "regret" and "detransition" are not the same.

Many young people who are coded in studies as having "detransitioned" have no regrets over their medication and may even stay on it; they have simply stopped identifying as binary *trans boy* or *trans girl*—which we know from that *Washington Post*/KKF poll accounts for only about one-third of all trans-identified youth.[522] [523] Ironically, this is the one really big difference between today's trans teens and previous generations, but

Bazelon and Ghorayshi largely miss it because they fail to foreground transgender kids.

So, while I said earlier that Real Regret Rates for teens are around 1% or so, using this more granular perspective, it's probably closer to about half of that, or 0.5%. That's equal to about 1-in-every-200 teens who transition. Base rates for Real Regret are so low that it is virtually impossible to develop any kind of "rigorous" medical testing or strict gatekeeping that would not misdiagnose vastly more transgender kids at the cost of identifying a single cisgender one. To provide a sense of what this means in practice, even if WPATH developed a validated, reliable new test that was 95% accurate at determining which kids were trans and which were cisgender, it would still be useless, because it would misdiagnose many more kids than it correctly identified.[524]

The fact is, there *is* no test for determining who is trans and who is cisgender. The best "test" is simply to believe kids when they tell us who and what they are—full stop—instead of looking for reasons to disbelieve them.

Although it presents itself as worrying about kids' health, the *Times'* concern tolling over and obsession with a tiny number of detransitions comes at the cost of denying or delaying care for a much larger population of kids who really are transgender. It is a deeply immoral abuse of journalistic privilege—one which harms the very young people it claims to help.

It falls to Ashley and their co-authors to state the simple truth that Sulzberger, Friedman, Ghorayshi, and Bazelon cannot or will not:

"Denying care to a large majority for the benefit of a small minority is unethical."

Part Three: A Brief History of Time(s)
Trans Articles by Year and by Desk

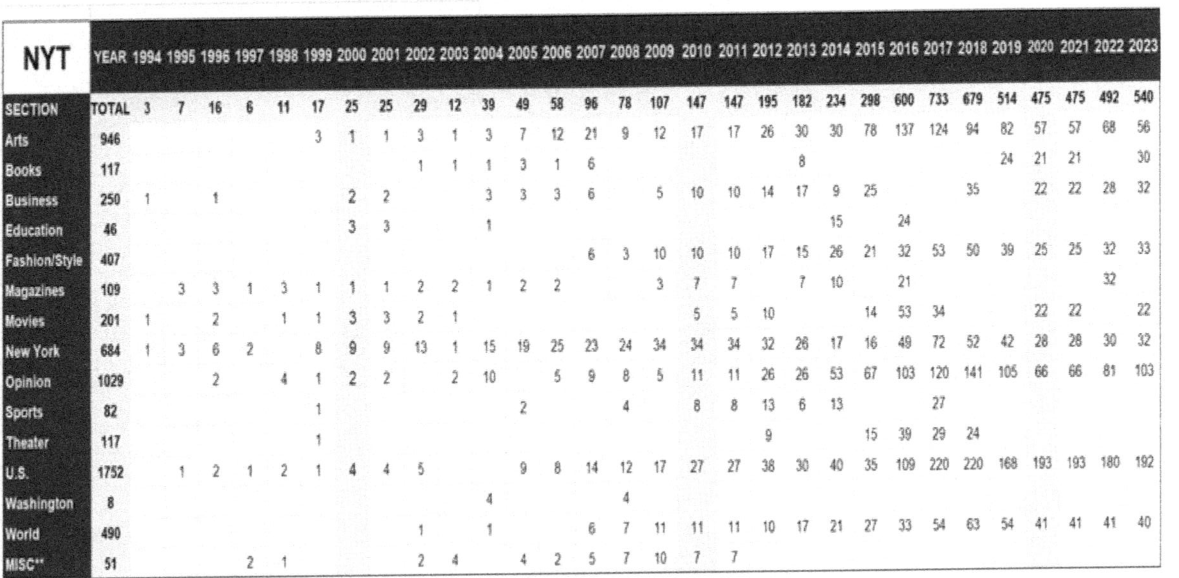

NYT	YEAR	1994	1995	1996	1997	1998	1999	2000	2001	2002	2003	2004	2005	2006	2007	2008	2009	2010	2011	2012	2013	2014	2015	2016	2017	2018	2019	2020	2021	2022	2023
SECTION	TOTAL	3	7	16	6	11	17	25	25	29	12	39	49	58	96	78	107	147	147	195	182	234	298	600	733	679	514	475	475	492	540
Arts	946						3	1	1	3	1	3	7	12	21	9	12	17	17	26	30	30	78	137	124	94	82	57	57	68	56
Books	117									1	1	1	3	1	6						8						24	21	21		30
Business	250	1		1				2	2			3	3	3	6		5	10	10	14	17	9	25			35		22	22	28	32
Education	46							3	3			1										15		24							
Fashion/Style	407														6	3	10	10	10	17	15	26	21	32	53	50	39	25	25	32	33
Magazines	109		3	3	1	3	1	1	1	2	2	1	2	2			3	7	7		7	10		21						32	
Movies	201	1		2		1	1	3	3	2	1							5	5	10			14	53	34			22	22		22
New York	684	1	3	6	2		8	9	9	13	1	15	19	25	23	24	34	34	34	32	26	17	16	49	72	52	42	28	28	30	32
Opinion	1029			2		4	1	2	2		2	10		5	9	8	5	11	11	26	26	53	67	103	120	141	105	66	66	81	103
Sports	82						1						2			4		8	8	13	6	13			27						
Theater	117						1													9			15	39	29	24					
U.S.	1752		1	2	1	2	1	4	4	5			9	8	14	12	17	27	27	38	30	40	35	109	220	220	168	193	193	180	192
Washington	8											4				4															
World	490									1		1			6	7	11	11	11	10	17	21	27	33	54	63	54	41	41	41	40
MISC**	51				2	1				2	4		4	2	5	7	10	7	7												

** Blogs/Health/Travel/Real Estate

Chapter Fifteen: The 1960s & 1970s

The *Times* coverage of trans subject matter had begun in the 1960s and 1970s, and it changed and grewn in unexpected ways even as the community being covered grew and changed in unexpected ways. Even in these early attempts, one could see journalistic tics, trends, and problems emerging. But prior to 2015's first deliberately anti-trans articles, they were mostly the mundane mistakes and casual transphobia that was common in almost any mainstream article trying to cover a community that—like homosexuals before them—it didn't know personally, didn't understand well, didn't feel entirely comfortable around, and thus towards whom it often projected a sense of implicit (and often quite explicit) journalistic condescension.

The 1960s

One of the *Times'* first 1960's mentions of trans was in a small, front-page article below the fold entitled, "A Changing of Sex By Surgery Begun at Johns Hopkins." In 1966 the article read:

> *"Johns Hopkins University has quietly begun performing sex change surgery... Although the controversial surgery has been performed in many European countries in the last 15 years... Johns Hopkins is the first American hospital to give it official support..."*[525]

The 1970s

In the 1970s, the tennis pro Renee Richards became the *Times'* first really big trans news story. Beginning in 1976, it carried dozens of largely-sympathetic pieces on her legal battle to play professional women's tennis, with titles such as "A Former Male Tennis Player Seeks to Join Women's Tour," and "Renee Richards Resolute, Angry."[526] [527]

This kind of coverage is impossible to imagine the *Times* affording any transsexual woman athlete today.[528]

Richards was then the most famous transsexual since Christine Jorgenson's 1952 coming out ("Ex-GI Becomes Blonde Beauty" screamed LIFE Magazine's cover)—which the *Times* strangely ignored, even though it was how much of the world first learned of this "new" phenomenon called "transsexuality."[529]

Unfortunately, in a harbinger of things to come, the *Times* publicly questioned Richard's womanhood, "Renee Richards Controversy: What Is a Woman?"—including one bitterly transphobic reader opinion, warning, Navratilova-like, that "…women's sports will be taken over by a giant race of surgically-created women."[530]

Given the *Times*' terrible treatment of swimmer Lia Thomas in the 2020s when it platformed the very same slurs against another trans woman, it is strange that it has never asked how this much-prophesied race of trans superwomen is always about to take over women's sports. Somehow, it has failed to do so for over half a century now—even as it keeps pushing the accusation. It is another dog that never barks.

In one sympathetic human-interest story, the *Times* writer couldn't resist adding this gratuitous, condescending evaluation of Richard's femininity: "But many of the masculine characteristics still remain: The bone-crushing handshake, the thick neck and shoulders, the deep voice…")[531]

A 1977 article announced the first U.S. phalloplasty preformed on a trans man capable of erection through "a tiny hydraulic system that permitted a fluid to be pumped from a reservoir in the abdomen… a procedure originally developed to treat men with impotence".[532] [533]

Two years later, in 1979, it would tap noted psychiatry critic Thomas Szasz to review Janice Raymond's notorious TERF screed, *The Transsexual Empire: The Making of the She-Male.*

In an eerie echo of Singal and Helen Joyce, it selected one transphobe to review the book of another. And similarly to Singal, Szasz ignored Raymond's book in favor of virulently attacking transsexuality generally, and female transsexuals specifically:

> "*In the old days, when I was a medical student, if a man wanted to have his penis amputated, my psychology professors said that he suffered from schizophrenia, locked him up in an asylum and threw away the key. Now that I am a professor, my colleagues in psychiatry say that he is a 'transsexual,' my colleagues in urology refashion his penis into a*

perineal cavity they call a vagina, and Time *Magazine puts him on its cover and calls him 'her.'"*

Long-time science writer Jane E. Brody wrote an update in 1972 on Johns Hopkins performing "one of the most radical forms of surgery—operations that change one's sex".[534] Yet then, as now, it was important to avoid transsexuality, and Brody noted approvingly that—despite almost no positive results—hospitals were still "trying to identify children who may be 'pre-transsexual,' and treat them [with reparative therapy] with the goal of reversing their gender misidentification before it is too late…"

In one credulous piece I suspect she would love to retract: "Doctors Report Transsexual Cure," Brody detailed the "reparative therapy" mistreatment of a Mississippi teenager who was almost certainly a young gay man through a combination of enforced behavior modification, electro-shock therapy, adult intimidation, and sexual abuse:[535]

"[T]he boy was first conditioned to stand, walk and sit in a more masculine manner, then taught to speak with a deeper voice and less feminine inflections. The therapists then tried to change his sexual fantasies, lavishly praising the patient's successful substitution of female for male figures... Using so-called aversive techniques, such as mild electrical shocks, the therapists were then able to diminish his sexual response to pictures of nude men. The successive treatments were carried out over a 10-month period with numerous follow-up visits afterwards... The researchers said they believed this case to be the first successful change in psychosexual orientation in

such person... Distortions in psychosexual identity could predispose the child to later homosexuality, transsexualism or other sexual deviations...'"

Brody's early detransition piece also included this bizarre anecdote:

"[T]he same issue of the journal... described the 'successful change in gender identity' of three persons through behavior modification... In an earlier report, Dr. Barlow described a transsexual 'well on his way to surgery' who was changed by a faith healer through exorcism, suggesting that methods short of surgery might help such people."

Looking up the actual faith-healing in the sometimes-controversial peer review journal *the Archives of Sexual Behavior*, it states:[536]

"The physician administered a total physical exam and said that he could live quite well as a woman, but told John the real problem was possession by evil spirits. After some discussion of this, John reported a session which lasted two to three hours, and involved exhortations and prayers over John by the physician, and laying on a hands-on John's head and shoulders. During this period, John reported fainting several times and arising to the continuing of the prayers and exhortations, resulting in the exorcism of 22 evil spirits, which the physician called by name as they left his body. During and after this session John felt waves of God's love coming over him, but was physically drained... The physician noted in his letter to us that he showed John that his life was a fake and that Jesus could redeem him and that a standard prescription of Scripture readings caused

the spirit of the woman in John to disappear.

"Immediately after the session, John announced he was a man, discarded his female clothes (hiding his breasts as best he could), and went to the barber shop to have his long hair cut into his current short, masculine style..."

Can I get an *Amen*?[537]

Chapter Sixteen:
The 1980s & 1990s

1980s

The 80s opened with the *Times*' positive review of Brian DePalma's *Dressed to Kill*, in which a reserved, middle-aged man unaccountably morphs into a demented, psychotic transgender killer by night, violently slashing females to death, presumably because he can never be a Real Woman[538] (we all do this of course).

Aside from Arts and Culture, the *Times'* first real transgender story of the 1980s would be the firing of combat vet and pilot Karen Ulane who was terminated by Eastern Airlines after transitioning on the job, and it would devote several articles to her legal battle for reinstatement and damages.[539]

The court ruled in Ulane's favor based on the Civil Rights Act of 1964, which forbade discrimination "because of sex." This was exactly the same basis on which, half a century later, in 2020, the Supreme Court would rule 6-3, in *Bostock v Clayton,* that gay and transgender people were indeed protected.[540] [541]

Alas, Eastern appealed, arguing that Ulane's transition posed an unspecified safety hazard in the cockpit—perhaps due to unproven fears that her new genitalia might spontaneously combust at higher altitudes—and the decision, although eventually proven correct, was overturned.[542 543]

The *Times* closed out the '80s with a quintet of articles, as trans people showed up in the first made-for-TV movies. Their article, about Vanessa Redgrave as Richards in the bio-pic "Second Serve - *He had it all, but there was a woman inside him, raging to get out*" noted, "…Miss Redgrave looks like the designer, Halston, trying to do an impersonation of Marlene Dietrich. But the emotional 'truth' is powerful…"[544 545 546]

In a1986 lifestyle article entitled, "Suburbs Are a Magnet to Many Homosexuals," the *Times* documented the strange mating habits of homosexuals, who "are now adopting more traditional lives outside the city… slipping into the fabric of suburban and small-town life… where they often live together as couples…" No doubt this was a shocking journalistic reveal to its hetero readers.

But the piece also contained a single casual aside about a "transgender counselling service." This was the *Times'* first use of the new term which would eventually displace the older, narrower, and more clinical "transsexual."[547]

Completing the decade were reviews of two of the all-time celebrated early trans vehicles, *Rocky Horror Picture Show* and Armistead Maupin's *Tales of the City*.

The second drew a deeply affectionate review from writer David Feinberg for this final installment of Maupin's long-running love-letter to the San Francisco boarding house run by Mrs. Madrigal—"the transsexual hophead"—and her extended gay family, including Michael "Mouse" Tolliver:

> *"I know I'm not the only one who was up until 2 in the morning with the latest installment, promising myself to stop after just one more chapter... I have no plans of leaving Manhattan for San Francisco, but I have to confess that I left my heart with Michael Tolliver. Thanks for the journey..."*[548] [549]

It wasn't a trans article, but as the decade drew to a close, in 1989 the *Times* published "Lesbian Partners Find The Means to Be Parents," which used the same kind of negative scaremongering it would later direct at transgender kids:[550]

> *"But some clinicians speculate that in the long term, girls might have difficulty in intimate relationships with men, and boys might be uncomfortable with their role as males. If lesbian parents are openly hostile toward men, these difficulties could be worsened.*
>
> *"Sidney Callahan, a psychologist and ethicist at Mercy College... had 'deep reservations'' about lesbian motherhood through artificial insemination. 'The ethical objection is the informed-consent issue. You are getting a child that is totally different from all other children. Do you have the right to do that? As perilous as it is to be brought into the world in a normal family, this is one step beyond that'' "*

1990s

The 1900s witnessed a huge expansion of *Times*' trans coverage, mostly in arts and culture at the beginning, before finally segueing into its first "hard news" coverage of the emerging transgender rights movement. It was first among major news outlets to do so.

From the 90s on, there would be so many articles that detailing it all would be a book in itself. So from here on, I'll just try to focus some of the high and low points.

The decade opened with a positive review of Jonathan Demme's Oscar-winning, *The Silence of the Lambs*, in which a reserved young man unaccountably morphs into a demented, psychotic transgender killer by night, violently slashing females to death for a *skin-suit*, presumably because he can never be a Real Woman[551] (which, once again, we all do, of course!).

The following month the *Times* positively reviewed Jennie Livingston's documentary, *Paris Is Burning*, about NYC's drag ball culture, its various *houses,* and the emergence of the dance craze *voguing,* which featured performers like Willie Ninja and Venus Xtravaganza.[552]

But by 1993, just two years later, theater critic Jesse Green posted a caring and bitter 3,000-word follow-up, "Paris Has Burned," about the consequences among the young queers of color who create the ball culture, once it had been strip-mined by popular culture and the lights had gone out. Even today, it remains an extraordinary dissection of the power dynamics inherent in white society's appropriation of an art form created by young, impoverished Black and Latina queens:[553] [554]

> *"Looking like endangered birds, the drag queens tottered on their heels as they entered — 'a bit early in the day for we girls,' said one. It was noon on a recent Saturday at the Sound Factory Bar on West 21st Street, and they were attending a memorial for Angie Xtravaganza. One of her children, Hector Xtravaganza, kept breaking down in tears. 'It's not just her, it's all of them,' he said. 'My entire gay childhood is disintegrating before my eyes...'*

"Though she was only 27, Angie had been a mother more than a dozen times. Not in the usual way; she was biologically male. 'But a mother is one who raises a child, not one who borns it,' Hector pointed out... And as mother of the House of Xtravaganza, Angie had taken many rejected, wayward, even homeless children under her wing; she had fed them, observed their birthdays, taught them all about 'walking the balls.'

"Drag balls... had been held in Harlem since the 1920's but [until 'Paris Is Burning'] no one outside that world knew much about them. By then it was almost too late. For Angie Xtravaganza, such fame as she achieved... could not be savored: the AIDS-related liver disease that eventually killed her was already destroying her hard-won femininity... Before filming was even completed in 1989, her 'main daughter,' Venus... was found strangled under a bed in a hotel... Of nine featured players, five are gone or going.

"Paris is no longer burning. It has burned... Once mainstream America began to copy a subculture that was copying it, the subculture itself was no longer of interest, and whatever new opportunities existed for the principals dried up...

"The mirror ball kept spinning at the Sound Factory Bar. It wasn't until after 3 o'clock that... the crowd went quiet. A man asked everyone to hold hands in a circle. 'Remember,' he said. 'We are all legends.'"

Yet in 1995, just two years later, the *Times* would revisit Black street queens in its "Hidden New York" series in a salacious and transphobic piece with unforgiveable slur for its headline: "Shantytown of the He-Shes:"[555]

> *"It's 4:30 P.M., the sky is litmus blue and the girls are still in bed. There are six in a single room, three to a bed, their wigs hanging on 16-penny nails. By gender they are male, but by profession they are ladies of the evening... The neighborhood is a shantytown sorority of crack-addicted prostitutes, buried in filth and refuse on an abandoned Hudson River pier between West 12th and West 14th Streets. It is the sometime brothel of J'avon English. 'Jesus don't come around here cause he ain't got no money,' J'avon purrs, 'and the Devil's just too plain scared...'"*

The City Desk continued to find Black transsexual street prostitutes irresistible, posting more pieces from Neighborhood Report that offered little in the way of context or explanation for the vicious rates of economic discrimination, racism, and family abandonment that had left so many young trans people of color on New York's streets, with nothing to sell but their bodies.

These were among the *Times'* earliest articles on trans people beyond the confines of entertainment or science/medicine, and this framing was an early warning of how unseriously it was already taking another new sexual minority, and how little it was invested in reporting about their lives beyond shallow, titillating, and condescending sketches.

The Christmas Eve murder of transgender man Brandon Teena in Falls City, NE in 1993 generated nationwide coverage—almost all of it transphobic—in mainstream outlets like the *New Yorker*, *Playboy*, and the *Village Voice*, but the *Times* ignored it.[556] Five years later, it devoted three pieces to the *entertainment* side of Brandon's murder, reviewing two movies released almost simultaneously: Susan Muska and Greta Olafsdottir's riveting documentary The *Brandon Teena Story*, and Kimberley Peirce's *Boys Don't Cry,* which was nominated for two Oscars, winning Best Actress for newcomer Hilary Swank and which finally broke the "gender ceiling" on Hollywood's unwillingness to consider serious films about trans people.[557] [558] [559]

In 1996, Natalie Angier broke the news of a study showing that the brains of transsexual women that had hypothalamuses 10% smaller than others assigned male at birth.[560] [561] [562] It was the precursor to Friedman's 2015 article with the neuroscientist who found minor morphological differences in trans women's subcortical connectivity.

The piece was also the *Times'* first mention of the emerging intersex rights movement. Its leader, Bo Laurent (*aka* Cheryl Chase)—a topic which Angier revisited in-depth in her follow-up, "Intersexual Healing: An Anomaly Finds a Group":

> *"When the doctors decided she was to be raised as a girl, they removed the entire clitoris and the inner labia. Today, she has no sensation left in her genitals, has never experienced orgasm and feels disfigured."*[563]

It was among the first coverage from a major news outlet on this new front in the gender wars, about a minority most had never heard of.[564]

An article on lesbian health clinics both misspelled and misidentified trans people as 'transgenders:' an umbrella term for transsexuals, cross-dressers, hermaphrodites, and others with unconventional sexual identities."[565] Angier called the group the "transgendered." It was another sign of the sloppiness and lack of editorial standards for writing about trans people.

In 1996, *Times* Boston Bureau Chief Carey Goldberg discovered the transgender rights movement just as the transgender right movement had begun discovering itself. Weirdly titled, "Shunning 'He' and 'She,' They Fight for Respect," it included a lot of archaic and inaccurate language—but it also captured the sense of a community just starting to recognize itself as a civil rights movement:[566 567]

> *"In Boston, Nancy Nangeroni is helping arrange a courthouse vigil for a slain male-to-female transsexual. In Washington, Dana Priesing lobbies for laws that would ban discrimination against ''transgendered'' people. And in Southern California, Jacob Hale and the rest of the local Transgender Menace chapter occasionally pull on their black Menace T-shirts and go for a group walkabout, just to look people in the eye with collective pride in who they are.*
>
> *"All see themselves as part of a burgeoning movement whose members are only now, nearly two decades after gay liberation took off, gathering the courage to go public and struggle for the same sort of respect and legal protections.*
>
> *"The name that scholars and organizers prefer for this nascent movement is ''transgender,'' an*

umbrella term for transsexuals, cross-dressers (the word now preferred over transvestites), intersexed people (also known as hermaphrodites), womanish men, mannish women and anyone whose sexual identity seems to cross the line of what, in 1990's America, is considered normal...

"[Said Wilchins] 'When you have people in isolation who are oppressed and victimized and abused, they think it's their own fault, but when you hit that critical mass that they see is happening to other people, they realize it's not about them. It's about a system, and the only way to contest a system is with an organized response.'"

The piece also covered the emergence of GenderPAC as the first national trans political organization and its first National Gender Lobby Day on Capitol Hill as well as the Transexual [sic] Menace's vigil outside the Falls City, NE courthouse where the men who murdered Brandon Teena were being sentenced.

Even in its inaugural coverage of trans rights, the *Times* was already turning to white Christian nationalists for the "other side"—an authoritative voice to "condemn the movement as decadent and unhealthy:"

"'This is yet another social pathology...' said Robert H. Knight [of] the Family Research Council... 'a deviant behavior...'" Knight was also known for denouncing homosexuals as pedophiles who recruited children, and condemning lesbians for being "at war with motherhood, femininity, family, and God."[568]

Goldberg also filed a human-interest piece on me, as part of the "Public Lives" series:

"There is no really right, widely accepted pronoun for

Riki Anne Wilchins. Nor is there the right honorific. For the sake of convenience, let it be "she," and "Ms.," since she is a post-operative, male-to-female transsexual… She began an interview amiably but firmly: "I'm not going to talk about when I got my surgery, you know. It's not about what's between my legs… It's a civil rights movement… People say I transgress gender. I don't. It's the gender system that transgresses all over me…'"[569]

Chapter Seventeen: The 2000s

At the turn of the century, *Times* coverage accelerated again, with perhaps 100 mentions—about one a month. Coverage which had been largely confined for 40 years to three sections—arts/culture/fashion (*aka* Styles), local human interest, profiles and Science/Medicine—finally broke out into regular news desks, just like politics, U.S. hate crimes, and sports.

The *Times* began its first international coverage as well with the story of a pioneering surgeon in LGBTQ-phobic South Korea, the plight of the Hijra in India, and so on. This was ahead of its time.

But a clear pattern was beginning to emerge for its selection of "other side" voices: the *Times* sought out the most virulently transphobic sources possible, particularly Christian nationalist hate groups like ADF, Focus on the Family, and Heritage Foundation, just as it does today. An analysis by Media Matters and GLAAD found that during a year of coverage, nearly one in five (18%) of political stories about transgender carried disinformation—often from WCN or TERF groups—that was never fact-checked or debunked.[570]

Politics & Society

Two thousand five previewed the first of many articles on how major corporations—an early backer of trans rights—had been dealing with trans employees, particularly women, who were transitioning on the job.

"An Employee, Hired as a Man, Becomes a Woman. Now What?" noted the increasing numbers of Fortune 500's that had added "transgender" to their employment nondiscrimination policies and the LGBTQ+ Employee Resource Groups (ERGs) pushing for such protections. Two thousand eights' "Smoother Transitions" also detailed the increasing impact of HRC's Corporate Equality Index, an annual "report card" on companies' LGBTQ+ policies. As a trans member of Ernst & Young's ERG declared: "[T]his is the next frontier for discrimination protections." And indeed it was.

By November 2007, "New York Plans to Make Gender Personal Choice" documented the city's proposal to allow birth certificate changes. The "other side" statements went to Johns Hopkins's Paul McHugh, a notoriously and proudly anti-gay homophobe and committee Catholic who reportedly had helped defend numerous priests credibly accused of pedophilia.

McHugh had arrived at John Hopkins some years earlier with the express intent of shutting down its gender program, and promptly did so—declaring that he didn't dislike transsexuals, he just considered them sick and wanted to get them the psychiatric help they needed. He thus introduced the exact rhetorical framework of *concern trolling* that Christian nationalist groups would employ decades later. In fact, McHugh's shutting down Hopkins was perhaps the first known instance of white Christian extremists mounting a successful institutional backlash against gender-affirming care.

In a first for the *Times,* McHugh offered one of those endless "somebody told me" stories about another sighting of that mythical unicorn, the transgender bathroom predator, to which the *Times* obligingly lent the full weight of its journalist authority: "'I've already heard of a 'transgendered' man who claimed at work to be 'a woman in a man's body, but a lesbian' and who had to be expelled from the ladies' restroom because he was propositioning women there.'"

"Liberal Base Proves Trying to Democrats" documented the trials of gay Rep. Barney Frank who opposed promoting transgender employment protections in a bill then in Congress, describing him as "under siege by gay rights groups… "—but apparently not by transgender groups, because while we heard from many other voices including two Republicans—trans voices were conspicuously absent, even though our rights were the topic. The word "gay" appeared 13 times and "Frank" 11 times; but "transgender" only four times.

So the *Times* had already adopted the enduring editorial tick of reducing trans people to spectators and/or relegating them to the bottom of articles about them. This was perhaps among the earliest entries in what would become that beloved, long-running *Times* series: Cisgender People Under Siege.

In 2004, "On Campus, Rethinking Biology 101" documented the emergence of more transmasculine students at the traditional women's colleges (Sarah Lawrence, Brown, Smith, and Barnard). This was among the first real coverage of trans men, and covered both the unfamiliar questions that colleges were grappling with around housing and roommate assignment, as well as those personal quandries this small group of transmasculine students were wrestling with around pronouns, hormones, and when to stop cohabiting with co-eds. It had an inevitable quote from Ken Zucker, who, paradoxically, became a sort of *Times* go-to expert on trans adolescence.

Two years later, 2006's "The Trouble When Jane Becomes Jack," was the *Times'* second in-depth coverage of trans men—but only by positioning them as a "problem" for lesbians and women's colleges: "Some lesbians view it as a kind of disloyalty bordering on gender treason… [and] conflict has raged at some women's colleges… [including an article] headlined with the question, 'Is Lesbianism Dead?'…"

Readers heard from one disgruntled lesbian from *The L Word*, one disgruntled lesbian music producer, one disgruntled gender theorist ("It's as if the category of "Lesbian" is emptying out,"), and one apparently random disgruntled lesbian chosen simply because she had broken up with her transitioning partner—all before they heard from an actual trans man.

If the piece seemed mainly an update of Roiphe's "The Trouble at Sarah Lawrence" a decade ago, with trans boys scaring cis girls playing the role of lesbians scaring straight girls, at least it showed a consistency of message.

Two thousand eight's "When Girls Will Be Boys" revisited the issue yet again in the *Sunday Magazine*, in which Alissa Quart actually devotes a significant portion of her 5,000 words to trans men. She built the piece around Rey, a young trans man with a tattoo, spiky hair, oversized tribal earrings, and very baggy jeans. While it often detoured into treating trans men as problems, it generally did so sympathetically. It also introduced *Times* readers to the growing number of youth "who identify as trans but are seeking not to simply change their sex, but to create an identity outside or between established genders… [without] modifying their bodies chemically or surgically," as well as to terminology like "gender nonconforming," "genderqueer," "gender-variant," "trans," "transmale," as well as gender neutral pronouns like *hir* and *ze*.

Unfortunately, it also included the slur "hermaphroditic" for intersex, although it was the last piece to do so. It was yet another example of the *Times* not taking emergent sexual minorities seriously enough to have basic editorial standards for writing about them.[571]

In 2008, "He's Pregnant You're Speechless" by Guy Trebay in Fashion treated pregnant men with all the sensitivity of a sideshow barker hawking tickets to view the Bearded Lady. The man in question was Thomas Beatie, who made headlines around the shocked-horrified-titillated cisgender world.

To be fair, Beattie leaned hard into his sensationalism, coming out on *Oprah* and "posing half-nude and very pregnant for *The Advocate*. We do not learn much about these unique and pioneering men, but we do learn that Beattie still "does not have a penis [and] his clitoris has been surgically reconfigured to mimic a phallus…" This is the kind of untoward interest in our genitalia that was all too common in early coverage by main mainstream outlets.

In 2007, trans author Jennifer Finney Boylan was hired as a contributing opinion columnist—a first for the *Times,* and to its credit, also first among major outlets.

Sports

Among the decade's first articles on trans women and sports was a 2004 piece by Selena Roberts, who was known for her coverage of performance-enhancing drugs and her pithy turns of phrase. But here both got away from her, and she seemed utterly incapable of recognizing the humanity of the women on the receiving end of all the rhetorical fun she was having.[572]

It was a disaster without a single redeeming sentence, a *tour de force* of every low-bottom TERF canard that could be slung at the few trans women struggling to compete in their proper sex:

> *"Given the intense political and judicial attention on drug cheats, given the International Olympic Committee's public abhorrence for artificial advantages, why would the I.O.C. tempt extreme risk-takers by approving performance-enhancing surgery? Out with THG, in with estrogen. Out with Stephen, and in with Stephanie... [T]he credibility of Olympic records is just as vulnerable by the inclusion of transgender athletes as it is by the racing of drug cheats... [S]teroids are fine as long as they are disguised as estrogen, as in therapy for male-to-female athletes."*

Hard to believe, but it gets worse. After comparing transgender women to *dirty athletes* and *cheats,* she mocks the *artificial alterations* they have for *surgically enhanced routes to the finish line,* introducing the oft-cited urban myth of East German male athletes who had sex-changes to win at the Olympics.

There would be two more nuanced articles by Boylan and by Dreger, making clear that sports participation was emerging as a new source of cisgender anxiety as transgender visibility grew.[573] [574]

Metro Color

Local color pieces in Metro and other desks continued to be mostly centered around salacious stories of drag, prostitution, and fashion—sometimes all three.

There was, by now, an evolving and not-so-subtle classism and racism going on in local pieces at the *Times*. Black trans women tended to show up in profiles of street prostitution or drag balls; white trans men tended to show up in long-form articles about students at exclusive eastern private colleges.

Two thousand two's abysmal "Tolerance in Village Wears Thin; Residents Up in Arms Over Drug Deals and Prostitution" was a particularly egregious example of the former.[575] We heard from two angry residents, the chairwoman of Community Board 2, one NYPD detective, the president of the Christopher Street Association, the Christopher Street Patrol, one NYC Assemblywoman, and one State Senator before finally getting to a single supportive quote from a wonderful trans woman named Melissa Sklarz of Community Board 2.

There is nothing from any of the impoverished young trans women of color who are the subject of the piece until the very end, when one is identified as among "a number of bulky Black women in high heels, wigs and thick makeup: ''I call myself a preoperative transsexual,' Dominque said. She said she was not a prostitute, but knew others who were. "'They just do it because it's easy money… Who's beeping me?' Ms. Bryant said, as she strode up to the car." Sneer received again, loud and clear.

It is journalistic malpractice to cover an embattled and marginalized racial and sexual minority while never examining the vicissitudes of their lives or actually letting them speak.

Two thousand two's "A Tender Woman and a Tough Advocate" was another Public Lives profile like my own. Melissa Sklarz was an enormously accomplished woman, but here's the *Times'* opening lead: "Let us now meditate on the errant black bra strap, slipped over the plump upper arm of Melissa Sklarz, a middle-aged woman who, for much of her life, was a man. Is it significant that the bra strap, for an hour or more, will be so exposed?… A reminder, lest you forget, of femininity? Though she has a deep mannish voice…" Sneer received again, loud and clear.

I reached out to Melissa and she emailed back that "I called Joyce Wadler to discuss this and she… said that, in the long run, people will only remember that I was featured in the New York *Times*." There it was: the legendary *Times* Arrogance. Forget we slimed you; just be grateful we noticed you at all.[576]

In 2004 Mireya Navarro's outstanding "Learning to Walk in Size 17 Pumps; Cross-Dressers Gladly Pay to Get in Touch with Their Feminine Side" was the rare mainstream article about the large but mostly-invisible crossdressing wing of the transgender community. Sympathetically, without judging, she surveys the world of a Staten Island "Male Image Consultant" and his crossdressing clients looking for helping hand, going out for the night *en femme.*

It was followed by another equally remarkable piece by Penelope Green in 2006 about the Casa Susanna: a "slightly run-down bungalow camp in Hunter, N.Y." that provided a refuge for downstate crossdressers in the mid-1950s and early 1960s: those "pre-Judith Butler, pre-Phil Donahue days when gender was more tightly tethered to biology."[577] Nominally about a hit picture book by Robert Swope and Michel Hurst, it is really a sensitive and loving retrospective of Casa Susanna's many habitués who are now in their 60s, 70s, 80s and even 90s.

The story included the tale of one guest being driven to her cottage there, who "turned to look in the back seat and froze: there lay a nightstick, handcuffs and other police paraphernalia… Her chauffeur was the sheriff of a small New Jersey town… The resort catered to hunters as well… and sometimes there was overlap… One day the hunters were there and [they] all had a great time discussing rifles."

Hate Crimes

By 2000, the *Times* began covering transgender hate crimes. Among the first was "Watershed of Mourning at the Border of Gender" a solid piece of reporting by Nina Siegal about the brutal slaying of Amanda Milan that was packed with detail and context.[578]

But a 2002 piece on the slaying of 17-year-old Gwen Araujo might as well have been published in a different paper. "Three Are Charged in Death of Man Who Dressed Like a Woman." Repeatedly misgendered, mispronouned, and deadnamed Gwen, the victim was identified as "Mr. Araujo… a 17-year-old man who frequently wore women's clothing."

But *that New York Times* could learn, and did learn, and three years later, when it covered the trial of Gwen's killers, her name, gender, and pronouns would all be correct.

It wasn't until 2008 that the *Times* would devote a trio of articles within months of each other which would finally put these killings into the context of a nationwide epidemic which continues to claim the lives of countless Black and Latina trans women.[579] [580] [581]

Arts & Culture

In "Genders That Shift, but Friends Firm as Bedrock," well-known film critic Elvis Mitchell sympathetically reviews Kate Davis' heartbreaking 2001 documentary *Southern Comfort,* about the untimely death of Robert Eads of "Toccoa, Georgia's trailer badlands," who died of cervical and ovarian cancer after unsuccessfully trying to find a single gynecologic oncologist willing to treat him. [582]"'The last part of me that is female is killing me,' Mr. Eads notes, dryly."

Mitchell sympathetically describes the "weathered, quiet dignity" of this "rocking-chair pappy," and the "lilt of his soothing speaking rhythms," and steadfast courage as he describes the medical establishment whose hostility contributed greatly to the impending death which he and his trans female lover, Lola Cola, face with a group of trans friends: "'I can't hate 'em. I feel sorry for 'em.'"

Children & Youth

The 5,000-word "About a Boy Who Isn't" in 2002, was by Benoit Denizet-Lewis who frequently covered

LGBTQ+ issues for the *Magazine*, and it shows. He sensitively documents "M." as "a well-liked and attractive 13-year-old with short-cropped black hair, brown eyes and a clear, soft complexion [whose] backpack is tied loosely around his thin frame, and his stylish, oversize gray sweater falls nearly to his knees…"[583]

Other kids assume "he is probably secretly gay or bisexual or maybe just confused [but] they all have it wrong. He isn't gay. He isn't confused. He isn't even a boy… [M]ost self-identified transgender teenagers can't hide their biological gender and face daily harassment and ridicule at school.." The article is woven around this young Latino child whose family lives in subsidized housing and who shares a bunk-bed with a younger 10-year-old sister who taunts him as "boy-girl."

This coverage of transgender kids was new for the *Times* and the nation, and it wouldn't be until five years later, in 2007, that Norman Spack would open the GeMS pediatric clinic in Boston. It is also among the few *Times* articles on trans children or adults that foregrounds low-income families of color.

The piece is only marred by the obligatory "other side" quote from disgraced Canadian sexologist/psychologist Ken Zucker, but then Denizet-Lewis does something unusual: he immediately quotes two counter opinions.

And there's this hard, cold-eyed view of the realities of trans life, which will be almost entirely absent from future *Times*' coverage: "If [M.] gets found out at school as having a vagina, he will probably be beaten or raped.'"

Denizet-Lewis also provides the reader with this remarkable exchange:

> *"Why would you want to take away what God gave you?" his mother says in Spanish, her voice soft and loving... It becomes clear that this is the first time that the subject of surgery has come up... M. leans forward and scratches the side of his head. He says finally. "I want to do it because I want to be a guy." I ask M. if he wants a penis as an adult, and he nods his head. I ask his mother if she would be supportive of that. "They can attach a penis?" she asks in Spanish, unbelieving. She looks at M. "Why would you want to do that?" To M., the answer is obvious: he is a boy, and he wants a boy's body..."*

There is so much here that is admirable and groundbreaking: the foregrounding of M's own voice, quotes from recognized experts on trans kids, the focus on a boy of color, and most importantly Denizet-Lewis's respectful willingness to take a 13-year-old's statements about his gender at face value.

It was equally notable for what was missing: the skepticism, disinformation from evangelical extremists, and the charge that adolescents were unreliable narrators of their own gender. That, and the dark and skeptical framing that "something must be very wrong here" that would characterize the stories of Friedman, Ghorayshi, Bazelon, and Twohey/Jewett when they covered teen transitions a decade later.

It is a model of what the *Times*' coverage of pediatric gender affirmation could have looked like. And what many other outlets, like the *Washington Post*, Reuters, the AP, and even CNN—which started out bad but mostly improved over time—would often look like. But it was also a decade before Sulzberger's plan to move to the right.

In 2006, "Supporting Boys or Girls When the Line Isn't Clear" was another 5,000-word piece on transitions from the *Magazine*'s Patricia Leigh Brown. It was a separate desk, and the only one that consistently produced solid and sometimes outstanding reporting on trans youth.[584]

This one would also be marred by the obligatory "other side" quote from Zucker—here described blandly as "helping these kids be more content in their biological gender." But Brown mainly offers a sensitive survey of how parents are reacting to, and coping with, children as young as five or six coming out as trans. As with "About a Boy Who Isn't," it's what the *New York Times* could have looked like... if it was still the *New York Times*.

> *"[A] growing number of professionals have begun to think of gender variance as a naturally occurring phenomenon rather than a disorder. 'These kids are becoming more aware of how it is to be themselves...' [But his parents] have carefully choreographed his life, monitoring new playmates, selecting a compatible school, finding sympathetic parents in a babysitting co-op... [and] 'there is still the stomach-clenching fear for your kid.' It is indeed heartbreaking to hear a child say, as J. did recently, 'It feels like a nightmare that I'm a boy.'"*

Chapter Eighteen: 2010 to 2015

As with the past decade, there were so many articles from so many desks being published that a meaningful analysis by category is impossible, so I'll provide a few topline highlights by year.

International Coverage

With a few exceptions, the *Times'* coverage of transgender had been generally been U.S.-centric, but in the in 2010s it became truly global. In 2010, the *Times* covered the Pakistani government's use of door-to-door transgender tax collectors to embarrass the rich into paying taxes.[585] In 2012, it covered Koovagam India's festival for which thousands of hijra, along with eunuchs, crossdressers, and male admirers gather annually for two weeks—undoubtedly the world's largest trans gathering, and also one of the single largest in all of India.[586] [587] And it covered the highest court in Malaysia overturning a religious law punishing trans women and encouraging Islamic religious police to abuse them.[588] [589]

In 2014, three pieces (two of them videos) documented Brazil's increasing acceptance of transgender women as models.[590] [591] [592] In South America, it covered a new Argentinian law making it the first Latin American nation to legalize gay marriage, and also among the first in the world to allow trans people to change their sex without a psychiatrist or surgery.[593] Tiny, arch-conservative Serbia had emerged as a global hub for affirming surgery because of its high surgical standards, combined with low prices.[594]

That same year, the *Times* Editorial Board saluted trans rights breakthroughs in Cuba, hailing Fidel Castro's daughter, Mariel, for almost single-handedly opening Cuban society to LGBTQ+ citizens.[595] And it would laud India for officially recognizing trans people as a third gender, so they were formally allocated public jobs and educational slots under its vast system of quotas—a small step for an enormous population often consigned to marginal lives of prostitution, abuse, and terrible poverty.[596]

2010

Among the *Times*' 2010 achievements was a full week devoted to Laura Erickson-Schroth's "Trans Bodies, Trans Selves" —an enormous resource guide for transgender and gender-expansive people, loosely modeled after 1970s landmark *Our Bodies Ourselves*. The book covered everything from medicine and law to history and language. It was a kind of *Whole Earth Catalog* for trans people. The first article introduced Laura and her work, and the next three articles featured her answering questions submitted by readers.[597] [598] [599] [600]

On the Arts desk, the *Times* devoted no less than seven pieces to the transploitation-slasher-comedy, "Ticked-Off Trannies With Knives." GLAAD and others had protested its trailer for "misrepresenting transgender women with "grotesque, exploitative depictions of violence"—which was the whole point of the movie.[601] (GLAAD might have also protested the *Times*, whose reviewer stooped to describe one actress as "male where it counts."[602])

Yet it was one of few movies to star trans women *as* trans women, and filmmaker Israel Luna initially defended it by explaining that it was actually inspired by the violence *against* trans women—before altering his trailer.[603] [604] [605] [606]

As perhaps the last person in the trans community who is still fond of sometimes using the word politically-incorrect term "trannie" to refer to myself, I was glad to at least see it back in print. However, a couple months later MTV apologized after GLAAD protested when two stars on its *Jersey Shore* show used the term.[607]

The T-word also showed up in a piece that mentioned Obama's transvestite nanny from his boyhood in Jakarta, Indonesia—his 'tranny nanny,'[608] It was also used by the gay mag *Out* in "Obama's Tranny Nanny," but no protest ensued.[609] (On the off-chance that GLAAD decides to to protest me over this book, I'd like to take this occasion to very earnestly and sincerely pre-apologize in print.)

In "When Boys Dress Like Girls for Halloween" published right after the holiday, a Kansas City mom defended her five-year-old's wearing the pink velvet dress of his favorite Scooby-Doo character from the outrage of other moms in their conservative community.[610] The picture of her son in costume she posted was viewed over a million times, drawing 26,000 responses.

> *"If you think that me allowing my son to be a female character for Halloween is somehow going to 'make' him gay then you are an idiot… If my son is gay, O.K., I will love him no less. I am not worried that your son will grow up to be an actual ninja, so back off. If my daughter had dressed as Batman, no one would have thought twice about it. No one. All I hope for my kids, and yours… is that they are happy. If a set of purple sparkly tights and a velvety dress is what makes my baby happy one night, then so be it. And my little man worked that costume like no other. He rocked that wig, and I wouldn't want it any other way."*

For her sudden celebrity, she was interviewed on CNN's Good Morning America, whereupon she was attacked by a clinical psychologist for "outing" her son. She very sensibly pointed out that he had *not* been outed, since he was only five and had not made any statement about his sexuality, much less expressed romantic attraction to anyone. America, we can do better.

2011

The *Times* brought in cultural critic Cintra Wilson to write a sympathetic review the documentary *Becoming Chaz* about Cher's child "Chastity" coming out as trans. In the middle, Wilson "had to ask [a] sticky batch of questions: "Could the fact that Chaz is now a man be somehow Cher's fault? Did the toxic culture of celebrity damage Chastity/Chaz's [female] gender identity? Did Cher's almost drag-queenlike hyper-female persona somehow devour Chastity's emerging femininity? Could Chaz's transition have been motivated by gender-bent Oedipal revenge? Is he reclaiming the childhood attention his superstar mother always diverted?... Is it remotely possible that he needed to make the transition because his mom is Cher?"[611]

Then, as now, one is struck by the *Times'* endless search for reasons young people who are transgender are not cisgender, and its endless search for the *cause* of being trans. Apparently the *Times* learned nothing from its ugly treatment of homosexuals and gay kids in the '80s.

This piece would be followed by an amazing one from the New York desk by investigative journalist Laura Rena Murray,"The High Price of Being a Woman." It focused on a 42-year-old Ecuadorian immigrant, Zaira Quispe, who arrived in New York at nine, determined to transition. Unable to afford proper medical care or insurance for implants, she settled for an illegal "pumper," working out of an anonymous Upper East Side apartment, who charged her $1,200 for her generous curves with injected silicon. Ecstatic at first, she then found the silicon had hardened and migrated all over her body.[612]

Tragic as her medical condition was, at least she was spared the ugly death the practice has inflicted on other immigrant trans women of color, as have illegal street hormones. It was an object lesson in the power of good journalism to help trans people, particularly those who are low-income and of color, and remains among the few anywhere detailing the huge black-market medical economy that serves often victimized, impoverished, undocumented trans people, desperate for safe medical care that is forever beyond their reach.

The following year, the City Room blog posted another *local color* piece about immigrant trans women. Jocelyn from Guatemala was literally buried alive by the *coyotes* smuggling her across the border to avoid the Border Patrol. It detailed her challenges and those of so many other Latinas who struggle to find work in America while avoiding drugs, assault, prostitution, and deportation to almost certain death.[613]

Good as some of this coverage was, there was also an unconscious racism threading through it. Of the few sympathetic articles documenting the lives trans people of color, they were almost always Latinx, and seldom Black. They were few if any articles focused on the lives and experiences of Asian Pacific Islander trans people or those who are Native Americans/American Indians.

Three columns in the Mother Lode blog were devoted to challenges of parents supporting gender-diverse children: "Navigating Gender in Pre-K," "When a Boy Wants a Tutu," and "In Praise of Pink Polish" and Fashion's "Boys Will Be Boys? Not in These Families."[614 615 616 617]

The latter two detailed the national right-wing outrage—which Jon Stewart called *Toemageddon* —which ensued after J. Crew's creative director included a carefree photo of her four-year-old son with pink-toenails in its annual catalog. The caption read: "Lucky for me, I ended up with a boy whose favorite color is pink. Toenail painting is way more fun in neon."[618 619] Cue the right-wing Outrage Machine. Interestingly, it was devoted almost entirely to gender diverse boys.[620] The three *Toemageddon* pieces helpfully consoled parents by advising them that gender-diverse kids may not grow up to be gay or (gasp!) transgender, and one therapist warned against an "aggressive rush" to affirming care: "'Whoa, not so fast.'"

2012

This attention to gender diverse boys continued the following year with Motherlode's "My Son Looks Like a Girl. So What?" and the Magazine's nearly 6,000-word "What's So Bad About a Boy Who Wants to Wear a Dress?"[621] [622] "What's So Bad" included this remarkable set-piece:

> *"Once when Jose was 3 and wearing a dress every day, his father pleaded: 'Jose! You're a boy! You're not a girl — you're a boy!' and then started to cry. Jose slipped out of bed, padded over to his weeping father and patted his head..."*

It also weirdly accused the transgender community of denying "gender is a spectrum"—even though I think we pretty much own the copyright on the phrase—and of trying to force gender-diverse kids into strict boy/girl binaries—exactly the accusation writer Pamela Paul would seize on a few years later in one of her vacuous op-eds: "Free to Be You or Me—Or Not." It also embarked on the usual mandatory snipe-hunt for the underlying cause of gender diversity in kids: hormones, genetics, culture, parental attachment issues, etc., etc..

None of these articles on gender diverse children used the term *nonbinary* yet, although that's probably what many of them were. But in four more years, 20-year-old Maria Munir would come out to Obama as nonbinary, effectively adding the phrase to the gender vocabulary and the journalistic dictionary.[623]

In a rare *Times* Editorial Board statement on the side of trans kids, it lauded the Girls Scouts of Colorado for welcoming "all girls," after one mother was mistakenly told her seven-year-old could join because she had "boy parts."[624]

Fashion once again revisited "Paris Is Still Burning" and the House of Xtravaganza—including famed drag queen Lady Bunny ("I'm here representing the International House of Pancakes")—and the *Xtras* campaign to engage a new generation in the ball culture.[625] [626]

The *Times* also did another tired and obligatory voyeuristic piece on predominantly Black trans women forced into sex work without a shred of background or insight. It quoted an exchange between a trans woman and a newcomer to the neighborhood who berated her for a past slight. She responded, "'The reason you buy your $2 million condo is because it is the historical West Village, and the reason it is the historical West Village is because of us…'" and "The screaming fight lasted for blocks, all the way to the river and into the night."[627] Sneer received, once again.

This consistent trivializing of the lives of young, often impoverished Black trans women rears up in yet another 2012 Metro article on the tragic burning death Lorena Escalera, "born male," which opened with this ugly lede: "She was 25 and curvaceous, and she often drew admiring glances in the gritty Brooklyn neighborhood where she was known to invite men for visits to her apartment…"—before going on to describe her being an escort, her adult website ads, and the contents of the debris pile outside her apartment.)[628] It was in such marked contrast to the respectful coverage the *Times* had recently afforded hetero white deaths-by-fire, that GLAAD, the Association of LGBTQ+ Journalists,

Laverne Cox, and an especially-incensed Janet Mock protested Metro Editor Carolyn Ryan, then one of the *Times'* highest ranking gay editors.[629] [630] [631] Rising to the task, Ryan defended the indefensible. This is the same Ryan who, becoming Managing Editor, lead the *Times* into its outrageous coverage of trans teens. In 2023 staffers, contributors, and subscribers rebelled.[632]

2013

The Sports section's "A Pioneer, Reluctantly" detailed the trials of Fallon Fox, the first openly trans athlete in mixed martial arts (MMA)—until Lia Thomas in the 2020s—probably the most visible trans professional athlete since Renée Richards in the 1970s.[633] In a sport that attracts many of the macho-MAGA boneheads who were no small part of MMP competitors and personnel, Fox would endure all manner of abuse, as well as many death threats.

"The Soldier Formerly known as Barry Manning" was one of scores of *Times* pieces about PVC Chelsea Manning: first for her trial, and then for her very public coming out as trans, and her struggle for affirming care from inside the prison cell of a government that wanted to make her an example.[634]

This particular piece was from Public Editor Margaret Sullivan, a position Sulzberger would eliminate just four years later as he was publishing "Our Path Forward," announcing that the *Times* connection to readers was so "important… [that it] cannot be outsourced to a single intermediary."[635] Loose translation: *I'm moving right to attract MAGA readership, and I don't need any critique from inside the castle gates when I do it.*

In explaining how the *Times* would cover someone

so well know for her previous name and gender, Sullivan provided the *Times*' style guide on coverage for guidance—evidence that the *Times* had grown and finally imposed such guidelines: ***"transgender** (adj.) is an overall term for people whose current identity differs from their sex at birth, whether or not they have changed their biological characteristics…"*[636]

"For 25 Days, Transsexual to the Core" in the Movies was one of many pieces devoted to the *Dallas Buyers Club* and Jared Leto's moving and sensitive portrayal of a doomed transgender man in small-town Nebraska.[637]

I'm sorry… that was Hilary Swank's moving and sensitive portrayal in *Boys Don't Cry.* Leto's was a moving and sensitive portrayal of a doomed transgender woman, as it just so happens, a prostitute. Leto noted that in "field testing" his role as Rayon, he walked into Whole Foods and got three quick reactions, "One was, 'What is that?' The second one was, 'Who is that?' and the other was, 'I dunno what the fuck that is, but I don't like it.'"[638] Welcome to our world.

2014

"Can Jill Soloway Do Justice to the Trans Movement?" was the Magazine's proflle of director and show-runner Jill Soloway of Showtime's series *Transparent*, a show apparently modeled after her trans father.[639] It ended on this lovely sentiment: "[He said] 'We're all trans. Don't you see that we're all trans?'"

But we aren't, except perhaps in the way we all struggle to become comfortable in the skin we were born into [and] to uncover an identity beneath what was assigned to us at birth.[640]

The three articles mentioned earlier about students transitioning at liberal women's colleges would serve as a kind of precursor to Ruth Padawer's outstanding 7,000-word piece in the *Magazine* titled, "When Women Become Men at Wellesley"—which remains to my mind the standard for thoughtful and sensitive explorations of college transition.[641]

Living on the cutting edge of gender roles, and often directly confronting binary gender relations, these transmasculine students were looked up to by many campus feminists as leaders, and it was exactly this influence and acceptance among young women that would so enrage the Eleanor Burkett in her op-ed just one year later in 2015.

2014 closed with a poignant obituary to transgender author and lifelong communist activist Leslie Feinberg, known for their best-selling book *Stone Butch Blues*. As writer Shauna Miller wrote of it on her website after Leslie's death, "It changed trans history. It changed dyke history. And how it did that was by honestly telling a brutally real, beautifully vulnerable and messy personal story of a butch lesbian."[642]

Part Four: Community Revolts

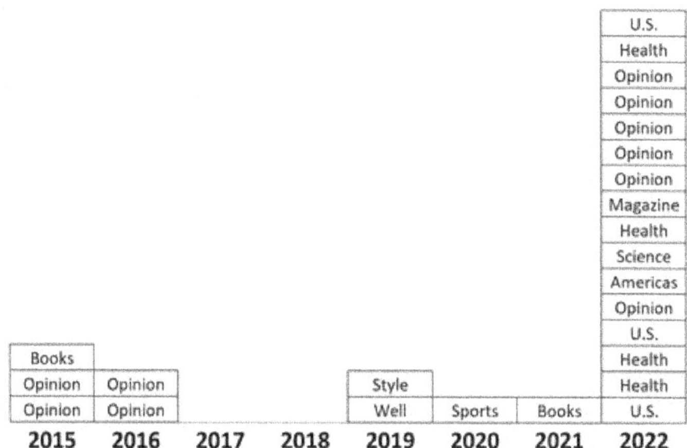

Times' articles from 2015-2022 by desk.

A Brief Honeymoon

There had been just 80 articles by the U.S. desk from 1994 through 2009— about three each year, but from by 2010 through 2023 there were 1,672, or about 88 each year: the *Times* was now publishing as many pieces on trans in a single week as it used to in an entire year. It was an astonishing amount of journalistic attention to about 1% of the population.

To be sure, in that high article count were more than a few that were not particularly trans-oriented, but once would have read "gay community" and now read "gay, lesbian, bisexual *and transgender* community." But beginning in 2016 or 2017, as the evangelical right began to prosecute its war on trans youth in earnest, articles mentioning "trans" increasingly had them as their subject.

If it was no longer possible to synopsize all of the *Times* pieces on trans, although it was possible to synopsize *how* the *Times* was covering trans.

The rhetorical space it had carved out was already clear. The coverage could be exemplary, but was too often bad, and sometimes trivializing.

There was also a frequent disrespect—especially from Arts, Fashion, Style, and local desks: too many pop culture lead-ins, and too many gratuitous descriptions about our looks and bodies. There was already a disturbing tendency to treat the new visibility of transgender as an imposition on cisgender people, and to create coverage around *their* feelings about *us*.

To its great credit, although it sometimes seemed to have a special fascination with it, the *Times* was one of the first mainstream outlets to take drag seriously as an art form. And increasingly often it would write with sensitively of crime and violence against the community and against trans people abroad. And as I've already noted, from 1995-96 it was also among the first major outlets to break the story of the new transgender rights movement taking hold, and to cover it as the *hard news* it was.

But there was also, already, an unfortunate tendency to promote the voices, as "experts," those who want to eradicate being transgender, In some of the issues surrounding transgender there have been legitimate arguments to be made from the "other side;" I don't agree with them, but there are people who can make them in the service of civil debate. White evangelical extremists are not this category.[643]

But during that brief honeymoon from 2000 to 2014, trans coverage seemed to settle into a regular news groove, as if the *Times* was growing up; as if trans people were going to be covered just as… news.

Editorial standards had arrived: gone were the mispronouncing and deadnaming, the descriptions of our failures to embody cisgender masculinity and femininity, the dehumanizing descriptions of our genitals. Gone, too, were the regular leering portraits of impoverished trans women engaged in commercial sex work. We'd broken out of Arts, Fashion, and Style sections—where we were entertainment; local profiles—where we were often colorful specimens; and Science or Medicine—where we were patients.

And because of all this these changes, there was a brief interregnum from around 2000 to 2012 when trans people were treated neither better nor worse than any other story.

In other words, the *Times* had begun rising to the challenge and learning like the sophisticated news organism that it was.

Ironically, despite Sulzberger's scorn towards trans advocates—who he has accused of wanting the paper to engage in advocacy journalism—*this* coverage was what it looked like when we were treated simply like every other issue, instead of dangled as click-bait for the evangelical right.

The End of an All-Too-Brief Era

But this brief period was already drawing to a close.

Sulzberger was promoted to Associate Editor for Newsroom Strategy in 2015, and began implementing his plan to ramp up the *Times'* digital subscriptions. And this coincided with the *Times* first blatantly transphobic op-eds, including Dobbs, Burkett, Friedman, Schuck, and Shulevitz.

Then there was another second brief pause, from the end of 2016 until mid-2019, which coincided with Sulzberger's competition with his cousins Sam Dolnick (now a Deputy Managing Editor) and David Perpich (now Head of Standalone Products) to lead the *Times.*[644]

But by 2018, Sulzberger would be named Publisher, and by mid-2019, the articles would start up again. But this time it wasn't a trickle, it was a flood.

The early errors of the *Times* of the 1970s to 1990s had been the common, casual bigotries of writers confronted with an unfamiliar minority that made them uncomfortable.

The errors of *Times* from 2015 on were something else entirely. This *Times* knew exactly what we were, and exactly what it was doing. And it wasn't just deadnaming or mispronouning, but directly attacking our legitimacy.

As Chu wrote in *New York* Magazine, Sulzberger was making himself and the *Times* into the leading U.S. voice for the twin propositions that "forcing the orthodoxy of gender down the public's throat… is censorship and intimidation," and that skepticism and disconfirmation of transgender kids' identities "was not only justified, but urgent."[645]

The two brief honeymoons—from 2000 to 2014, and then from the end of 2016 to mid-2019 were over. An old-fashioned newspaper crusade was on.

Chapter Nineteen: The Pamela Paul-ization of the *Times*

Troll-in-Chief

Two Thousand twenty-two was the year when Sulzberger's vision of transforming a "liberal rag" into a digital platform that could attract readers from the right as well as the left seems to have really kicked in. One piece after another—fifteen in all, one every three weeks—attacked trans children on nearly every front.

But then, having tagged all the bases that the Christian nationalist right had just laid out through a cascade of lawsuits, state policies, and new laws: bathroom use, sports, blockers and hormones, top surgery detransition, it was as if intellectual exhaustion set in. Having run dry on new "vexing problems" and "wrenching conflicts" to platform for its new right-wing subscribers, instead of major "think" pieces or investigative reporting, it turned to publishing drive-by hit-pieces by new opinion writer Pamela Paul.

Paul had been married to a right-wing *Times* trans-denialist, Bret Stephens, who used *his* own inaugural op-ed to attack the science behind global warming.[646]

Previously best known for writing "Pornified," a long, hysteric screed against adult eroticism, for ten years

Paul had served as Editor of the *Times'* Book Review, eventually greenlighting Jesse Singal's admiring column on Helen Joyce, the woman who had declared trans was a "crazy delusion," and that trans acceptance was being promoted by Jewish billionaires.[647] [648]

To get a flavor of the damage to trans people that Paul had already done from Book Review posts, one writer reported that she had asked that he change his original lede about how transgender children were under attack into something less political and "more focused on the book." But while his original first paragraph read, "The culture wars have come for your transgender children," the opening sentence published the *Times* read: "Now here is a beautiful little book that carries a great, great weight on its shoulders."[649]

So Sulzberger knew exactly what he was getting when he moved her to the op-ed pages only weeks after the *Times* terminated its 15-year contract with its first and only openly trans opinion writer, and only its second active LGBTQ+ columnist—Jennifer Finney Boylan.

According to *Xtra*, Boylan claimed that she left on good terms, but she and many of her editors decamped to the *Washington Post* and—along with his termination of the post of Public Editor—it had all the earmarks of Sulzberger clearing the decks for what was to come.[650]

He needn't have bothered.

Boylan's writing was often delightful and engaging, but as her community was being consumed in one of the most vicious legislative assaults in recent memory, she used her position as the highest-ranking, highest-profile trans journalist in the country to continue publishing poignant columns, often devoted to life's little challenges and personal vistas.

During her final two years at the *Times*, nearly 1,000 bills were being filed in 49 states, but her op-eds were typical, including profiles on Jimmy Carter, losing her hearing, trans ally-ship, rudeness, and the meaning of a trans person winning *Jeopardy!*. A community reeling under near-daily legislative attacks might be in need of strong and uncompromising voice to champion their cause. But Boylan was not to be it.

Once hired—as others have noted—Paul sought to position herself like every anti-trans bigot as a brave teller of the inconvenient truths which others dared not speak. Or, as the *Times* itself would crow in March 2022, "Pamela impressed us with her keen desire to write about what people really think and believe, but are often too afraid to say… [and] to help people question what has often become the received point of view."[651] Un-huh. To quote FAIR, a loose translation of this would be: "bringing on a hired gun to take the *Times*' side in this "culture war."

Book-Burning & Tweets

As FAIR also noted, Paul's hiring coincided with one of the more outrageous articles from the *Times* Editorial Board a week later, "America Has a Free Speech Problem," *both-sides-ing* the attempts by the right and the left to push back on opinions they didn't like:[652]

Right-wing extremists were literally burning books, banning school textbooks, making teaching or training of DEI or systemic racism illegal, passing laws that prevented teachers from saying "gay" or "transgender" in classrooms, and practicing a brand of domestic terrorism that saw armed right-wing militia shutting down drag book-readings, and bomb threats shutting down to least 33 schools, libraries, and hospitals.[653] [654] [655] [656] [657]

Meanwhile the left was writing hundreds, maybe *thousands,* of very angry tweets and blog posts which made some people really uncomfortable. So, you know, *both sides* are at fault.

The Editorial Board accused social media of being "awash in speech of the point-scoring, picking-apart, piling-on, put-down variety," which it considered a serious threat to free speech. Although the reader might be forgiven for thinking that this is *exactly* what free speech looks like once it slips the bounds of institutional actors like the *Times,* and the *great unwashed* finally enjoy access to the massive reach that was once the sole domain of newspapers and other media giants.

Paul's pieces tended to be so lightweight that they could not even be properly characterized as attacks—more like stones skipped across the intellectual surface of culture war ponds. They were less op-eds than exercises in marketing, recycling attacks that seemed calculated to pander to the new outrage wing of *Times* readers without breaking a sweat in the way of critical thinking or challenge their existing prejudices. And there would be bonus points if the piece was really so naughty and so politically incorrect that would piss off lefties. The subhead on every Paul column could have read: "Owning the libs *yet again*!"

The LA *Times* described her as "churning out low-effort reactionary garbage piece after piece," and *Gawke*r as "the new worst columnist at the Times," with its Editor-in-Chief noting, "Usually it takes a columnist a few years to get to a certain level of asininity; Paul, who started at the opinion desk in April, has summited the highest peak on column five."[658] [659]

Paul was effectively a kind of Troll-in-Chief, writing for the *Times'* new, if unannounced, Cancel Culture desk—which, as Froomkin noted, now included writers like Powell and Singal of course.[660]

Paul devoted her inaugural columns—six in the space of just eight months—to repeatedly criticizing transgender people for any number of imagined harms, just in case anyone has missed Sulzberger's "*Out with the trans/ In with the anti-trans*" hire.

The Anti-Woke Desk

Among Paul's first columns was, "She Wrote a Dystopian Novel. What Happened Next Was Pretty Dystopian," which attacked that ever-reliable straw man, the Horde.[661]

As usual, transgender advocates were so successful in cancelling sci-fi writer Sandra Newman, that her book *The Men* was punished with glowing reviews in the *Financial Times*, *Publishers Weekly*, the *Spectator*, the *Telegraph*, and the *Times of London*, and—her one-glowing career left in tatters—she was reduced to a personal invitation from the estate of the late George Orwell to write the long-awaited sequel to his landmark classic, *1984.*[662]

Paul's second anti-trans column was a rehash of Powell's, "Vanishing Abortion Word—'Woman'"—which was followed exactly three weeks later by "There's More Than One Way to Ban a Book," another cancel culture piece about the Horde.[663] The accompanying graphic literally showed books being tortured and dismembered by fire, arrows, buzzsaws, and dynamite (I am *not* making this up).

Pauls' main example was the American Booksellers Association getting pushback for promoting a new book.

What she doesn't say is that it was full of pseudoscience and disinformation, and authored by Abigail Shrier, a key TERF figure and subtitled, "The Transgender Craze Seducing Our Daughters."[664] It was also published by Regnery Publishing, best known for "Unfit for Command"—which maligned John Kerry's war record and made "Swift Boating" a verb, as well as books on COVID-denial and the "science" of intelligent design.

Psychology Today condemned Shrier's book as "bizarre and full of misinformation." American Booksellers pulled the book, apologized, and conducted its own internal review. Paul denounced this as "self-censorship" and "repression."[665]

Her column "Let's Say Gay" weirdly positioned Paul as defending of all the poor gay, lesbian, and bisexual people who—like cisgender women—feel the deep pain of erasure from inclusive language like the acronym "LGBTQ"—"which sometimes includes additional symbols and letters and represents so many identities unrelated to sexual orientation that gays and lesbians can feel crowded out, [as well as] 'queer' which can mean almost anything… Confused? You should be!" [666]

She closes by cheering on all those neglected "Gay people, lesbians, and bisexuals who fought for a long time to be open and clear about who they are. That's why they call it pride."

There is nothing quite like having a privileged, straight, cisgender white woman instruct you on the joys and pains of queer identity. One can only imagine the future columns that will ensue once Paul discovers "LGTBQIA+" and her head explodes.

"Free to Be You or Me—Or Not" was exceptionally airheaded even for Paul, who used the 50th anniversary of

Marlo Thomas's child-affirming "Free to Be… You and Me" album *cum* book to attack educators and presumably trans people for "not liberating children from gender, [and instead] offering them a smorgasbord of labels—gender identity, gender role, gender performance and gender expression… and gender stereotypes like in the 1970's [when] it didn't matter whether you were a boy or a girl, because neither could limit your choices."[667]

This counterfactual reverie about the carefree 1970s is only steps removed from white racists pining for the good old 1950s when *it didn't matter if you were Black or white, because we were all just people.*

But while Paul may have been the main problem, she wasn't the only problem.

As the queer community was already seething over the monthly drumbeat of biased and phobic articles, there would be two new scaremongering pieces on three new issues.

However, by then, the LGBTQ+ groups and the queer community and the *Times'* contributors had all finally had enough.

Chapter Twenty: How to Scare Parents

Title:	**“They Paused Puberty, but Is There a Cost?”[668]**
Date:	**November 14, 2022**
Byline:	**Megan Twohey & Christina Jewett**
Section:	**Front Page (print) / Health (digital)**
Words:	**5,764**

0.33% of Trans Kids

Megan Twohey and Christina Jewett essentially staged a replay of Bazelon’s “battle” over gender therapy just five months earlier, but focused entirely on puberty blockers. As FAIR noted, it was a front page “investigation so lengthy it spilled across three pages after the jump, incorporating 18 quoted sources.”[669]

And as with Bazelon’s piece, it glides through the obligatory positive notes before devoting the bulk of attention to cascades of warnings and life-threatening consequences.[670] So, instead of a balanced discussion of the quite modest, rare, and manageable side-effects of blockers, it pushed the idea that blockers shouldn’t be given at all.

Bazelon had noted two risks of blockers: possible

bone density loss and possible fertility problems. Twohey/Jewett run with the first, mentioning the word "bone" 55 times in 5,764 words—or once every 100 words. They mention "concern," "harm", "risk," and "danger" 24 times in total—or once every 200 words.

Again, there is a strong medical consensus around blockers, but the *Times* simply prefers to ignore it because it is trying to appeal to right-wing readers. This is clearly demonstrated in a pre-buttal slide-show titled "Behind Our Reporting on Puberty Blockers" below:[671]

Behind Our Reporting on Puberty Blockers

Megan Twohey and Christina Jewett
Reporting for the Investigations Desk

Doctors who treat transgender patients typically describe the use of puberty blockers as **a safe, reversible way to press pause**.

Republican politicians and other critics say the treatment is dangerous, even likening it to child abuse.

[Graphic courtesy of the New York Times.]

So there you have it. This captures Sulzberger's editorial posture in a single sentence: experienced pediatricians who regularly treat transgender kids and stay close to the data and medical standards say it is safe… *but on the other hand*, MAGA politicians say… Instead of debunking the right's lies and pseudoscience, the *Times* was *using* them to debunk the doctors.

A parallel slide around abortion might read: "Doctors who treat patients seeking abortions typically describe it as a safe and effective private procedure… but Republican politicians say it is murder and liken it to killing an unborn child."

It only rubbed salt in the wound that the front-page

piece was published during Trans Awareness Week, which it is hard to believe was not an intentional slap in the face or attempt to harvest outrage clicks—probably both.

Like Bazelon and Ghorayshi, Twohey/Jewett offer all of the *Times'* usual evidence-free assertions as to why trans kids aren't really trans, and thus shouldn't get blockers:

a) They have "psychiatric issues" and "psychiatric disorders"
b) Blockers are a *gateway drug* that will "lock" them into a "treatment pathway"
c) They have been swept into inappropriate medical interventions too quickly.

The groundbreaking Trans Youth Project study which found that 40% of trans-identified kids *still hadn't* gone on blockers five years later is not mentioned in the article: why offer facts when you can offer supposition?

As always, the big scary numbers come right up front: [A]s an increasing number of adolescents identify as transgender — in the United States, an estimated 300,000 ages 13 to 17 and an untold number who are younger — concerns are growing among some medical professionals about the consequences of the drugs…" Reading this, readers might be forgiven for thinking that all 300,000 of those trans kids aged 13 to 17 were getting blockers.

They are not. As the Komodo Health study found, only about 1,000 of the 300,000 are actually being prescribed blockers each year. That's just 0.33%.[672]

To put this in perspective, here's what it looks like (I've actually inflated the numbers getting care a bit by adding both those getting blockers *and* hormones):

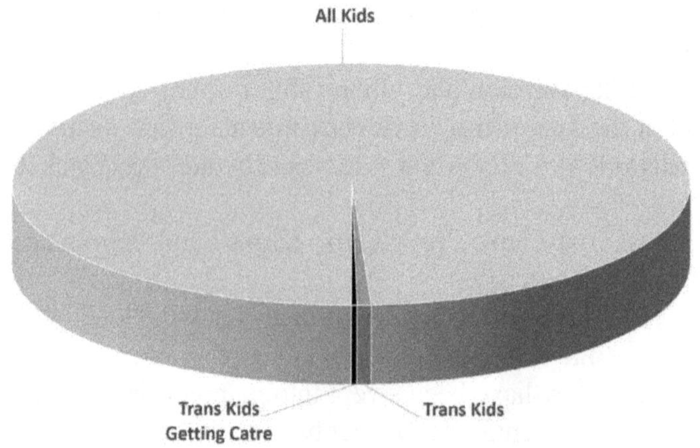

1% Equal Two-Thirds

Twohey/Jewett frame their piece with the stories of three adolescents: one trans girl for whom puberty blockers were right; one cis girl for whom they clearly were a mistake and who now has "a voice that sounds like man's;" and one trans girl who never had the recommended scans and had to stop blockers after one showed low bone density.

They also point to an anomalous case of a Swedish adolescent who also did not have the recommended scans, developed osteoporosis and compression fractures of the spine, and has developed a lifelong disability.

Since neither this teen nor the trans girl had bone scans *prior to* blockers, it is impossible to say if their osteoporosis predated the treatments—which would certainly help explain their highly anomalous bone problems.

Moreover, studies have found that trans girls are already especially vulnerable to low bone density issues because of a combination of lack of exercise, poor nutrition, anorexia/bulimia, and the vitamin D and calcium deficiencies that result from these—all of which are *caused* by the gender dysphoria which blockers would *help relieve.*[673 674]

Similarly, the website Science-Based Medicine noted that trans teens are more than twice as likely to suffer from anorexia/bulimia, with 63% "reporting weight manipulation for gender-affirming purposes,[675] adding, correctly, that "eating disorders have a more significant effect on bones than puberty blockers ever will."

Twohey/Jewett also threw in the story of Keira Bell, whose detransition and lawsuit against England's National Health Service essentially ended its pediatric gender care nationwide overnight. Bell later claimed that she had breast reduction and was left with facial hair and a deep, masculine voice.[676]

None of this is even slightly relevant to a story about puberty blockers, which merely pause pubertal effects temporarily: it's just gratuitous scaremongering.

To sum up, we have just one single happy story against two unhappy stories, plus two awful detransitions. Any poor parent reading this for medical guidance about their trans child on blockers might easily think that that they would be insane to do so, given that odds for a positive outcome look like only one in three.. Or even worse one in five, counting the Bell and the Swedish story. So the *Times* makes it seem that the regret rate, as provided from Twohey/Jewett's examples, is 66% or 80%.

Within four months, even the stuffy Associated Press corrected the record in a piece titled, "How Common Is

Transgender Treatment, Regret, Detransitioning?" noting that in "a review of 27 studies involving almost 8,000 teens and adults who had transgender surgeries, mostly in Europe, the U.S and Canada, 1% on average expressed regret."[677]

Twohey/Jewett cite doctors' opinions 13 times: three positive and 10 negative ones.[678] They also quote doctors discussing the side effects of blockers—while omitting that these doctors fully support blockers, and are vehemently opposed to any attempt to limit them.

Ominously, Twohey/Jewett note that "seven pediatric endocrinologists and pediatric endocrine nurse practitioners in Florida recently wrote to the state health department that evidence to support the use of those treatments in adolescents 'is simply lacking'..."

This sounds pretty serious. Until you consider that Twohey/Jewett neglected to mention that *300* of their fellow pediatric endocrinologists and nurse practitioners in Florida also wrote their own letter to the state health department in support of affirming care.[679] This misrepresentation of the real facts is a consistent method of tilting the scales their own way.

"Zero Bone Loss" But Very Dangerous

Twohey/Jewett commissioned a review of the research on blockers from a cardiology epidemiologist who now had apparent clinical expertise in transgender health, pediatrics, or transgender youth.

Nonetheless, even he finds that, "The change in bone density while adolescents were on blockers was observed to be zero." [*Emphasis added.]*

Yet Twohey/Jewett introduce his findings by saying

that they show that "it's increasingly clear that the drugs are associated with deficits in bone development" and could cause "debilitating fractures" in middle age.

But how can they do that?

Here's the rhetorical footwork involved.

All the examples they've offered are of *actual bone loss.*

But the "deficit" they're warning about here isn't actual bone loss at all, but lower rates of bone growth compared with other kids not on blockers.

This makes sense, because during puberty bones grow and lengthen, and blockers are designed to pause puberty. But once kids move on to hormones their bones get back on track. And this is true of cisgender kids who take blockers as well.

But by moving the goalposts, Twohey/Jewett can frame a positive finding as a negative one. Even worse, the finding of "zero bone loss" only appears in a housekeeping section after the article titled "Methodology." All those unproven risks of "debilitating factures" go right up front, but an actual finding from seven studies doesn't warrant a mention.

Reading between the lines, Twohey/Jewett commissioned their own meta-analysis to find evidence of harm, and when that failed, they buried the finding. The irony is the *Times* is still too good a news organization simply to expunge the finding entirely. But you can bet if it *had* found a negative result, it would have been right up front.

That trans adolescent they cited in the beginning whose bone density plummeted by 15% to prove the risks of blockers turns out to be total outlier, even among the among 500 kids in seven studies examined by their own reviewer.[680]

Which brings us to their other horror story: that Swedish adolescent who ended up with a lifelong disability. But his case was not drawn from peer review journals, or even a clinical case study. The unverified "Leo's" story was taken from a segment broadcast a year earlier by a Swedish right-wing news channel well-known for promoting anti-trans stories.[681]

To recap: Tens of thousands of American transgender kids have received puberty blockers for years with few problems, and cisgender kids since the 1980s, and the *Times*' own meta-analysis of 500 kids found "zero" bone loss, so Twohey/Jewett were reduced to digging up this one story from over a year ago carried by a right-wing Swedish television station to make the argument that blockers are harmful—a result apparently so rare they had to go abroad because they couldn't find a single case among the U.S's own 42 million adolescents or in any of scores of academic journals.[682]

But Wait... There's More!

But Twohey/Jewett weren't done scaring parents yet.

Along with bone density issues, osteoporosis, and permanent disability, they also added in brain damage because "some doctors and researchers are concerned that puberty blockers may some how disrupt a formative period of mental growth... [and] brain development."

Some doctors and researchers are also concerned that vaccines are causing cancer and autism, that hydroxychloroquine should be used to cure COVID, and that induced abortions causes breast cancer.[683] [684] [685] But I digress.

Twohey/Jewett charge that medical consensus is

based on "limited studies" and "low-quality research," that blockers are an "off-label" use, may not be "safe," have "little documentation of outcomes," "no government approval," and no "official tracking," which has led to a "false sense of security" about "'permanent damage.'"

I don't know where to begin with this kind of "flood the zone with shit" journalism, so I won't try here. As with Bazelon, there's the same massive contradiction: if puberty blockers were the cause mental impairment and permanent damage, we would have seen these effects from the tens of thousand of cisgender kids who have also taken them since the 1980s. And this is why, despite all these imminent health risks and the specter of "permanent damage," nearly every Republican bill introduced to ban trans kids from getting blockers has contained a specific exemption that ensures cisgender kids with precocious or contrasexual puberty continue getting their blockers uninterrupted.

Apparently this must be because—despite their superficial similarities—cisgender kids have *entirely different* physiologies from their transgender peers. We know this, because just six months earlier beneath a brightly-colored cartoon of a little girl in her backpack, the *Times*' own Science desk published a piece on cisgender kids and blockers.[686]

Titled, "Puberty Starts Earlier Than It Used To. No One Knows Why," it included zero warnings about osteoporosis, zero warnings about bone loss, and zero warnings of permanent damage or brain impairment. In fact, the words "danger," "bone density," "disability," "damage," and "concern" didn't even appear in it.

The piece only mentioned the word "risk," in connection with the risks of *not taking blockers* because that might cause cisgender girls to develop "depression, anxiety, substance abuse, and other psychological problems…"

So it looks like the physiologies of trans kids' bodies must be *totally* different.

Despite all this, somehow Twohey/Jewett have the colossal *chutzpah* to close their piece on trans kids and blocker with a plea for "less vitriol, more science."

Chapter Twenty-One: Pronouns & Hairstyles Are Dangerous

Title:	**"When Students Change Gender Identity, and Parents Don't Know"[687]**
Date:	**January 22, 2023**
Byline:	**Katie J. M. Baker**
Section:	**Front Page (print) / U.S. (digital)**
Words:	**3,217**

"Stabbed in the Back"

After eight years of questioning the judgment of parents who affirm their transgender children, in another front-page story the *Times* reversed course completely and came out strongly in support of the judgment of parents with trans kids… as long as they were skeptical and and/or opposed to their kids' transitions.

It was a new front in the anti-care culture war which had just been teed up by ADF in its efforts to expand the "parental right" of Christian parents, just as it had done with teen abortion.

The thrust of the Baker's article was that trans kids all over the country are transitioning socially without their parents' knowledge and school administrators are keeping this from them.

Or as one parent put it, they were being *stabbed in the back.*

It's a violent metaphor, and the violence here was directed at parents, despite the fact that non-metaphoric and very real violence against trans kids by hostile and rejecting parents is well-documented, but was unmentioned. As one student explained in a *Washington Post* piece on the same topic: "'I have many friends whose parents would kick them out if they found out they were queer, or beat them so badly they could wind up dead. That's not an exaggeration — that's the environment that LGBTQ+ teens exist in.'"[688] A UK study found that 43% of trans kids had been abused by their families.[689]

There's also the real specter of family abandonment—of which the *Times*' many articles on trans street kids are evidence. Although LGBTQ+ youth are less than 10% of young people, they comprise 20-40% of homeless youth.[690] The Trevor Project has found that nearly 6% of LGBTQ+ youth are abandoned by their families, and even more are *housing insecure*.[691 692 693 694]

Baker also ignored the dangers of trans-skepticism, although studies of gay and trans kids who have experienced parental rejection found they were eight times more likely to attempt suicide, and an NIH study found that 40% of trans kids have tried to kill themselves—with parental rejection being among the main contributing factors.[695 696]

But this attitude goes all the way back to Friedman's 2015 question—*What's wrong with a little skepticism?*—and the *Times* continued to refuse to consider the costs for trans kids.

Instead, Baker focused on "dozens of parents whose children have socially transitioned at school, [who said] they felt villainized by educators who seemed to think they—not the parents—knew what was best…" They have become ADF plaintiffs, which has formed a special Child and Parental Rights Campaign to "defend children" from the "existential threat" posed by being transgender.[697]

In response to the notion that kids are just trying to be themselves, Baker parroted Christian Nationalists' rebuttal, including the vile slurs of those who call transgender advocates "groomers."[698]

Weirdly, she quoted one ADF plaintiff who said, "I don't know why the school decided to hide this from us"—and then, in the very next sentence quoted him declaring that he was a Catholic who remained morally opposed to his trans child being trans. Boyfriend! *That's* why it was hidden from you.

Baker provided the by-now-inevitably *Times* list of reasons that trans kids aren't really trans, which had now mutated and added new entries, including that they:

a) Have mental health conditions
b) Are mistaken and will change their minds
c) Have been "influenced by classmates to ask for hormone treatments and surgery"
d) Aren't really being "serious."
e) This omits several of Bazelon's hypothetical reasons, including that they are:
f) Trying to avoid aspects of themselves they dislike
g) Dealing with past traumas
h) Feeling "confined by gender stereotypes
i) Too ashamed to admit they that really want to detransition.

Although Baker interviewed more than 50 people, including parents and their children, she was totally disinterested in affirming parents and their kids. Her sympathies lay entirely with trans-skeptical/rejecting parents and their need to assert their rights over their child's body and identity. In other words, another article taken from ADF talking points.

The "Irreparable Harms" of Social Transition

Baker made wild claims of "potentially life-altering decisions," with their "irreparable harms" caused by social transitions. These are exactly the claims that Ghoryashi, Edwards-Leeper, and Anderson made earlier in the "Doctors Debate…" piece in relation to hormones almost one year previous, to the day. The Times has been relentless in platforming every possible risk that might be associated with medical transition, but now downshifted to even social transitions—hair length, clothing, gendered names and pronouns—as being dangerous.

When our daughter was eight, she asked us to call her by the gender-neutral name "DJ." We'd kept her hair short, and also encouraged her to wear jeans instead of dresses when playing outside. I am just hoping we didn't do any "irreparable harm." I mean, she's 18 and about to start college, but you can never tell.

In a follow-up op-ed the following day, columnist Michelle Goldberg would suggest that we all ought to embrace ADF's trans-rejecting parents/plaintiffs, so they aren't sent "careening rightward" to right-wing websites where they will be seduced by extremists.[699] Which to me sounds an awful lot like the *social contagion* of Rapid Onset MAGA Extremism (ROME).

Explained one parent, "'It's politically weird to be a very liberal Democrat and find yourself shoved in bed with the governor of Texas. Am I supposed to listen to Tucker Carlson?" But since they're already plaintiffs for the world's largest anti-LGBTQ+ hate group, it's unclear how much farther right they could go.[700]

Baker herself had previously been sharply critical of anti-trans denialism, but here she sympathetically defended anti-trans parents and their right to force schools to drop dime on their kids. As Xtra's Jude Ellison Doyle noted, these kinds of abrupt *volte-face* by a *Times'* reporter "bore all the hallmarks of work being forced into pre-ordained editorial conclusions in service of an agenda set from above."[701]

Baker ended on this quote from another ADF plaintiff who remains staunchly unwilling to accept their child's gender identity: "'There is only so much and so far that I'm willing to go right now, and I would hope that, as a parent, that would be my decision.'"

But it isn't: it's their child's.

As *Assigned Media*'s Urquhart summarizes:

> *"An in-depth investigative look into the parents' rights movement would have been eye-opening, but this isn't that. Likewise, an honest examination of the question of why some public schools decided that the best interests of children are served by allowing youth to socially transition regardless of their parents' wishes would be useful and illuminating... but this isn't that, either. Instead it is a misleading, one-sided picture that will leave* Times' *readers less informed, and more primed to participate in the ongoing moral panic about transgender youth."*[702]

For three years, Sohn has warned about the dangers of chest-binding, Bazelon the dangers of medical transition, Ghorayshi the dangers of top surgery, Twohey and Jewett the harms of blockers, and now Baker the harms of changing pronouns and hair style.

The goalposts have been moved so many times they could be on rollers. Apparently *anything* a trans kid does to manifest their gender is potentially lethal.

By my count, by this point *Times* had devoted 50,000+ words across 25 articles to attacking trans people generally, and 30,000 words to attacking trans kids specifically—16 articles in 2022 alone.

The narrative thrusts of all these articles align closely with the message platform developed and promoted by Christian nationalist organizations and contradicts broadly-accepted medical consensus. Many are front page stories and/or multi-page spreads, even though the total number of kids transitioning are about half of 1% of all youth, and studies have found their transitioning experiences are almost entirely positive.[703]

So perhaps it's no wonder that only a week after this article appeared, over 1,000 *Times*' contributors, tens of thousand of subscribers and readers, and the LGBTQ+ national organizations—already seething under a sustained and unprecedented assault—finally exploded.[704]

Chapter Twenty-Two: A Community Revolts

Seeds of a Brushoff

The seeds of Sulzberger's hard-edge response to the revolt may have been laid because of the humiliating about-face the *Times* had been forced to perform after the op-ed by Republican Sen. Tom Cotton that called for turning federal troops loose on Black Lives Matter, which ignited fury across the office.[705]

Upper management first attempted to ignore the growing firestorm. But when staff tweeted out that "Running this puts Black *New York Times* staff in danger," followed by 800 staffers who had signed a letter of protest, and then 300 more who held an online virtual walk-out, it had no choice.[706] Heads had to roll, and Sulzberger, infuriated by the public embarrassment, called Bennett at home and icily fired him.[707]

Sulzberger reportedly abhorred both embarrassment and having *Times* staffers airing the firms' dirty linen in public. As one reporter told me privately, it was likely he determined then, that management would never again be put into the position of having staff dictate policy to them.

As in almost every bottom-up uprising today, social media—and especially multiple conversations going on over the company's Slack channels—had been a key instrument.

Following the Cotton debacle, management had killed the Slack channels employees used to share their thoughts and feelings. Now it was all one-way only, from management down; no criticism allowed. As one employee put it, "You can reply with an emoji. They are obsessed with collegiality. If I have feedback one minute before a piece is published it's like, 'Thank you for your feedback." Once it goes up, it's, 'How dare you attack a colleague.'"

According to *Xtra*'s Doyle, Joe Kahn was the first Executive Editor hired afterwards with orders to impose stricter social media policies, less patience for criticism, and less tolerance for those who wanted consideration of "the impact of its reporting on the marginalized communities it covered."[708] Things would get so bad that in May, 2024 *Times*' staffers would circulate a letter complaining of Kah's "unwillingness to tolerate dissent." It was a posture presumably dictated by Sulzberger that translated roughly to: *Shut up and write.*[709]

As Froomkin has explained, "Since Kahn's appointment [his] defense of the *status quo* has been aggressive to the point of belligerence."[710]

Or as the *The Nation*'s Jack Mirkinson put it: "[T]hirty years after [Abe Rosenthal], the *Times* is still trapped in the same bunker when it comes to LGBTQ+ issues. There are clear echoes of [Rosenthal's] blinkered loftiness in Joseph Kahn's acid references to 'advocacy groups' in his staff memo about trans coverage and the *Times* is still at pains to distance itself from what it clearly believes to be an activist mob that doesn't understand what Real Journalism is all about.[711]

"It is still so instinctively appalled at the notion that its critics might be right, that it is choosing the path of aristocratic contempt."

The Wheels Come Off

There isn't a lot of reporting on what it was like from inside the *Times* in the runup to the February 15th explosion, in part because the *Times* clamped down hard on information and threatened punishing for anyone who talked.

So much of what *is* publicly known comes from the Black, trans-led new group TransLash Media, and a remarkable long-form interview it conducted with a number of folks close to the *Times,* including a *Times* journalist called "Harper " who was a young person of color on the rise at the time, and also a leader of TimesOut, the employee group for LGBTQ+ employees.[712]

What follows from that piece has been edited for brevity and clarity.

In Harper's telling, the wheels first started coming off with Sohn's longform piece on the supposed dangers of binding.

> *"It's hard to read it because the writer did not have experience with this. And the article basically makes the argument that there are all these risks to it. Moreover, it cites a website, 4thWaveNow, that we investigated earlier in this series that spreads fears about a trans* social contagion. *But the Times story didn't provide that context. It was laughable to me, because binding has been around forever: It's something I'm doing now."*

The next issue for Harper was a short piece that cited, as a source, the venomous anti-LGBTQ+ group Family Research Council, an SPLC designated hate group, which was also not identified as such.

When Harper brought this to management's attention, they were told, "We don't blindly follow all the SPLC's designations." But as TransLash points out, the *Times does* tend to mention SPLC's designations when hate groups are quoted in other contexts that are not about transgender people.

The publication of Singal's hit-piece was a breaking point:

> *"I wake up to messages, 'Oh my God, did you see it? Did you see it?' Everyone was speaking out and everyone was DMing me... I read a paragraph or two in and my stomach dropped. It's just hard to read as a trans person. I'm immediately realizing that this fury is reaching crisis mode and we've gotta move on it ASAP. The Times has given Singal this soapbox to say things that are factually wrong. I feel like it came to a head with this piece."*

In desperation, Harper sent a note directly to Managing Editor Dean Banquet, another Black employee whom Harper had seen show leadership in the aftermath of the Cotton op-ed:

> "*Hi Dean. You may remember me as the controversial blazer-wearing Ugly Sweater Contest winner of 2018... I'm reaching out today as a trans nonbinary NYT employee who has been deeply hurt by this week, by the actions of my own employer...*

> *Reviewing this book was absolutely the right call. Picking a cisgender, transphobic person who has a history of denying gender identity is real and who has hurt and defamed transgender journalists was not... This is actively doing harm to trans and queer folks in the building. I don't know how to defend this place that I love, the people and reporters and editors I love, when my existence as a trans person is up for debate... I want to know that the Times hears me and sees me as a queer and trans person of color and is taking my experience seriously..."*

But Dean's response is just to confirm that there's no problem at all:

> *"Of course I remember this sweater. I'm glad you wrote. I have to tell you, I disagree with you. I know Pamela worked hard to find someone to review the book. There was not a long line of people who were willing to do so, to be honest... I think she* worked tremendously *hard..."*

So management's posture was that Paul had to work hard to find a writer willing to review a blatantly transphobic book, and so she found one who had just penned a transphobic piece himself, and as one of those most directly affected by this bile, Harper should shut up and get with the team by sympathizing with her struggles and applauding all her hard work.

> *"I was heartbroken. 'Betrayal' is the word... Because I wanted someone, anyone, to see me and see what was happening at the paper. I've spent the*

> *last three years playing Whack-A-Mole with all these articles. This is not the place that I thought it was."*

Harper was right.

This *Times* was a different place. And it was going to shed Harper and people like Harper, who was now considered a troublemaker.

Harper suddenly realized this when they was put up for another promotion. Harper had a sterling record, and the interview would be with Deputy Managing Editor Sam Dolnik, one of the two Sulzberger cousins who had also been considered for Publisher, and with the promotion he would now be Harper's new boss.

The interview was going well until Dolnik asked them point-blank about their private note to Banquet, and their feelings about the Singal piece—and all the wheels suddenly came off.

> *"It was as if all the air left my body. It felt like a trauma response. So many wheels started turning in my mind at once and I felt frozen. My immediate response was to joke and deflect: 'Oh Sam, are you trying to get me in trouble? Ha, ha, ha.' And he said, 'No, no, I really want to know what you think? You know, Dean shared with us at the masthead your note.'*
>
> *"At that point my heart sunk. First, because I realized that Dean had shared my personal note with him. And second, this was a test. For the first time it starts to sink in that the career I still believed was possible for me at the Times no longer was—I was going to be marked as long as I stayed there."*

Their once promising *Times* career over, Harper quietly withdrew their application for promotion, and shortly after accepted a job elsewhere.

It's easy to overlook how radical this is.

Imagine the *New York Times* publishing a series of front-page articles that are not only used in multiple legislative attacks on gay, disabled , undocumented, or Black kids, but which the community under fire denounces as homophobic, ableist, xenophobic, or racist—including those among its own staff. And then not only ignores them, but suggests that they stop complaining and tow the company line as a condition of further promotion.

It appears that management was determined to pursue Sulzberger's vision of using anti-trans content to appeal to the right, even if that meant weaponizing hiring and promotion to squash dissent, even in the case of entirely internal dissent that is private, sincere, and respectful.

Press Watch's Froomkin distilled Sulzberger's message to the *Times*': "'One, you will earn my displeasure if you cross me and take a position with which I disagree. And two, you prove your value to me by trolling our liberal readers.' That explains a lot of the *Times*'s aberrant behavior, doesn't it?"[713] [714]

"Heck of a Job, Brownie"

Sulzberger was also ready to reward bigotry. For one of his sought-after Publisher's Awards given for outstanding journalism, Sulzberger selected Bazelon's "The Battle Over Gender Therapy," applauding its "rigorous, meticulous, and fair-minded explanatory reporting about gender therapy for young people." This was for a piece that was already being wielded by white Christian nationalist groups and cited by state legislators in anti-care bills.

For anyone who thought that Sulzberger wasn't fully aware of what was going on, or that all this didn't originate from his office, this should have permanently disabused them of that notion. That message couldn't have been any clearer: *We are not your friends. We're a business. And we sell what we can to whom we can.*

According to *Vanity Fair*, after calling an all-hands meeting after the contributor's protest broke, Managing Editor Carolyn Ryan told the newsroom, "I want to talk to you briefly about journalistic independence."[715] She was seated with the other brass, between fellow Managing Editor Marc Lacey and the Executive Editor Kahn. "We don't do our work in an effort to please organizations, governments, presidents, activist groups, ideological groups."

Among the examples she cited of such outstanding journalism was Twohey and Jewett's awful "They Paused Puberty, But Is there a Cost?" she underscored the importance of not "reflecting an activist-group way of looking at an issue…"

She added that being as "panoramic as possible" was not only "good journalism," but a "key to how we think about attracting new, [and] more readers and satisfying a need that's really out there." This was the digital rightward push in a nutshell: find stories that appeal across the spectrum so we can attract right-wing readers. Kahn would later apply this to defending democracy, saying that it was important, but not among readers' top concerns.[716]

Applause from both Lacey and Kahn:

"'Great,' said Kahn. 'Marc?'"

"'Very nicely put, Carolyn,' said Lacey."

They did everything but give one another high-fives.

It was Ryan and Lacey who reportedly had some signatories to the protest letter hauled into meetings described in the Daily Beast as “tongue-lashings.” They would also send written warnings accusing other signatories of endangering co-workers and harming them personally—a strange mirror of exactly what the queer signatories were trying to warn the *Times* that it was doing to them.[717]

As someone noted, if only the *Times* was as rigorous in hunting down errors into its trans coverage as it was in hunting down any sign of dissent among its own employees. As Bloomberg Editor Graham Starr tweeted, “It is unfortunate to see reporters and editors respond to a letter defending trans people affected by coverage with insistence that journalists were the ones harmed.”[718]

But Sulzberger, Ryan and Lacey appeared determined to ensure that the trans-denialist coverage did not end up having to be repudiated like the Cotton op-ed because younger, more outspoken, and more liberal staffers were not going to be able to make management respond to their concerns.

This time, the ivory tower would stay on lockdown.

What made this all weirder was that Ryan’s pedigree was the *Times’* first openly-gay Managing Editor and its highest-ranking LGBTQ+ employee.

Going back to GLAAD’s protest of her Metro desks’ horrendous coverage in the 1980s of the tragic burning death of a Black trans woman, Ryan had long ago shown she was no *friend of the trannies.*[719]

What likely made this all the more head-spinng for LGBTQ+ staffers was just as the *Times* management was busily defending dozens of prominent articles attacking trans teens' medical care, it was also ignoring the news of Arkansas, Kentucky, Mississippi, Tennessee, and West Virginia enacting anti-care laws that impacted thousands of them.

Said one staffer, "The way that the masthead talks about activists, you would think that activists only exist on the left." Or as another put it, "By being so explicit about not wanting to appear left-leaning, the masthead is in fact picking a side."

But that had been clear 25 articles, and 50,00 words ago.

And those two staffers were wrong about one thing: Sulzberger wasn't really picking the side of the anti-trans extremist right, or even picking the side of journalistic independence and objectivity.

He was picking the side of doubling digital revenues.

Chapter Twenty-Three: Timeline of a Debacle[720]

February 15, 2023

On February 15, an open letter from 200 *Times* contributors was sent to Philip B. Corbett, Associate Managing Editor for Standards, and was also published.[721] Sadly, only a few signatories are current, active *Times* reporters, so apparently most of the newsroom kept its head down.[722] That same day, a coalition led by GLAAD and including HRC and PFLAG, delivered its own letter. A *Times* spokesperson released a statement conflating the two, thus allowing it to dismiss both of them as "advocacy," and asserting that it is "proud of" its anti-trans reporting.

February 16, 2023

.Further intentionally conflating the two letters, the following day Executive Editor Joe Kahn and Opinion Editor Kathleen Kingsbury send a staff memo which was leaked to the press, declaring that they "do not welcome, and will not tolerate, participation by *Times* journalists in the protests of outside advocacy groups.

As Froomkin explained, "Their main attack line was that there is a clear distinction between journalism and activism, with the *Times* newsroom representing journalism and critics being activists."[723]

This prompted the NewsGuild leadership to jump in and assert that workers have a right to organize, and that the first letter, from *Times* contributors, addressed the workplace environment.

Right in the midst of all this, in what can only be read as yet another effort to "own the libs," former Book Review Editor and current Troll-in-Chief Pamela Paul published a piece titled, "In Defense of J. K. Rowling," condemning the "dangerous" campaign against her by the "powerful transgender rights activists and LGBTQ lobbying groups." The Horde was back.

When asked about the pain caused by being cancelled, Rowling tweeted that, "I read my most recent royalty cheques and find the pain goes away pretty quickly"—a sentiment she apparently lifted directly from the text of Our Path Forward.[724]

By way of background, Rowling had recently accused one trans woman of "cosplaying a misogynistic male fantasy of what a woman is;" donated £70,000 to a Scottish group whose woman cofounder apparently referred to trans women as "sick, pathetic fucks;" mocked gender inclusive language; equated trans women in restrooms with sexual predators; retweeted #SayYesToHate in response to an anti-LGBTQ+ killing on Transgender Day of Remembrance; and joked coarsely about trans women that "The emperor is naked. He might be wearing lipstick, but his balls are swinging in plain sight."[725] [726] [727] [728]

She also used her writing to attack trans women: one book contained a male killer with a troubled past who unaccountably morphs into a demented, psychotic transgender killer by night who violently murders women and masturbates into their clothing—presumably because he can never be a Real Woman[729] [730] [731] (we all do this of course). In other words, she is an author after Paul's own heart.

Once again, the *Times* staff was showing itself fully capable of stooping to get a little payback when it was feeling wounded or aggrieved.

February 17, 2023

As watchdogs and media watches chimed in on the revolt, *The Onion* published its *can-you-top-this?* takedown, "It is Journalism's Sacred Duty To Endanger The Lives Of As Many Trans People As Possible," including this summary of Sulzberger's defense of *Times* journalism:[732]

"Good journalism is about finding those stories, even when they don't exist. It's about asking the tough questions and ignoring the answers you don't like. Then offering misleading evidence in service of preordained editorial conclusions. In our case, endangering trans people is the lodestar that shapes our coverage. Frankly, if our work isn't putting trans people further at risk of trauma and violence, we consider it a failure…"

February 23, 2023

A number of *Times* journalists led by Jeremy Peters send a letter pushing back on the NewsGuild, declaring that "We welcome robust and respectful critical feedback from colleagues… Factual, accurate journalism… does not create a hostile workplace"[733]—thus overlooking the fact that no one is protesting factual, accurate journalism.

February 27, 2023

In *Vanity Fair*, *Times* spokesperson Danielle Rhoades bizarrely claimed that the anti-trans coverage was "providing a vital service to the LGBTQ+ community." She did not clarify the LGBTQ+ community in which country she was referring to, since all the U.S.'s main LGBTQ+ organizations were busily protesting the supposedly *vital service* being provided to them.[734]

In fact, *Xtra* reported that, only a couple of years earlier, the *Times* reached out to the Trans Journalist Association in an attempt to hire more trans writers, but never granted so much as an interview to any journalist the Association recommended.[735] [736]

February 28, 2023:

Denouncing transgender as "a false ideology [and] pseudo science pushed onto our children," Mississippi enacted a ban on affirming care: the *Times* did not cover it until a month later on March 30.[737]

March 1 2023

Associate Managing Editor for Standards Corbett sent an email claiming that the *Times* was doing a great job on its coverage of trans issues which "was entirely in keeping with our journalistic standards [and was] reported deeply and empathetically." In other words, this wasn't the Cotton op-ed, and we're not budging an inch.[738]

March 2, 2023

Tennessee banned care for trans children, but the *Times* ignored it until nearly a month later on March 30.[739]

Sulzberger futher defended the reporters under fire, saying they had been "attacked for sensitive reporting" and the complaints "overlook how thoughtfully and broadly we've explored this topic." The *Times* repeatedly defended itself with words like "sensitive" "thoughtful," and "empathetically," which were irrelevant. Today's Mystery Word is "accurate."

March 3 2023

Multiple speakers at the annual MAGA-oriented CPAC conference, a major venue for Republican presidential hopefuls, launched into vile verbal assaults on transgender people with one even declaring, to rousing applause: "[T]here can be no middle way… It is all or nothing… Transgenderism must be eradicated." The *Times* ignores this genocidal rant until a week later.

March 6, 2023

An extraordinary piece from *Daily Beast* media writer Corbin Bolies titled "The New York Times' Trans Coverage Debacle Was Years in the Making" broke the news that TimesOut has been trying to address the problem of journalistic bias through regular channels for years. But Carolyn Ryan was its executive sponsor, and refused to put anything in writing "because she was afraid of it becoming public and 'being used against her.'[740] When Jesse Singal's awful 2021 book review of Helen Joyce's book was published, an enraged TimesOut tried to schedule a meeting with her, but Ryan refused to meet with them..

So two days later TimesOut drafted a letter for the masthead, but it was never sent after Ryan and other brass agreed to meet with them and preparatory meetings were held with a transgender DEI consultant S. Leigh Thompson. But the planned DEI sessions never happened. Instead, management met with TImesOut, listened, and left.

Said Thompson afterwards, "I do not believe they are trying to adequately or responsibly reflect the trans community, trans lives, or trans issues. I believe they're using trans people as a political pawn to maintain a centrist reputation to keep from being seen as too liberal of a paper."

March 17, 2023

GLAAD issued a statement clarifying once again that its letter from the coalition of gay organizations was separate from the Times' contributors' letter. *Times* spokespeople continued to ignore the distinction.

March 11-16 2023

West Virginia passed a ban on affirming care, but the *Times* did not cover until two seeks later, when it was signed into law.[741]

Kentucky passed a ban the ACLU called "the worst anti-trans bill in the country," but the*Times* didn't cover that either until the legislature overrode the governor's veto nearly two weeks later on March 29.

March 17, 2023:

Wyoming passed a sports ban and the governor refused to veto it, allowing it to become law. The *Times* did not report it.[742]

April 6, 2023

The *Times* contributors sent a second letter, this one directly to Sulzberger, noting that management had "repeatedly and falsely" conflated their letter with GLAAD's, "in a cynical effort to dismiss its own contributors and staff as 'advocates' and justify attempts to intimidate and retaliate against *Times* staff."

Moreover, it noted that the *Times* had "long been hostile to its few trans, nonbinary, and gender-nonconforming employees" and was now engaged in "combing through the 1,200 contributor signatories… to find staffers to intimidate."[743] At the *Washington Post*, media critic Eric Wemple broke the story that the NewsGuild had accused the *Times* of calling signatories into "investigatory meetings" and beginning "disciplinary proceedings" against them.[744]

Vanity Fair reported that after mulling over serious punitive measures for signatories, management eventually settled for telling signatories that a letter *would* be placed in their permanent file, with consequences if they even did so again.[745]

The *Times* engaging in this witch-hunt is the same *Times* whose Editorial Board, almost exactly a year previous, had decried attempts to silence public debate, and declared that America had a "free speech problem."

May 9, 2023

GLAAD hired a digital billboard truck and parked it outside the *Times*' front office entrance. One side read: "Every major medical association SUPPORTS healthcare for trans youth. The science is settled. Why is the NYT ignoring this fact?" On the back it read: "Dear *New York Times*: Stop questioning trans people's right to exist & access to medical care."[746]

May 16 2023

The Pulitzer Prizes are announced: the *Times* failed to receive a single award for individual or investigative journalism.[747]

As the *Nation* would note a year later, "The New York *Times* is Repeating One of Its Most Notorious Mistakes." One person who was heartened by the contributors' letter was a former copyrwriter, Donna Cartwright, who had pinned a notice on all of the company bulletin boards in March, 1998 announcing her transition, and becoming the first out transgender person at the *New York Times*.

"'That was wonderful. I was very glad that there was some group of people… who are saying that the *Times* and society generally need to do more, not less."

Cartwright added that the letter would help remind trans people that there is a community willing to fight alongside them: "I think there are a lot of trans people who kind of look for support. It can be pretty scary when you think you're alone, even if you weren't."[748]

Epilogue

The explosion contained, the *Times* went back to business as usual. Turning to Ghorayshi yet again, six months later in August, 2022 the *Times* published "How a Small Gender Clinic Landed in a Political Storm" on its front page, documenting claims of Jamie Reed, identified as a former case manager at Washington University's youth gender clinic.[749]

It came just months after the publication Project 2025, the Trump campaign's official transition guide, which denounced "transgender ideology" as a form of pornography that sexualized children, and transgender advocates as "child predators" who should be imprisoned along with sympathetic teachers, who it suggested must be registered as sex offenders.[750]

Reed's job was to simply collect medical histories and handle appointments, but she began compiling a private list of patients, including some who had detransitioned or had had psychiatric issues, eventually filing an explosive complaint with the state and airing it in the reliably transphobic *Free Press* in an article titled, "I Thought I Was Saving Trans Kids. Now I'm Blowing the Whistle."

Her main accusation was that the Missouri clinic was prescribing hormones and blockers too freely, not tracking detransitions, and not offering enough mental health care.

Missouri's Republican Attorney General, running for election and presumably eager for such an opportunity, immediately announced an investigation, which he soon expanded to clinics state-wide—even opening a "tip line" to report affirming care abuse.

As a FAIR analysis found, Ghorayshi was playing the usual game of stacking the deck, 175 words to a single unhappy detransitioner—two more than the 173 she devoted to two trans kids and a parent who had positive experiences.

Ghorayshi doesn't mention that out of 1,165 youth, the clinic provided blockers to 67 and hormones to 531—about half in total—which is tough to square with her accusation that the clinic was shoving medication at too many kids too quickly.

As for all those detransitioners the clinic was ignoring, Ghorayshi mentions only three out of a total of 598 who were prescribed medication. That would be 0.5%—even lower than usual rate of 1%.

Ghorayshi reported that "Some of Ms. Reed's claims could not be confirmed, and at least one included factual inaccuracies. But others were corroborated..." As *Assigned Media*'s Evan Urquhart would point out, it's a telling paragraph. The biggest news organization on the planet with 5,900 employees was saying in a front-page piece that it didn't do its homework.[751]

So relying on his enormous investigative staff of one (himself), Urquhart went through all 86 complaints contained in Reed's affidavit (his spreadsheet and findings are available online).[752] He found just seven claims that could be considered corroborated by the *Times,* or anyone else—*none of which* referred to allegations of medical wrongdoing. So Ghorayshi's claim that Reed's allegations had been partially confirmed, while literally true, was irrelevant to the medical care being provided, and completely misleading.

And, in fact, the claims would start to fall apart quickly on closer inspection. Local in-depth reporting by the *St. Louis Post Dispatch* and by the *Missouri Independent* directly contradicted Reed's claims—but this would go unreported by the *Times*.[753] [754]

Even an internal investigation launched by Washington University could find no medical misconduct or violations of the Standards of Care. This was widely reported by the A/P, CBS, NBC, and others—but again, not by the *Times*.[755] [756]

Yet the *Times* would take an apparent "victory lap" three weeks later, when the clinic was closed as Urquhart has noted, with Health and Science Editor Virginia Hughes continuing to promote Reed's claims even as they were falling apart under press scrutiny.[757]

And then came the *coup de grace*: FAIR reported that both Ghorayshi and Hughes neglected to mention that Reed was affiliated with Genspect—the rabidly anti-trans UK TERF group Bazelon had quoted calling trans a "gender cult"—and that her lawyer was associated with ADF and had once compared LGBTQ+ people to "cockroaches."[758] [759]

About a half year later, Paul offered another of her poison-pen op-eds, this one nearly 5,000 words across two printed pages, and that was even preceded by a prebuttal by Opinion Editor Kathleen Kingsbury, who defended Paul's constant trolling of trans people by calling for more "humanity, nuance and empathy."[760] According to news reports, shortly after typing this, her laptop spontaneously burst into flames.

Since Paul generally struggled to generate ideas on

her own, the piece was a retread of Katie Herzog's awful piece for the *The Stranger,* "The Detransitioners: They Were Transgender, Until They Weren't" and Singal's piece for the *Atlantic*, "When Children Say They're Trans." Only this time it was retitled, "As Kids, They Thought They Were Trans. They No Longer Do."

Unable to find any new sources, she returned to Edwards-Leeper, an outlier in her own profession, who has now been a *Times* source in eight articles between January 2022 through August 2023. She also recycled Stephanie Winn, *aka* the "Needle Lady," who had suggested parents help discourage their trans boys by putting them through acupuncture so "[t]hey can see how they like having needles put in them…"

In a sign of how sloppy the *Times* still is about trans reporting, she even managed to get the Trans Youth Project study data wrong, showing either sloppy fact-checking or perhaps no fact-checking at all.[761]

Pushing the *social contagion* theory, she mentioned blandly that "a group of professional organizations put out a statement urging clinicians to eliminate the term,"—without mentioning that these include the American Psychiatric Association and the American Psychological Association.

Paul claimed that 80% of trans kids de-transition based on an old Dutch study in which most of the kids were not trans, which claimed that 30% of adults also de-transition. That was based on study of military families who stopped refilling prescriptions through a military health program when Trump banned trans service members, and it cites SEGM (Society for Evidence Based Medicine)—mentioned earlier as part of that secret working group crafting anti-trans legislation—as "one of the most reliable nonpartisan organizations dedicated to the field," although it *is* partisan and is funded by some of the same Christian nationalist sources as ADF and Family Research Council, is one of the most prolife distributors of anti-trans pseudoscience, lobbies across the U.S. for states to ban care, and has declared, "It might take years, but we're going to get them."[762] [763] [764] [765]

Oh… in June 2024, SPLC classified SEGM as an anti-LGBTQ+ hate group.[766] This is what the *Times is still* quoting as a source on trans kids.

As evidence of how quickly the Christian right weaponizes *Times* columns, 48-hours later ADF cited Paul's article in a legal brief to keep care illegal in Idaho as proof of the "pain and lifelong regret" that result from affirming medical care.[767] [768]

As always with Paul, trying to critique writing this vacuous and deceptive ends up making my eyes bleed, so I'll just close with my favorite quote in all her writing, with which she also closes that piece:

> *"Instead of promoting unproven treatments for children, which surveys show many Americans are uncomfortable with, transgender activists would be more effective if they focused on a shared agenda... [such as] legal protections and more research... A shift in this direction would model tolerance and acceptance. It would prioritize compassion over demonization. It would require rising above culture-war politics and returning to reason. It would be the most humane path forward."*

Paul is suggesting that by continuing to insist on access to safe and effective medical care— recommended by physicians and endorsed by 17 medical associations—it is actually transgender people and gender-affirming parents who are picking a fight. And their continuing to insist on getting medical care for transgender kids displays insensitivity and intolerance towards the feelings of cisgender people: the moral thing for parents and advocates to do is to outsource decisions on trans kids' bodies care to the cisgender public.

Reading this, if you just replace the words "transgender" with "pro-choice," you get almost exactly the framework employed by Christian right organizations on ending abortion.

Almost exactly one month after Paul's piece, NIH published news of another pediatric follow-up study. This time it was of 552 Australian kids, 35% of whom went on blockers or hormones and 1%, of whom desisted (detransitioned)—just as expected. It even had more boys than girls, as Bazelon and Ghorayshi wanted. The *Times* did not cover it.[769]

Other legacy news organizations have mostly learned from their mistakes, and —while they still run the odd transphobic op-ed—they have acknowledged science in their news reporting, and moved on.

But the *Times'* institutional war on trans continues, as does its commitment to dishonest and prejudicial journalism.

But not quite as before.

For 2023, and so far in 2024, it has not been anything like the onslaught of 2022, when anti-trans articles averaged more than one a month.

It may be because Christian nationalists have stopped teeing up any new issues to cover.[770] [771] [772] With the *Times* pushing 70,000 words of trans-denialism over nearly 30 articles, there simply isn't all that much that hasn't been said and re-said.

After the public rebellion, it may also be that Sulzberger has realized the limits of what staff and contributors will tolerate, and another humiliating public protest with the *Times* being a national pinata for scores of other national outlets is just not is not worth the cost.

It's impossible to know.

In a recent long-form interview in Politico, an anonymous *Times* journalist discussed the *Times'* apparent fixation on harming Biden with one story after another about his age. He explained that "It's A.G. He's the one who is pissed [that] Biden hasn't done any interviews and quietly encourages all the tough reporting on his age."[773] [774]

Although this says nothing directly about trans, it does make it seems entirely plausible that Sulzberger is not just chasing profits but—like Abe Rosenthal with the "homosexuals"—uses the paper to pursue his own piques and prejudices, elevating editors and encouraging storylines that promote trans-denialism.

Whatever the reason, time will not be kind to all of Sulzberger's carefully curated denialism, just as the last 50 years haven't been to Rosenthal's homophobia. For all the dozens of fearmongering articles, none of the nearly 100 peer reviewed studies published to date has ever found that affirming care—blockers, hormones, social transition, surgery—harms transgender kids or transgender adults, and almost all of them found significant benefit. As new studies appear every few months now, with findings that prove that the medical consensus was right all along, science will continue whittling away at the *Times* reporting until eventually it will become untenable.

Part of me remains glad that Sulzberger's financial plan worked. I just wish that he'd found another way to balance the company books than on the backs of a tiny and already-beleaguered group of kids, who can't fight back.

Because it's a good thing that the *Times* has survived. I believe we need a *New York Times*.

I just don't believe we need this *New York Times.*

Endnotes

[1] https://www.washingtonpost.com/dc-md-va/2023/03/23/takeaways-post-kff-survey/

[2] https://www.komodohealth.com/perspectives/komodo-findings-point-to-rising-healthcare-needs-for-transgender-youth

[3] https://www.reuters.com/investigates/special-report/usa-transyouth-data/

[4] Of course, this does not count those who might have paid out of pocket or gone abroad for care, so the numbers might be somewhat understated.

[5] https://www.cnn.com/2023/09/13/media/christiane-amanpour-cnn-reliable-sources/index.html

[6] https://cronkitenewslab.com/digital/2023/01/26/beyond-objectivity/

[7] https://www.nytimes.com/2023/05/15/opinion/christian-nationalism-election-2024.html

[8] https://newrepublic.com/article/156415/faith-militant

[9] https://twitter.com/RpsAgainstTrump/status/1760780642671845629

[10] https://www.mediaite.com/trump/welcome-to-the-end-of-democracy-trump-booster-jack-posobiec-vows-to-finish-what-began-on-jan-6-as-steve-bannon-cheers-on/

[11] TERF or Trans Exclusionary Radical Feminists started as a neutral descriptor coined by described cishetero, feminist trans-ally Viv Smythe to describe those committed to biological determinism and the exclusion of trans women from women-centered spaces, activities, and laws. See: https://www.theguardian.com/commentisfree/2018/nov/29/im-credited-with-having-coined-the-acronym-terf-heres-how-it-happened

[12] TERF was at first adopted by many anti-trans feminists themselves. But as it was increasingly wielded by transgender activists, they began denouncing it as derogatory and referring to themselves as Gender Critical Feminists. Simple respect for any group's right to decide what they will be called might seem to be in order here. However, the anodyne misnomer Gender Critical is a bit of intentional misdirection: TERF feminists aren't engaged in a broad intellectual critique of gender but in very specific political attacks on the presence of transgender women. For example, anti-trans TERF activists carry signs that read, "Judith Butler Was Wrong: All Gender Is NOT Drag!" They carry signs like

"Real Women DON'T Have Penises!" See:
https://en.wikipedia.org/wiki/Gender-critical_feminism
[13] "It's Strategy People!," Parents With Inconvenient Truths About Trans (PITT), February 1, 2022. https://pitt.substack.com/p/its-strategy-people.
[14] https://www.splcenter.org/captain/introduction
[15] https://en.wikipedia.org/wiki/Hands_Across_the_Aisle_Coalition
[16] Southern Poverty Law Center. "Family Research Council," n.d. https://www.splcenter.org/fighting-hate/extremist-files/group/family-research-council.
[17] "Before You Continue to YouTube," n.d. https://www.logotv.com/news/r5h7ca/martina-navratilova-transphobic-op-ed-cited-conservative-lawmakers
[18] https://en.wikipedia.org/wiki/Robert_H._Knight
[19] https://www.theguardian.com/us-news/2023/feb/17/new-york-times-contributors-open-letter-protest-anti-trans-coverage#:~:text=Nearly%201%2C000%20New%20York%20Times,and%20gender%20non%2Dconforming%20people.
[20] https://www.splcenter.org/captain/disinformation
[21] https://fair.org/home/nyts-anti-trans-bias-by-the-numbers/
[22] https://xtramagazine.com/power/what-went-wrong-at-the-new-york-times-246409
[23] https://twitter.com/AriDrennen
[24] https://twitter.com/assignedmedia
[25] https://glaad.org/medical-association-statements-supporting-trans-youth-healthcare-and-against-discriminatory/
[26] https://www.assignedmedia.org/breaking-news/promo-alert-discourages-families-from-nyt-podcast
[27] https://fair.org/home/nyts-anti-trans-bias-by-the-numbers/
[28] https://www.mediamatters.org/new-york-times/new-york-times-helped-fuel-anti-trans-panic-2022-will-2023-be-any-better
[29] Journalism's Essential Value CJR A. G. Sulzberger May 15 2023
[30] For instance, see: https://www.reuters.com/article/usa-lgbt-health-idUSL8N2TU2P2/
[31] https://www.ncbi.nlm.nih.gov/pmc/articles/PMC8099405/?utm_source=substack&utm_medium=email#R36
[32] https://www.nytimes.com/2020/06/03/opinion/tom-cotton-protests-military.html
[33] https://www.politico.com/news/magazine/2023/12/14/james-bennet-nyt-firing-00131826
[34] https://xtramagazine.com/power/what-went-wrong-at-the-new-york-times-246409
[35] https://translash.org/the-new-york-times-responds-to-translash-media/
[36] https://www.newyorker.com/culture/the-new-yorker-interview/a-g-sulzberger-on-the-battles-within-and-against-the-new-york-times

[37] American Academy of Child and Adolescent Psychiatry, American Academy of Dermatology, American Academy of Family Physicians, American Academy of Nursing, American Academy of Pediatrics, American Academy of Physician Assistants, American College Health Association, American College of Nurse-Midwives, American College of Obstetricians and Gynecologists, American College of Physicians, American Counseling Association, American Heart Association, American Medical Association, American Nurses Association, American Osteopathic Association, American Psychiatric Association, American Psychological Association, American Public Health Association, American Society of Plastic Surgeons, Endocrine Society, National Association of Nurse Practitioners in Women's Health, National Association of Social Workers, National Commission on Correctional Health Care, Pediatric Endocrine Society, Society for Adolescent Health and Medicine, World Medical Association, World Professional Association for Transgender Health.

[38] https://whatweknow.inequality.cornell.edu/topics/lgbt-equality/what-does-the-scholarly-research-say-about-the-well-being-of-transgender-people/

[39] https://apnews.com/article/transgender-treatment-regret-detransition-371e927ec6e7a24cd9c77b5371c6ba2b#:~:text=Some%20studies%20suggest%20that%20rates,1%25%20on%20average%20expressed%20regret.

[40] https://www.voanews.com/a/how-common-is-transgender-treatment-regret-detransitioning-/6993101.html

[41] https://en.wikipedia.org/wiki/Voice_of_America

[42] https://www.nytimes.com/2024/02/02/opinion/transgender-children-gender-dysphoria.html

[43] In the U.S. the main service was the Associated Press (AP) which was later joined by Reuters and United Press International (UPI) and the International News Association.

[44] https://en.wikipedia.org/wiki/News_agency

[45] https://www.frc.org/abortion

[46] https://www.them.us/story/new-york-times-detransition-youth-op-ed-pamela-paul-chase-strangio?utm_social-type=owned&utm_brand=them&utm_medium=social&utm_source=twitter&s=03

[47] https://ago.mo.gov/docs/default-source/press-releases/2023-04-13---emergency-reg.pdf?sfvrsn=7f78d4fc_2

[48] https://glaad.org/new-york-times-inaccurate-coverage-transgender-people-being-weaponized-against-transgender/

[49] https://www.texasobserver.org/emily-bazelon-transgender-healthcare-debate-new-york-times/

[50] https://www.youtube.com/watch?v=TYekckkVcC0&t=6927s

[51] https://www.youtube.com/watch?v=TYekckkVcC0&t=6920s

[52] https://www.alabamaag.gov/wp-content/uploads/2023/05/AG-Marshall-Leads-Appellate-Court-Brief-Defending-Arkansas-Ban-on-Experimental-Transgender-Treatments-for-Children.pdf

---

[53] https://www.hawley.senate.gov/senator-hawley-demands-answers-washington-university-transgender-center-after-further-evidence
[54] https://xtramagazine.com/power/politics/missouri-gender-care-centre-closure-256740
[55] https://www.splcenter.org/captain/introduction
[56] https://www.splcenter.org/captain/disinformation
[57] https://www.splcenter.org/captain/defining-pseudoscience-network#_ftnref73
[58] https://www.splcenter.org/fighting-hate/extremist-files/group/american-college-pediatricians
[59] https://www.splcenter.org/hatewatch/2023/06/05/documents-reveal-adf-requested-anti-trans-research-american-college-pediatricians
[60] https://www.splcenter.org/sites/default/files/adf_research_requests_to_acpeds.pdf
[61] "It's Strategy People!," Parents With Inconvenient Truths About Trans (PITT), February 1, 2022. https://pitt.substack.com/p/its-strategy-people.
[62] https://www.splcenter.org/captain/disinformation
[63] https://www.youtube.com/watch?v=ahS0VjJNaew
[64] https://www.transgendermap.com/politics/media/bridget-phetasy/
[65] https://twitter.com/transscribe/status/1532675450589396993
[66] https://www.thepinknews.com/2022/06/03/helen-joyce-transgender-lgbtq/
[67] https://www.youtube.com/watch?v=ahS0VjJNaew
[68] https://www.sometherapist.com/read/yourkidwantstoliveastheoppositesex
[69] https://www.advocate.com/transgender/nyt-trans-article-debunked#:~:text=Fact%3A%20Stephanie%20Winn%20suggested%20the,good%20reasons%20to%20be%20wary.
[70] She seemed unaware that estrogen does not require needles but is most often provided orally or by transdermal patch.
[71] https://twitter.com/sometherapist/status/1753838943613997224
[72] https://www.sometherapist.com/read/yourkidwantstoliveastheoppositesex
[73] It was not until Rosenthal retired that the ban was lifted in 1986—five years into the AIDS epidemic. See: https://www.nytimes.com/2017/06/19/us/gay-pride-lgbtq-new-york-times.html#:~:text=It%20was%20not%20until%20after,the%20ban%20on%20%E2%80%9Cgay.%E2%80%9D
[74] As journalists Michael Signorile would recall on Huffpo: "[t]he next day he raced into the office and assigned reporter Robert Doty a story that would forever take a place in the paper's history. On Dec. 16, 1963, a headline blared from the front page: 'Growth of Overt Homosexuality in City Provokes Wide Concern:' The overt homosexual -- and those who are identifiable probably represent no more than half of the total -- has become such an obtrusive part of the New York scene that the phenomenon needs public discussion…'" See: https://www.huffpost.com/entry/new-york-times-gays-lesbians-aids-homophobia_n_2200684
[75] https://timesmachine.nytimes.com/timesmachine/1953/11/03/92763522.html?pageNumber=28

[76] https://timesmachine.nytimes.com/timesmachine/1967/10/29/121513539.html?pageNumber=27

[77] https://www.nytimes.com/1965/04/16/archives/cuban-government-is-alarmed-by-increase-in-homosexuality.html?searchResultPosition=17

[78] https://www.nytimes.com/1963/12/17/archives/growth-of-overt-homosexuality-in-city-provokes-wide-concern-growth.html

[79] https://www.thenation.com/article/society/new-york-times-trans-coverage-gay-rights-history/

[80] https://www.advocate.com/media/new-york-times-transgender-coverage

[81] https://www.aei.org/op-eds/in-2022-reality-has-a-conservative-bias/#:~:text=%E2%80%9CReality%2C%E2%80%9D%20Stephen%20Colbert%20remarked,and%20the%20line%20rolled%20out

[82] https://jabberwocking.com/the-truth-has-a-liberal-bias/

[83] https://www.aei.org/op-eds/in-2022-reality-has-a-conservative-bias/#:~:text=%E2%80%9CReality%2C%E2%80%9D%20Stephen%20Colbert%20remarked,and%20the%20line%20rolled%20out

[84] https://journals.sagepub.com/doi/10.1177/14778785231162779

[85] https://www.cnn.com/2021/11/16/media/steve-bannon-reliable-sources/index.html

[86] E.g. Amy Sohn's, "Chest Binding Helps Smooth the Way for Transgender Teens, but There May Be Risks," and E.G. Megan Twohey & Christina Jewett's "They Paused Puberty, but Is There a Cost?"

[87] E.g., Katie J. M. Baker's "When Students Change Gender Identity, and Parents Don't Know"

[88] E.g., Gillian R. Brassil and Jeré Longman's "Who Should Compete in Women's Sports: There Are 'Two Almost Irreconcilable Positions'" and Michael Powell's "What Lia Thomas Could Mean for Women's Elite Sports" both of which cite clams that trans women will destroy women's sports;

[89] E.g. Katie J. M. Baker's "When Students Change Gender Identity, and Parents Don't Know" which recycled, without comment, the vile canard that trans advocates are grooming children.

[90] E.g. Azeen Ghorayshi's "More Trans Teens Choosing 'Top Surgery'" which recycled unrebutted Republican claims that affirming surgeries is *disfiguring mutilation.*

[91] E.g. Megan Twohey & Christina Jewett's "They Paused Puberty, but Is There a Cost?"

[92] E.g. Gillian Brassil and Jeré Longman's "Who Should Compete in Women's Sports: There Are 'Two Almost Irreconcilable Positions'" and Michael Powell's "What Lia Thomas Could Mean for Women's Elite Sports," both of which are about trans athletes but feature few quotes from any, reducing them to little more than coat racks on which to hang stories of "conflict" and cisgender opinions about them.

[93] E.g., Julie Shulevitz's "Is It Time to Desegregate the Sexes?"

[94] E.g. Shulevitz in "Is It Time to Desegregate the Sexes?" in which she blandly identifies ADF as "a Christian legal advocacy organization with mostly evangelical clients"—omitting that ADF's goal is making the U.S. officially a white Christian nation ruled by Biblical principles and has fought in fought or filed in every important gay and transgender case in the U.S., including the leading the fight to keep gay marriage illegal and being a prime mover in the 1,000+ anti-trans laws introduced in 49 states. ADF has defended laws criminalizing homosexual activity in the US, Belize, India, Jamaica, and Uganda; combatted transgender rights in France, Bulgaria, Russia, in Macedonia; and fought to maintain the compulsory sterilization of trans people in the 20+ countries which still require it before official sex can be changed

[95] E.g. Amy Sohn in "Chest Binding Helps Smooth the Way for Transgender Teens, but There May Be Risks" identifying Rethink Identity Medicine Ethics as "examining standards of care for gender-variant children," when actually it is devoted ending medical care for trans kids and promotes "conversion therapy" to "cure" them of being transgender, and compares pediatric care to Nazi eugenics experiments as well as "alien mind control."

[96] E.g., Megan Twohey & Christina Jewett's "They Paused Puberty, but Is There a Cost?"

[97] E.g., Emily Bazelon's "The Battle Over Gender Therapy"

[98] For a particularly good rundown of many of these, check out Science Based Medicine's in-depth debunking of the *Times*'s 2022 Front page journalism attacking puberty blockers. https://sciencebasedmedicine.org/what-the-new-york-times-gets-wrong-about-puberty-blockers-for-transgender-youth/

[99] E.g. Michael Powell's "What Lia Thomas Could Mean for Women's Elite Sports," which quotes just three people unambiguously supportive of trans participation in sports while quoting three athletes, two physiologists, one biologist, one law professor, one philosophy professor, and one angry mom—10 in all—who are antagonistic to it, with seven o the "official" quotes from academics or researchers against.

[100] E.g. Megan Twohey & Christina Jewett's "They Paused Puberty, but Is There a Cost?"

[101] E.g. Richard Friedmans, 'How Changeable Is Gende?" in which he dismisses a very positive meta-analysis of 28 different studies with nearly two thousand participants because some of them were supposedly "suboptimal," but then diagnoses all transsexuals based on a single obscure 2014 study of just 23 transsexual women by a Viennese neuroscientist with no apparent expertise in transgender people generally or transsexuality specifically.

[102] E.g. Richard Friedman in "How Changeable Is Gender?" citing only the earliest cohort to received care in the Swedish Study which had higher suicidality, omitting that the later cohort had suicidality rages comparable to the average population.

[103] E.g. Azeen Ghorayshi's More Trans Teens Choosing 'Top Surgery'" i

[104] E.g. Gillian R. Brassil and Jeré Longman's "Who Should Compete in Women's Sports: There Are 'Two Almost Irreconcilable Positions'" which buries the single sentence, "Contrary to fears expressed by some, there has been no large-scale dominance of transgender athletes in women's sports…" below the fold, 1,000 words down.

[105] https://translash.org/transcript-capturing-the-new-york-times/

[106] Thanks to Andrea James at Transgender Map for his useful encapsulation. See: https://www.transgendermap.com/politics/media/john-mcdermott/

[107] Julia Serano identifies and dissects this narrative device and its use against populations that are actually severely marginalized. See: https://juliaserano.medium.com/the-dregerian-narrative-or-why-trans-activists-vs-276740045120

[108] https://www.theguardian.com/us-news/2023/feb/17/new-york-times-contributors-open-letter-protest-anti-trans-coverage

[109] https://www.transgendermap.com/issues/topics/media/outlets/the-new-york-times/

[110] Jennifer Finney Boylan was hired in 2007 and left in 2022; she was replaced by resident transphobe Pamela Paul, who wrote many of the worst stories. In addition, unfortunately even during her tenure as arguably the highest-profile trans writer in the U.S., Boylan wrote only intermittently about trans issues and almost never about trans politics.

[111] https://www.cjr.org/special_report/ag-sulzberger-new-york-times-journalisms-essential-value-objectivity-independence.php/

[112] https://web.archive.org/web/20161218072736/http://www.nationalreview.com/article/439126/transgender-teens-parents-cry-foul-doctors-and-educators-ignore-them.

[113] https://www.splcenter.org/captain/foundations#_ftnref71

[114] https://www.nytimes.com/by/david-french

[115] https://cbmw.org/nashville-statement/

[116] https://www.assignedmedia.org/breaking-news/erik-wemple-doesnt-think-the-new-york-times-is-biased

[117] https://www.nytimes.com/2022/06/10/science/transgender-teenagers-national-survey.html#:~:text=The%20analysis%2C%20relying%20on%20government,0.5%20percent%20of%20all%20adults.

[118] A study by Jack Turban would find about 13% of adults detransitioned at some point, but also that much of this was not due to regret or mistakes but due to stigma and discrimination, and family rejection. The number appears to have dropped signification with young generations in a perhaps a less-discriminatory time. See: https://fenwayhealth.org/new-study-shows-discrimination-stigma-and-family-pressure-drive-detransition-among-transgender-people/

[119] https://www.hrc.org/resources/attacks-on-gender-affirming-care-by-state-map

[120] https://www.ncbi.nlm.nih.gov/pmc/articles/PMC8099405/?utm_source=substack&utm_medium=email

[121] https://www.nytimes.com/2022/09/26/health/top-surgery-transgender-teenagers.html
[122] https://www.americanjournalofsurgery.com/article/S0002-9610(24)00238-1/abstract?utm_source=substack&utm_medium=email
[123] Conversely, when Legionnaire's disease struck in 1976, the *Times* repeatedly put it on its front page, helping to focus media and government attention .
[124] https://www.huffpost.com/entry/new-york-times-gays-lesbians-aids-homophobia_n_2200684
[125] Executive Editor A M Rosenthal was notorious for having banned the word "gay" from the *Times* pages and often promoting homophobic story lines. It was not until he retired that the ban was in 1986—five years into the AIDS epidemic, See: https://www.nytimes.com/2017/06/19/us/gay-pride-lgbtq-new-york-times.html#:~:text=It%20was%20not%20until%20after,the%20ban%20on%20%E2%80%9Cgay.%E2%80%9D
[126] https://translash.org/transcript-capturing-the-new-york-times/
[127] https://www.nytimes.com/2024/02/28/technology/news-media-industry-dying.html?smid=nytcore-android-share
[128] https://www.huffpost.com/entry/new-york-times-gays-lesbians-aids-homophobia_n_2200684
[129] https://www.nytimes.com/2024/02/28/technology/news-media-industry-dying.html
[130] https://en.wikipedia.org/wiki/A._G._Sulzberger#cite_note-MurphyHa-12
[131] https://www.niemanlab.org/2017/01/this-is-the-new-york-times-digital-path-forward/
[132] https://www.buzzfeednews.com/article/mylestanzer/exclusive-times-internal-report-painted-dire-digital-picture
[133] https://www.niemanlab.org/2014/05/the-leaked-new-york-times-innovation-report-is-one-of-the-key-documents-of-this-media-age/
[134] One fascinating find was that A1, the home page, the peak of the news hierarchy and for centuries the print editors' Holy-of-Holies worldwide, was not even particularly popular online: "only a third of readers ever visit it, and those who do visit are spending less time: page views and minutes spent per reader dropped by double-digit percentages…"
[135] https://www.niemanlab.org/2024/02/the-new-york-times-made-more-than-1-billion-from-digital-subscriptions-in-2023/
[136] https://thesocialtalks.com/news-analysis/pamela-paul-arch-opportunist-returns-to-the-new-york-times/
[137] https://news.yahoo.com/facebooks-amoral-algorithms-095213923.html
[138] https://9to5mac.com/2022/12/20/how-tiktoks-algorithm-works/
[139] https://apnews.com/article/misinformation-anonymous-accounts-social-media-2024-election-8a6b0f8d727734200902d96a59b84bf7
[140] https://www.axios.com/2023/03/07/gannett-changes-leadership-workers
[141] https://www.nytimes.com/wirecutter/reviews/best-vibrators/?smtyp=cur&smid=tw-nytimes

[142] https://www.nytimes.com/wirecutter/reviews/dansk-kobenstyle-butter-warmer-review/

[143] https://www.nytimes.com/2024/02/06/well/ear-wax-clean.html

[144] https://www.nytimes.com/2023/11/08/style/sex-drive-disparity-relationships.html

[145] https://www.thedailybeast.com/how-the-new-york-times-trans-coverage-debacle-was-years-in-the-making?utm_medium=socialflow&utm_source=twitter_owned_tdb&via=twitter_page&utm_campaign=owned_social

[146] https://en.wikipedia.org/wiki/Reality-based_community#:~:text=Reality-based%20community%20is%20a,reporter%20Ron%20Suskind%20in%202004

[147] Two-thirds of this demographic tell pollsters that they are actively waiting for the Rapture, when the living and the dead are resurrected to meet Christ , after which unbelievers will be killed and believers ascend see: Audrey Barrick, "Poll: What Evangelical Leaders Believe about the End *Times*." *The Christian Post*, March 9, 2011. https://www.christianpost.com/news/poll-what-evangelical-leaders-believe-about-the-end-times.html.

[148] https://www.nytimes.com/2020/06/03/opinion/tom-cotton-protests-military.html

[149] https://www.nytimes.com/2017/11/25/us/ohio-hovater-white-nationalist.html

[150] https://fortune.com/2017/11/28/nyt-nazi-next-door/

[151] The *Times* model is actually subscriptions-based and not oriented towards maximizing eyeballs or clicks like many news websites. See: https://www.nytimes.com/projects/2020-report/index.html

[152] Riki Wilchins and Chloe Souchere, "Analysis of ACLU Transgender legislation," unpublished raw data, 2023 https://www.aclu.org/legislative-attacks-on-lgbtq-rights.

[153] 61% (11) of these organizations spoke out against bathroom bills and about the same number against school sports laws.

[154] Our list, which is a decidedly unscientific sample, included the American Association of University Women (AAUW), Anti-Defamation League (ADL), AFL-CIO, Color of Change, Lawyers Committee for Civil Rights, Legal Momentum, Mexican American Legal Defense and Educational Fund, NAACP & NAACP Legal Defense Fund, National Education Association (NEA), National Partnership for Women and Families, National Urban League, National Council La Raza (NCLR), National Organization for Women (NOW), National Women's Law Center (NWLC), People for the American Way, Race Forward, Service Employees International Union (SEIU), and Southern Poverty Law Center (SPLC).

[155] In fact, the only organization among the 18 we could find that issued more than a single statement in support of young people's access to affirming care was the National Partnership for Women and Families, with three.

[156] There were about 30 for bathrooms and for sports from these same organization.

[157] https://thesocialtalks.com/news-analysis/pamela-paul-arch-opportunist-returns-to-the-new-york-times/

[158] https://www.wired.com/2017/02/new-york-times-digital-journalism/

[159] https://www.wsj.com/articles/facebook-knows-instagram-is-toxic-for-teen-girls-company-documents-show-11631620739#:~:text=For%20the%20past%20three%20years,them%2C%20most%20notably%20teenage%20girls.

[160] https://www.wired.com/2017/02/new-york-times-digital-journalism/

[161] https://www.wired.com/2017/02/new-york-times-digital-journalism/

[162] https://gitnux.org/new-york-times-readership-statistics/#:~:text=The%20most%20prominent%20age%20group,media%20consumption%20and%20consumer%20influence.

[163] https://www.nytimes.com/2009/02/09/business/media/09times.html

[164] https://www.niemanlab.org/2017/01/this-is-the-new-york-times-digital-path-forward/

[165] https://www.wired.com/2017/02/new-york-times-digital-journalism/

[166] As I write this, David French the anti-trans, anti-gay e-ADF lawyer has just posted a column on Justice Clarence Thomas—that walking judicial conflict of interest whose wife helped lead the effort to overthrown the election—beginning with the words: "Clarence Thomas Is a Kind Man…"

[167] https://www.nytimes.com/2015/09/12/insider/1896-without-fear-or-favor.html

[168] https://www.nytimes.com/2015/04/19/books/review/galileos-middle-finger-by-alice-dreger.html

[169] https://www.nytimes.com/1999/06/11/nyregion/public-lives-issues-of-gender-from-pronouns-to-murder.html

[170] https://www.nytimes.com/1996/09/08/us/shunning-he-and-she-they-fight-for-respect.html

[171] Intersexuality is also often referred to as *differences of sexual development* or DSD.

[172] https://www.transgendermap.com/issues/history/alice-dreger/differences-of-sex-development/

[173] https://juliaserano.medium.com/making-sense-of-autogynephilia-debates-73d9051e88d3

[174] https://www.juliaserano.com/sexedup.html

[175] https://www.nytimes.com/2015/04/19/books/review/galileos-middle-finger-by-alice-dreger.html

[176] https://juliaserano.medium.com/the-dregerian-narrative-or-why-trans-activists-vs-276740045120

[177] https://www.washingtonpost.com/news/morning-mix/wp/2015/04/17/what-happened-when-a-medical-professor-live-tweeted-her-sons-sex-ed-class-on-abstinence/

[178] https://alicedreger.com/oprah/

[179] https://www.nytimes.com/2015/05/04/opinion/the-quest-for-transgender-equality.html
[180] https://www.nytimes.com/2015/05/04/opinion/the-quest-for-transgender-equality.html
[181] https://www.advocate.com/politics/media/2015/06/09/why-new-york-times-suddenly-focused-transgender-people
[182] https://www.mediamatters.org/new-york-times/seen-not-heard-new-york-times-failed-quote-trans-people-over-60-2023-stories-anti
[183] https://www.nytimes.com/2015/06/07/opinion/sunday/what-makes-a-woman.html
[184] https://www.cnn.com/2023/04/24/opinions/anti-trans-rhetoric-strategy-turban/index.html
[185] https://vancouversun.com/news/oscar-interrupted-the-story-behind-elinor-burketts-kanye-moment
[186] https://en.wikipedia.org/wiki/Music_by_Prudence
[187] Because it was a short documentary, Steve McQueen is often listed as the first Black director to win an Oscar (for "12 Years a Slave"). See: https://www.thewrap.com/black-director-nominated-for-oscar-john-singleton-jordan-peele/
[188] https://www.huffpost.com/entry/short-film-producer-elino_n_489893
[189] Although Burkett had had her credit as producer removed from the film, she was still on the Oscar nomination credits, and thus present for the ceremonies. l
[190] Burkett would later go on the Joy Behar Show to declare *herself* the wounded party, "He tried to make sure I couldn't get there before him…He just didn't seem to think I would be so rude to interrupt him…I think you get up and wait for me to get up, and we go up together graciously [but] he starts talking when I'm halfway up." See: http://www.cnn.com/2010/SHOWBIZ/Movies/03/09/oscar.speech.interrupted/index.html
[191] https://www.statista.com/statistics/241488/population-of-the-us-by-sex-and-age/ (with this estimate ~128,000,000 women over 20)
[192] https://williamsinstitute.law.ucla.edu/publications/trans-adults-united-states/
[193] https://www.salon.com/2015/06/08/memo_to_crotchety_feminists_caitlyn_jenner_is_a_woman_and_we_must_embrace_her_its_whats_feminist_and_whats_right/
[194] https://www.salon.com/2015/06/08/the_new_york_times_bungles_transgender_rights_what_its_caitlyn_jenner_op_ed_gets_wrong_about_feminism_and_gender_identity/
[195] https://www.cosmopolitan.com/politics/news/a41641/caitlyn-jenner-feminism/
[196] https://medium.com/@TedPillow/the-18-greatest-craziest-cosmo-headlines-ca7d5c34fd0d
[197] https://www.thepinknews.com/2015/10/27/watch-rare-footage-of-bette-midler-performing-in-a-gay-bathhouse/

---

[198] https://twitter.com/BetteMidler/status/1543979948611981313
[199] https://you.com/search?q=continental+baths+gay+men&utm_source=vivaldi_browser
[200] https://www.nbcnews.com/nbc-out/out-pop-culture/bette-midler-defends-social-posts-criticized-transphobic-rcna36893
[201] https://www.nytimes.com/2015/08/23/opinion/sunday/richard-a-friedman-how-changeable-is-gender.html
[202] https://pressthink.org/2022/06/he-used-to-edit-political-stories-at-the-chicago-tribune-now-he-says-the-press-is-failing-our-democracy/
[203] https://www.splcenter.org/captain/foundations#_ftn25
[204] These mainly attacked access to school bathrooms and sports; 3 of them would pass into law.
[205] https://translegislation.com/learn
[206] https://en.wikipedia.org/wiki/Richard_A._Friedman
[207] https://weillcornell.org/richardfriedman
[208] https://gaycitynews.com/dr-richard-friedman-key-in-normalizing-homosexuality-dies-at-79/
[209] https://www.nytimes.com/2018/10/22/health/transgender-trump-biology.html
[210] See: https://www.researchgate.net/profile/Andreas-Hahn-7 and also https://www.emedevents.com/speaker-profile/georg-s-kranz and https://www.polyu.edu.hk/mhrc/people/mhrc-people/dr-georg-kranz/
[211] https://academic.oup.com/cercor/article/25/10/3527/387406
[212] Curiously Friedman never cites the study or the author, but his description is consistent with a meta-study by Murad, *et al.* See: https://onlinelibrary.wiley.com/doi/abs/10.1111/J.1365-2265.2009.03625.x
[213] https://www.splcenter.org/captain/disinformation
[214] https://journals.plos.org/plosone/article?id=10.1371/journal.pone.0016885&utm_source=mandiner&utm_medium=link&utm_campaign=mandiner_202101
[215] https://www.erininthemorning.com/p/debunked-the-swedish-study-doesnt
[216] https://archive.thinkprogress.org/new-york-times-op-ed-encourages-people-to-be-skeptical-of-trans-identities-75e46d46869f/
[217] https://www.erininthemorning.com/p/debunked-the-swedish-study-doesnt
[218] In fact, not only does it not show anything about gender care. but lead author Cecilia Dhejne has publicly denounced TERF's repeated misuse of her work. She points out that similar studies show higher suicide rates after cisgender people receive care for bipolar disorders and schizophrenia, but no ethical scientist asserts that this suggests that bipolar or schizophrenia care is ineffective or should be withheld. See: https://www.splcenter.org/captain/disinformation#_ftnref26
[219] https://www.transadvocate.com/the-ny-times-goes-concern-trolling_n_15397.htm
[220] https://whatweknow.inequality.cornell.edu/topics/lgbt-equality/what-does-the-scholarly-research-say-about-the-well-being-of-transgender-people/

[221] For studies on mental health outcomes with kids, see Jack Duban's survey in Psychology Today, in which several studies predate Friedman's piece: https://www.psychologytoday.com/us/blog/political-minds/202201/the-evidence-trans-youth-gender-affirming-medical-care
[222] https://www.vox.com/2015/8/24/9197789/new-york-times-transgender-research
[223] https://www.vox.com/2015/8/24/9197789/new-york-times-transgender-research
[224] https://www.statnews.com/2023/11/28/fda-gender-affirming-care-estrogen-approval/?utm_campaign=morning_rounds&utm_medium=email&_hsmi=284258856&utm_content=284258856&utm_source=hs_email
[225] https://www.motherjones.com/politics/2024/05/cass-review-transgender-health-care-nhs-gender-affirming-care/
[226] The right continues to make much of the lack of RCTs in affirming care, since they are the gold standard for evidence of clinical efficacy, but only a tiny fraction of medical practice has been actually tested by RCTs since recruiting randomize groups for every medicine or surgical procedures would be impossibly difficult, expense, and often unethical—not to mention unnecessary.
[227] https://casetext.com/case/dekker-v-weida-1
[228] https://www.acluga.org/sites/default/files/gand-1_2023-cv-02904-00106.pdf
[229] PITT even calls children continuing to identify as trans a "relapsing."
[230] https://psychnews.psychiatryonline.org/doi/full/10.1176/appi.pn.2022.07.7.16
[231] https://store.samhsa.gov/sites/default/files/sma15-4928.pdf
[232] https://publications.aap.org/pediatrics/article/142/4/e20182162/37381/Ensuring-Comprehensive-Care-and-Support-for?autologincheck=redirected
[233] https://www.apa.org/topics/lgbtq/sexual-orientation-change
[234] See also this useful roundup by HRC: https://assets2.hrc.org/files/documents/SupportingCaringforTransChildren.pdf
[235] For instance, see: https://bmcpublichealth.biomedcentral.com/articles/10.1186/s12889-015-1867-2
[236] https://www.jstor.org/stable/jj.5973186
[237] https://www.nytimes.com/2016/05/18/opinion/a-bathroom-of-ones-own.html
[238] https://www.nytimes.com/2016/10/16/opinion/sunday/is-it-time-to-desegregate-the-sexes.html
[239] In fact, In 1966, the first Black college student to be murdered in the struggle for civil rights was 21-year-old Sammy Younge, Jr. of the Student Non-Violent Coordinating Committee (SNCC), who was shot and killed by a white gas station attendant for trying to desegregate a Tuskegee AL gas station restroom in 1966. 68-year-old Marvin Segrest would be acquitted of the murder by an all-white jury. See: https://sncclegacyproject.org/in-memoriam-samuel-leamon-younge-jr/?utm_source=rss&utm_medium=rss&utm_campaign=in-memoriam-samuel-leamon-younge-jr
[240] https://rewirenewsgroup.com/2016/05/20/no-obama-administration-doesnt-need-public-weigh-trans-bathroom-equality/

[241] Neil J Young, How the Bathroom Wars Shaped America, Politico
[242] https://www.thepinknews.com/2016/09/06/anti-equality-conservative-phyllis-schlafly-dies-aged-92
[243] Schlafly also claimed that the ERA would lead to legalizing gay marriage and turned her Eagle Forum on gay rights—even after her son John came out as gay, and Anti-ERA forces also claimed women would be drafted into the armed forces and lose alimony in cases of divorce—both of which were untrue. See: https://www.thepinknews.com/2016/09/06/anti-equality-conservative-phyllis-schlafly-dies-aged-92/ and https://eagleforum.org/publications/psr/sept1974.html and also /https://thesocietypages.org/socimages/2015/11/10/protecting-white-women-in-the-bathroom-history/
[244] https://en.wikipedia.org/wiki/Equal_Rights_Amendment#:~:text=Not%20ratified-,Ratifications,constitutional%20amendment%20within%20a%20year.
[245] https://fedsoc.org/contributors/peter-schuck
[246] https://fedsoc.org/commentary/fedsoc-blog/hhs-s-proposed-nondiscrimination-regulations-impose-transgender-mandate-in-health-care-1
[247] https://www.nytimes.com/2016/05/13/us/politics/obama-administration-to-issue-decree-on-transgender-access-to-school-restrooms.html?_r=0
[248] https://medium.com/gender-2-0/is-the-new-york-times-collaborating-with-anti-trans-lawmakers-f22aaddb4c98
[249] https://www.cbsnews.com/philadelphia/news/survey-transgender-public-restroom/
[250] https://www.ncbi.nlm.nih.gov/pmc/articles/PMC5685206/
[251] https://publications.aap.org/pediatrics/article/143/6/e20182902/76816/School-Restroom-and-Locker-Room-Restrictions-and?autologincheck=redirected
[252] https://www.nbcnews.com/feature/nbc-out/lgbtq-rights-fight-reignited-4-years-after-n-c-s-n1250390
[253] https://www.thenation.com/article/society/new-york-times-trans-coverage-gay-rights-history/
[254] https://www.nytimes.com/1977/03/20/archives/the-trouble-at-sarah-lawrence-sarah-lawrence.html
[255] https://www.thenation.com/article/society/new-york-times-trans-coverage-gay-rights-history/
[256] https://www.splcenter.org/hatewatch/2023/06/05/documents-reveal-adf-requested-anti-trans-research-american-college-pediatricians
[257] https://www.charlottemagazine.com/the-growing-war-over-the-restroom-thing/
[258] https://www.splcenter.org/fighting-hate/extremist-files/group/alliance-defending-freedom
[259] https://www.washingtonpost.com/investigations/2023/09/24/alliance-defending-freedom-wedding-lawsuit/

[260] https://www.splcenter.org/fighting-hate/extremist-files/group/alliance-defending-freedom
[261] https://blackstonelegalfellowship.org/
[262] https://www.advocate.com/law/gender-affirming-care-idaho-blocked
[263] https://www.splcenter.org/hatewatch/2017/07/27/anti-lgbt-hate-group-alliance-defending-freedom-defended-state-enforced-sterilization
[264] This was finally repealed in 2017.
[265] https://www.au.org/the-latest/church-and-state/articles/exporting-extremism-backed-by-u-s-christian-nationalist-groups-african-nations-are-enacting-a-wave-of-oppressive-anti-lgbtq-laws/
[266] https://archive.thinkprogress.org/new-york-times-shulevitz-transgender-80686781b4c3/
[267] https://www.mediamatters.org/new-york-times/seen-not-heard-new-york-times-failed-quote-trans-people-over-60-2023-stories-anti
[268] https://www.splcenter.org/news/2020/04/10/why-alliance-defending-freedom-hate-group
[269] https://www.splcenter.org/hatewatch/2017/07/24/alliance-defending-freedom-through-years
[270] https://en.wikipedia.org/wiki/Women%27s_Liberation_Front
[271] Shulevitz does note violence against trans people, the social difficulties of transitioning, etc.
[272] https://www.vox.com/identities/2019/9/5/20840101/terfs-radical-feminists-gender-critical
[273] Shulevitz does quote a phase she lifted from an ACLU press release.
[274] https://en.wikipedia.org/wiki/List_of_court_cases_involving_Alliance_Defending_Freedom and https://www.washingtonpost.com/investigations/2023/09/24/alliance-defending-freedom-wedding-lawsuit/
[275] https://www.washingtonpost.com/investigations/2023/09/24/alliance-defending-freedom-wedding-lawsuit/
[276] https://archive.thinkprogress.org/new-york-times-shulevitz-transgender-80686781b4c3/
[277] https://www.aclu.org/cases/doe-v-boyertown-area-school-district
[278] http://www.nytimes.com/2016/03/25/opinion/transgender-law-makes-north-carolina-pioneer-in-bigotry.html
[279] https://www.nbcnews.com/feature/nbc-out/no-link-between-trans-inclusive-policies-bathroom-safety-study-finds-n911106
[280] https://www.mediamatters.org/new-york-times/why-wont-new-york-times-tell-truth-about-bathroom-predators-its-reporting
[281] http://www.nytimes.com/2016/03/29/us/north-carolina-anti-discrimination-lawsuit.html?rref=collection%2Ftimestopic%2FNorth%20Carolina
[282] http://www.nytimes.com/2016/03/30/us/north-carolina-governor-attacks-critics-of-law-curbing-protections-from-bias.html

283 http://www.nytimes.com/2016/04/02/us/politics/north-carolina-anti-discrimination-law-obama-federal-funds.html
284 http://www.nytimes.com/2016/04/12/us/rights-law-deepens-political-rifts-in-north-carolina.html?rref=collection%2Ftimestopic%2FNorth%20Carolina
285 https://www.nytimes.com/2019/05/31/well/transgender-teens-binders.html?searchResultPosition=1
286 When I was head of GenderPAC, for years we would get calls every few months like clockwork from outlets wanting us to put them in touch with some young person who was transitioning so they could follow them through the whole process and air it for their audience. I would always pitch some fresh angle on transgender rights and they would listen politely before hanging up.
287 For instance, see: https://www.ncbi.nlm.nih.gov/pmc/articles/PMC9873819/#:~:text=For%20trans%20women%2C%20gender-affirming,is%20permanent%2C%20resulting%20in%20infertility
288 https://www.cosmopolitan.com/sex-love/news/a55546/how-to-bind-your-chest/
289 https://www.buzzfeed.com/skarlan/all-the-questions-you-had-about-chest-binding-but-were-afrai
290 https://www.heritage.org/gender/commentary/protect-good-medicine-stop-the-censorship-good-counseling
291 https://translegislation.com/learn
292 https://www.nytimes.com/2018/04/27/t-magazine/times-journalists-aids-gay-history.html
293 https://rethinkime.org/facts-about-gac/
294 https://www.transgendermap.com/politics/regret/reime/
295 https://www.transgendermap.com/politics/academia/gender-critical/jane-wheeler/
296 https://www.splcenter.org/captain/foundations#_ftn26
297 https://www.splcenter.org/captain/foundations#_ftn26
298 https://4thwavenow.com/2015/05/09/breast-binders-and-the-helpful-strangers-pushing-them-on-your-son/
299 https://www.nytimes.com/2019/06/17/reader-center/chest-binding.html
300 https://www.nytimes.com/2019/11/02/style/what-is-cancel-culture.html
301 https://xtramagazine.com/power/politics/missouri-gender-care-centre-closure-256740
302 https://newrepublic.com/article/155606/fixating-cancel-culture-age-transphobia
303 https://www.thestranger.com/features/2017/06/28/25252342/the-detransitioners-they-were-transgender-until-they-werent
304 Full disclosure: Katie interviewed me for her piece a couple times, most of which I devote to trying unsuccessfully to talk her out of, and in the end I refused to be quoted in it. s
305 https://twitter.com/JamesCantorPhD/status/1071499969910198274

[306] https://adflegal.org/article/psychologist-dr-james-cantor-details-harms-transitioning-kids
[307] https://epgn.com/2020/06/03/biases-and-bad-theories/
[308] https://www.assignedmedia.org/breaking-news/proponents-of-rogd-remove-rapid-onset-aspect?ss_source=sscampaigns&ss_campaign_id=658588c2d90bb179736e0c48&ss_email_id=658596afc92b86324eebf2a1&ss_campaign_name=ROGD+Proponents+Ditch+%E2%80%9CRapid%E2%80%9D+and+more%E2%80%A6&ss_campaign_sent_date=2023-12-22T14%3A06%3A38Z
[309] https://twitter.com/ErinInTheMorn/status/1739714017776796008
[310] For example, see: https://www.blockedandreported.org/p/premium-hormones-headlines-and-chatgpt
[311] https://www.transgendermap.com/politics/media/katie-herzog/
[312] https://thespectator.com/topic/pride-lost-public-lgbt-trans-children/
[313] https://www.youtube.com/watch?v=ahS0VjJNaew
[314] https://www.transgendermap.com/politics/media/bridget-phetasy/
[315] https://newrepublic.com/article/155606/fixating-cancel-culture-age-transphobia
[316] https://www.hrc.org/resources/violence-against-the-transgender-community-in-2019
[317] https://www.nytimes.com/2022/05/29/us/lia-thomas-women-sports.html?searchResultPosition=1
[318] https://www.si.com/sports-illustrated/2020/06/30/idaho-transgender-ban-fighting-back
[319] https://www.si.com/college/2022/03/03/lia-thomas-penn-swimmer-transgender-woman-daily-cover
[320] https://www.cnn.com/2023/11/15/media/2024-election-horse-race-stakes-nyu-professor/index.html
[321] https://fair.org/home/nyts-anti-trans-bias-by-the-numbers/
[322] https://apnews.com/general-news-1db9278e3349c21d2951ffc9147f98f0
[323] https://newrepublic.com/article/161425/trans-student-athletes-white-supremacy-mothers
[324] Trudy Ring, "How Runner Lindsay Hecox Is Fighting for Trans Athletes." *Advocate.Com*, August 3, 2021.
https://www.advocate.com/exclusives/2021/8/03/how-runner-lindsay-hecox-fighting-trans-athletes.
[325] https://www.si.com/sports-illustrated/2020/06/30/idaho-transgender-ban-fighting-back
[326] Sarah Mervosh, Remy Tumin, and Ava Sasani. "Biden Plan Sets New Rules for Transgender Athletes and School Sports." *The New York Times*, April 7, 2023. https://www.nytimes.com/2023/04/06/us/transgender-athletes-title-ix-biden-adminstration.html.
[327] -who-rose-to-prominence-for-competing-against-women-it-took-a-toll-on-me-191642125.html.

---

[328] https://www.aclu.org/news/lgbtq-rights/four-myths-about-trans-athletes-debunked
[329] Jeremy W. Peters, "A Conservative Push to Make Trans Kids and School Sports the Next Battleground in the Culture War." The New York *Times*, November 3, 2019. https://www.nytimes.com/2019/11/03/us/politics/kentucky-transgender-school-sports.html?
[330] In the coming protest, Peters would help lead the pushback in defending the *Times.*
[331] David Crary, "Lawmakers Can't Cite Local Examples of Trans Girls in Sports." *AP NEWS*, March 3, 2021. https://apnews.com/article/lawmakers-unable-to-cite-local-trans-girls-sports-914a982545e943ecc1e265e8c41042e7.
[332] Karleigh Webb, "Chelsea Mitchell Wins Second Title in Two Weeks at CIAC Open." *Outsports*, February 25, 2020. https://www.outsports.com/2020/2/25/21151031/transgender-chelsea-mitchell-terry-miller-adf-lawsuit-connecticut-track-and-field.
[333] https://www.fox61.com/article/news/local/transgender-athlete-loses-track-race-lawsuit-ciac-high-school-sports/520-df66c6f5-5ca9-496b-a6ba-61c828655bc6
[334] https://www.npr.org/2023/08/18/1194593562/chess-transgender-fide-pushback
[335] https://www.assignedmedia.org/breaking-news/dutch-darts-dames-ditch-dart-games
[336] https://apnews.com/article/transgender-roller-derby-nassau-new-york-a918953e0063760c9d00372f322b7765
[337] https://www.assignedmedia.org/breaking-news/world-sailing-bans-trans-women
[338] https://www.foxnews.com/us/trans-girl-wins-girls-u14-dance-competition-sparking-both-fury-praise-riley-gaines-weighs
[339] https://en.wikipedia.org/wiki/Katie_Ledecky
[340] https://people.com/sports/katie-ledecky-finishes-14-seconds-ahead-of-competition-at-world-championships-wins-17th-world-title/
[341] https://www.si.com/olympics/2024/02/09/katie-ledecky-13-year-800-meter-freestyle-streak-ends-summer-mcintosh
[342] https://fair.org/home/in-media-framing-trans-kids-are-problems-to-be-solved-not-people-with-rights/
[343] As with the *Times*, FAIR would note that Hobson interviewed an army of 17 experts and academics—endocrinologists, cultural anthropologist, lawyers, psychiatrists—but only two trans athlete, and one of these is only heard from only in passing.
[344] The Post's accompanying graphic would show two girls running down the track leaving a (white) girl behind with the track snarled before her, literally making movement impossible—as if trans runners presented some kind of insurmountable barrier to cis girls.

[345] In 2020, New Zealand's Laurel Hubbard made history by competing in women's weightlifting, although she was unable to complete any of her lifts. See: https://www.nbcolympics.com/news/transgender-pioneer-laurel-hubbard-makes-history-competing-olympic-weightlifting#:~:text=New%20Zealand's%20Laurel%20Hubbard%20made,competitor%20in%20the%20weightlifting%20field.
[346] https://www.nytimes.com/2021/09/07/books/review/trans-helen-joyce.html?searchResultPosition=1
[347] https://translash.org/transcript-capturing-the-new-york-times/
[348] https://jessesingal.substack.com/p/i-have-to-admit-i-still-dont-fully
[349] https://www.theatlantic.com/magazine/archive/2018/07/when-a-child-says-shes-trans/561749/
[350] source: https://www.jezebel.com/whats-jesse-singals-fucking-deal-1826930495
[351] https://www.newstatesman.com/politics/2019/01/maria-miller-called-me-fake-feminist-over-gender-self-id-now-she-says-i
[352] https://www.jezebel.com/the-atlantic-has-a-transphobia-problem-1833677331
[353] https://www.thetimes.co.uk/article/a-man-can-t-just-say-he-has-turned-into-a-woman-m5lltcgv7
[354] As journalist Edie Miller would explain in Outline, it is was one of the alarming aspects of UK politics that many of those expressing wildly transphobic views understood themselves to be members of the left. See: https://theoutline.com/post/6536/british-feminists-media-transphobic?zd=1&zi=sidko7ng
[355] https://www.nationalreview.com/2014/05/laverne-cox-not-woman/
[356] source: https://www.mediamatters.org/new-york-times/kevin-williamson-also-said-his-podcast-people-whove-had-abortions-should-be-hanged
[357] https://www.politico.com/story/2018/04/05/atlantic-kevin-williamson-writer-abortion-504244
[358] https://slate.com/news-and-politics/2018/03/the-atlantics-bad-reasons-for-hiring-kevin-williamson.html
[359] https://www.transgendermap.com/issues/topics/media/outlets/the-atlantic/masthead/
[360] https://www.nytimes.com/2018/02/13/business/media/quinn-norton-new-york-times.html
[361] https://www.bbc.com/news/uk-england-57853385
[362] www.newsweek.com/lily-cade-transphobic-rant-full-transcript-1645922
[363] https://www.theguardian.com/media/2021/nov/01/bbc-rejects-complaints-that-it-published-transphobic-article
[364] https://www.thepinknews.com/2021/11/04/lily-cade-bbc-trans-porn/
[365] https://www.statista.com/statistics/330638/politics-governement-news-social-media-news-usa/

---

[366] https://slate.com/human-interest/2018/06/desistance-and-detransitioning-stories-value-cis-anxiety-over-trans-lives.html
[367] How nuanced and humane the story was could be seen in its cover art, which managed to both misgender its 22-year-old trans model Mina Brewster while also outing him to his family before he had told them he was trans (first reported by Poynter's Syndey Bauer). See: https://www.poynter.org/ethics-trust/2020/the-atlantic-tried-artistically-show-gender-dysphoria-cover-instead-damaged-trust-transgender-readers/
[368] https://en.wikipedia.org/wiki/Kenneth_Zucker
[369] https://www.theglobeandmail.com/news/national/ontario-passes-ndp-bill-to-ban-conversion-therapy-for-lgbtq-children/article24811878/
[370] https://web.archive.org/web/20150320203815/http://metronews.ca/news/toronto/1315743/outcry-prompts-camh-to-review-its-controversial-treatment-of-trans-youth/
[371] https://boingboing.net/2018/06/19/the-atlantic-again-concern-tro.html
[372] https://www.amazon.com/Trans-When-Ideology-Meets-Reality/dp/0861540492
[373] https://nymag.com/intelligencer/article/trans-rights-biological-sex-gender-judith-butler.html
[374] The actual quote from Matthew is, "But whoso shall cause one of these little ones who believe in Me to fall, it were better for him that a millstone were hung about his neck, and that he were drowned in the depth of the sea." See: https://www.biblegateway.com/verse/en/Matthew%2018%3A6
[375] https://www.assignedmedia.org/breaking-news/helen-joyce-misquotes-bible-to-say-rachel-levine-should-kill-herself
[376] https://www.youtube.com/watch?v=ahS0VjJNaew
[377] https://twitter.com/GBBranstetter/status/1532690051527806978?lang=en
[378] https://www.adl.org/resources/blog/what-grooming-truth-behind-dangerous-bigoted-lie-targeting-lgbtq-community
[379] https://www.pbs.org/newshour/politics/what-is-great-replacement-theory-and-how-does-it-fuel-racist-violence
[380] https://popula.com/2023/01/29/the-worst-thing-we-read-this-week-why-is-the-new-york-times-so-obsessed-with-trans-kids/
[381] https://www.mediamatters.org/new-york-times/new-york-times-helped-fuel-anti-trans-panic-2022-will-2023-be-any-better
[382] Total bills: 2015 = 19; 2016 = 55; 2017 = 45; 2018 = 26; 2019 = 19; 2020 = 66; 2021 = 143, 2022 = 174; 2023 = 589; and so far 539. TOTAL= 1,675 as of April 1, 2024. See: https://translegislation.com/learn
[382] Total bills: 2015 = 19; 2016 = 55; 2017 = 45; 2018 = 26; 2019 = 19; 2020 = 66; 2021 = 143, 2022 = 174; 2023 = 589; and so far 539. TOTAL= 1,675 as of April 1, 2024. See: https://translegislation.com/learn
[383] Healthcare bills only: 2015 = 2; 2016 = 0; 2017 = 3; 2018 = 8; 2019 = 9; 2020 = 36; 2021 = 38; 2022 = 50; 2023 = 185; 2024 = 137. TOTAL = 468 as of April 1, 2024. See: https://translegislation.com/learn

[384] https://www.nytimes.com/2023/06/27/us/transgender-laws-states.html
[385] https://nytletter.com
[386] https://www.nytimes.com/2023/02/18/opinion/trans-gender-missouri.html
[387] https://www.nytimes.com/by/azeen-ghorayshi?page=4
[388] https://www.assignedmedia.org/breaking-news/nyt-takes-victory-lap-after-mo-clinic-closure
[389] https://www.assignedmedia.org/breaking-news/promo-alert-discourages-families-from-nyt-podcast
[390] source: https://read.dukeupress.edu/tsq/article-abstract/9/3/407/319361/Insidious-ConcernTrans-Panic-and-the-Limits-of
[391] All numbers are approximations. The family abuse numbers are based on a UK study.

A) 0.1% Playing competitive school sports is based on Idaho runner Lindsay Hecox, who was the only one of the state's approximately 1,000 trans teens playing sports. See: https://williamsinstitute.law.ucla.edu/publications/trans-adults-united-states/ and also https://newrepublic.com/article/161425/trans-student-athletes-white-supremacy-mothers

B) 1% Detransition: https://fenwayhealth.org/new-study-shows-discrimination-stigma-and-family-pressure-drive-detransition-among-transgender-people/.

C) 8% Abandoned by Families. See: https://www.thetrevorproject.org/wp-content/uploads/2022/02/Trevor-Project-Homelessness-Report.pdf

D) 23% Sexually Assaulted in School Restrooms: https://www.cbsnews.com/philadelphia/news/survey-transgender-public-restroom/ and also https://www.ncbi.nlm.nih.gov/pmc/articles/PMC5685206/

E) Have Attempted Suicide: https://publications.aap.org/pediatrics/article-abstract/123/1/346/71912/Family-Rejection-as-a-Predictor-of-Negative-Health?redirectedFrom=fulltextf and also https://pubmed.ncbi.nlm.nih.gov/32345113/

F) Abused by Their Families: https://galop.org.uk/wp-content/uploads/2022/04/Galop-LGBT-Experiences-of-Abuse-from-Family-Members.pdf

[392] https://scholar.google.com/scholar?start=10&q=Ann+Haas+suicide&hl=en&as_sdt=0,10&lookup=0
[393] https://scholar.google.com/scholar?start=10&q=Ann+Haas+suicide&hl=en&as_sdt=0,10&lookup=0
[394] https://www.nytimes.com/2024/02/07/health/trangender-survey-harassment-poverty.html?searchResultPosition=1
[395] "It Is Journalism's Sacred Duty To Endanger The Lives Of As Many Trans People As Possible." *The Onion*, February 17, 2023. https://www.theonion.com/it-is-journalism-s-sacred-duty-to-endanger-the-lives-of-1850126997
[396] https://www.nytimes.com/2022/01/13/health/transgender-teens-hormones.html

[397] https://www.transgendermap.com/guidance/medical/psychotherapy/usa/oregon/laura-edwards-leeper/
[398] https://www.washingtonpost.com/outlook/2021/11/24/trans-kids-therapy-psychologist/
[399] Anderson has also worked with ADF and in cases involving forcibly outing trans youth to their parents. See:
https://www.splcenter.org/captain/disinformation#_ftnref100 part of "parental rights" movement
[400] https://www.dailywire.com/news/chris-cuomo-hosts-first-national-news-coverage-of-detransitioners
[401] https://www.washingtonpost.com/outlook/2021/11/24/trans-kids-therapy-psychologist/?ref=quillette.com
[402] Deutsch, M. B. (2012). Use of the informed consent model in the provision of cross-sex hormone therapy: A survey of the practices of selected clinics. International Journal of Transgenderism, 13(3), 140–146.
https://doi.org/10.1080/15532739.2011.675233
[403] https://psycnet.apa.org/record/2024-16010-001
[404] Three of the 17 later retransitioned to trans, which is not uncommon, thus lowering the rate further.
[405] https://www.tandfonline.com/doi/figure/10.1080/15532739.2011.675233?scroll=top&needAccess=true
[406] https://www.nytimes.com/2022/07/28/health/transgender-youth-uk-tavistock.html
[407] Regret rates at the NHS were actually extremely low. The notorious Cass Report, which resulted in care being banned, found "less than 10" detransitions out of thousand of kids treated. They do not specify the actual number, note how many retransitioned, or provide any details. See:
https://www.erininthemorning.com/p/opinion-englands-anti-trans-cass
[408] https://www.thepinknews.com/2022/07/13/alice-litman-trans-nhs-care/
[409] https://www.thepinknews.com/2022/11/25/finn-hall-trans-teen-suicide-nhs-funding-crisis/
[410] https://www.nytimes.com/2022/05/04/health/transgender-children-identity.html?searchResultPosition=2
[411] https://www.census.gov/quickfacts/fact/table/US/RHI825222#RHI825222
[412] https://www.smithsonianmag.com/innovation/why-are-finlands-schools-successful-49859555/#:~:text=Ninety%2Dthree%20percent%20of%20Finns,student%20than%20the%20United%20States.
[413] https://www.thetrevorproject.org/blog/new-poll-illustrates-high-support-among-parents-for-transgender-nonbinary-children/
[414] The actual number may be smaller since there is like overlap because of kids who received both blockers *and* hormones.
[415] Obviously this different from the Trans Youth Project study, which found that 40% did not go on to blockers. But that was a five-year follow-up study, and it was of only 31.

[416] https://www.nytimes.com/2024/02/16/health/adolescents-drugs-polypharmacy.html
[417] https://www.nytimes.com/2024/02/21/health/chronic-fatigue-syndrome-long-covid.html
[418] https://www.transgendermap.com/issues/psychiatry/richard-green/
[419] https://www.transgendermap.com/issues/psychiatry/richard-green/
[420] https://www.nytimes.com/2024/02/10/opinion/transgender-detransitioning.html
[421] https://thinkprogress.org/transgender-children-desistance-a5caf61fc5c6/
[422] https://www.nytimes.com/2022/06/08/us/women-gender-aclu-abortion.html
[423] https://www.nytimes.com/2022/07/03/opinion/the-far-right-and-far-left-agree-on-one-thing-women-dont-count.html
[424] https://www.nytimes.com/2022/07/20/world/americas/argentina-gender-neutral-spanish.html
[425] https://www.salon.com/2015/06/08/memo_to_crotchety_feminists_caitlyn_jenner_is_a_woman_and_we_must_embrace_her_its_whats_feminist_and_whats_right/
[426] https://presswatchers.org/2022/07/who-hates-inclusivity-the-question-answers-itself/
[427] https://www.nytimes.com/live/2024/04/02/opinion/thepoint?smid=nytcore-android-share#scotlands-censorship-experiment-threatens-free-expression
[428] In response to the law, J. K. Rowling would immediately misgender 10 trans women online, group trans women with rapists and sex offenders and defiantly boast of looking forward to being arrested. When she was not, UK TERFs would celebrate this as a great moral victory. See: https://www.msnbc.com/top-stories/latest/jk-rowling-scotland-hate-crime-laws-transphobic-rcna146183
[429] https://www.nytimes.com/2024/04/03/opinion/sex-assigned-at-birth.html?smid=nytcore-android-share
[430] Even uber-liberal columnist Nicholas Kristoff would jump in with a 2023 column fretting that inclusive terms were just playing into the hands of the right. https://www.nytimes.com/2023/02/01/opinion/inclusive-language-vocabulary.html
[431] https://www.nytimes.com/live/2023/12/06/us/republican-debate-fact-check?searchResultPosition=1#i-did-a-bill-in-florida-to-stop-the-gender-mutilation-of-minors-its-child-abuse-and-its-wrong-she-opposes-that-bill-she-thinks-i
[432] https://www.nytimes.com/2023/06/14/world/canada/girl-athlete-trans-gender.html?searchResultPosition=1
[433] https://www.nytimes.com/2022/03/01/us/texas-child-abuse-trans-youth.html?searchResultPosition=2
[434] https://www.nytimes.com/2022/12/10/us/politics/anti-transgender-lgbtq-threats-attacks.html?searchResultPosition=6
[435] https://www.nytimes.com/2023/03/30/us/nebraska-filibuster-transgender-bills.html?searchResultPosition=9

---

[436] https://www.nytimes.com/2022/07/22/us/politics/after-roe-republicans-sharpen-attacks-on-gay-and-transgender-rights.html?searchResultPosition=13
[437] https://www.nytimes.com/2022/09/26/health/top-surgery-transgender-teenagers.html?searchResultPosition=1
[438] https://www.nytimes.com/2022/09/13/magazine/ron-desantis.html?searchResultPosition=12
[439] https://www.nytimes.com/2023/11/10/opinion/abortion-trangender-culture-war-republican-party.html?searchResultPosition=1
[440] https://www.nytimes.com/2022/03/08/health/texas-transgender-clinic-genecis-abbott.html?searchResultPosition=4
[441] https://www.nytimes.com/2022/04/08/us/alabama-transgender-law-ivey.html?searchResultPosition=6
[442] https://www.nytimes.com/2023/06/03/us/transgender-care-bill-abbott-texas.html?searchResultPosition=2
[443] https://www.nytimes.com/2022/12/03/us/lgbtq-patients-doctor-threatened-boston.html?searchResultPosition=8
[444] https://www.nytimes.com/2022/06/10/science/transgender-teenagers-national-survey.html
[445] https://www.nytimes.com/2022/09/26/health/top-surgery-transgender-teenagers.html
[446] https://www.splcenter.org/captain/disinformation
[447] https://theconversation.com/why-rapid-onset-gender-dysphoria-is-bad-science-92742
[448] Theorist and author Julia Serano has developed an incredibly detailed timeline and background on the origins of RODG. See: https://juliaserano.blogspot.com/2019/02/origins-of-social-contagion-and-rapid.html
[449] https://www.aap.org/en/news-room/aap-voices/supporting-our-transgender-and-gender-diverse-youth/#:~:text=Some%20providers%20may%20worry%20that,phenomenon%2C%20Rapid%20Onset%20Gender%20Dysphoria.
[450] https://publications.aap.org/pediatrics/article/150/3/e2022056567/188709/Sex-Assigned-at-Birth-Ratio-Among-Transgender-and?autologincheck=redirected
[451] https://www.nbcnews.com/nbc-out/out-health-and-wellness/social-contagion-isnt-causing-youths-transgender-study-finds-rcna41392
[452] Also see Florence Ashley's widely-quoted dissection of RODG here: https://www.florenceashley.com/uploads/1/2/4/4/124439164/ashley_a_critical_commentary_on_rapid-onset_gender_dysphoria.pdf
[453] https://www.huffpost.com/entry/trump-calls-out-crowd-anti-trans_n_64854d49e4b0756ff85e0b40
[454] They actually cheat here, using 25 and under which inflates the percentage to 43%, when it should be 18 and under.
[455] The actual numbers are 4.5% and 22.3% and 1.9% and 15.3% respectively

---

[456] https://news.gallup.com/poll/611864/lgbtq-identification.aspx
[457] https://www.assignedmedia.org/breaking-news/university-of-california-transgender-nonbinary
[458] https://thehill.com/changing-america/3811406-new-studies-find-millions-of-young-nonbinary-and-transgender-americans/
[459] https://time.com/6275663/generation-z-gender-identity/
[460] https://files.kff.org/attachment/Topline-KFF-Washington-Post-Trans-Survey.pdf
[461] https://www.thepinknews.com/2024/05/01/transition-regret-detransitioners/
[462] More cisgender boys and young men are requesting breast reductions mostly as a result of obesity. For instance, see: https://www.theplasticsurgerycenterofnashville.com/why-is-male-breast-reduction-becoming-popular/
[463] Ghorayshi lists only cisgender girls' breast augmentations for ages 18-19. There many who get them earlier, but she excludes them because it is not medically recommended. The 4,700 cisgender breast reductions for cis girls which she cites are between the ages of 13 and 19.
[464] Ghorayshi says "teens," which is actually somewhat more accurate. Although cis breast reductions are almost all girls, a very small number are also boys, often as a side effect of the increase in obesity. See: https://my.clevelandclinic.org/health/symptoms/16227-enlarged-male-breast-tissue-gynecomastia
[465] Similarly, a study published in 2024 by the American Medical Association found that of 151 breast reductions performed on U.S. teen boys, 97% (146) were on *cisgender* boys, and just 3% (5) on transgender ones. See: https://www.advocate.com/health/gender-affirming-surgery-minors-rate
[466] https://www.newsweek.com/theres-no-standard-care-when-it-comes-trans-medicine-opinion-1603450
[467] https://thatweirdolee.medium.com/my-resignation-letter-to-gender-care-consumer-advocacy-network-gccan-59596eb53f96
[468] https://search-prod.lis.state.oh.us/cm_pub_api/api/unwrap/general_assembly_134/chamber/134th_ga/ready_for_publication/committee_docs/cmte_h_families_aging_1/testimony/cmte_h_families_aging_1_2022-05-19-0900_1395/hb454.corinna.cohn.proponent.pdf
[469] https://www.them.us/story/60-minutes-platforms-detransitioners-trans-healthcare
[470] https://www.them.us/story/60-minutes-platforms-detransitioners-trans-healthcare
[471] https://www.cbsnews.com/news/transgender-health-care-60-minutes-2021-05-23/
[472] https://www.newsweek.com/theres-no-standard-care-when-it-comes-trans-medicine-opinion-1603450
[473] https://www.nytimes.com/2022/06/15/magazine/gender-therapy.html

[474] https://fair.org/home/nyt-centers-trans-healthcare-story-on-doctors-not-trans-people/
[475] Jules Gill-Peterson Histories of the Transgender Child Paperback, University Of Minnesota Press; 2018
[476] https://www.nytimes.com/2019/11/03/us/politics/kentucky-transgender-school-sports.html
[477] https://www.nytimes.com/2023/04/16/us/politics/transgender-conservative-campaign.html
[478] https://www.washingtonpost.com/nation/2024/04/29/lgbtq-legislation-trans-bills/
[479] https://www.liberalcurrents.com/the-actual-ubiquity-of-gender-affirming-care/
[480] https://www.liberalcurrents.com/the-actual-ubiquity-of-gender-affirming-care.
[481] https://glaad.org/new-york-times-inaccurate-coverage-transgender-people-being-weaponized-against-transgender/
[482] https://ago.mo.gov/docs/default-source/press-releases/2023-04-13---emergency-reg.pdf?sfvrsn=7f78d4fc_2
[483] https://www.texasobserver.org/emily-bazelon-transgender-healthcare-debate-new-york-times/
[484] https://en.m.wikipedia.org/wiki/Gish_gallop?utm_medium=email&utm_source=substack#:~:text=The%20Gish%20gallop%20(%2F%CB%88%C9%A1,or%20strength%20of%20those%20arguments.
[485] https://www.tandfonline.com/doi/full/10.1080/26895269.2022.2100644
[486] https://glaad.org/new-york-times-inaccurate-coverage-transgender-people-being-weaponized-against-transgender/
[487] https://www.texasobserver.org/emily-bazelon-transgender-healthcare-debate-new-york-times/
[488] https://www.splcenter.org/captain/disinformation
[489] https://www.wpath.org/soc8
[490] https://www.erininthemorning.com/p/detransitioner-wave-fails-to-materialize?utm_medium=email
[491] https://www.cnn.com/2023/06/06/politics/states-banned-medical-transitioning-for-transgender-youth-dg/index.html
[492] https://www.nytimes.com/2023/12/01/opinion/politics/life-without-regret.html
[493] https://www.plasticsurgery.org/news/press-releases/american-society-of-plastic-surgeons-weighs-in-on-growing-popularity-of-teen-plastic-surgery
[494] https://www.plasticsurgery.org/news/articles/redefining-masculinity-the-growing-appeal-of-plastic-surgery-among-men
[495] https://abcnews.go.com/GMA/Wellness/teens-turn-cosmetic-surgery-study-outlines-age-guidelines/story?id=57432332
[496] https://www.nimh.nih.gov/health/statistics/any-anxiety-disorder
[497] https://www.ncbi.nlm.nih.gov/pmc/articles/PMC8868033/

[498] https://www.cdc.gov/ncbddd/adhd/data.html
[499] https://www.cnn.com/2023/06/13/health/lgb-people-mental-health-substance-use/index.html
[500] https://www.mediamatters.org/new-york-times/new-york-times-helped-fuel-anti-trans-panic-2022-will-2023-be-any-better
[501] https://neurodivergentinsights.com/autism-infographics/trans-autism
[502] She puts this in the mouth of rabidly anti-trans columnist Andrew Sullivan, whom Bazelon identifies simply as a "gay commentator" but who has written many deeply transphobic columns, including one claiming that trans "ideologues" were "coming for the kids." For instance, see: https://nymag.com/intelligencer/2019/09/andrew-sullivan-when-the-ideologues-come-for-the-kids.html
[503] https://www.hrc.org/news/new-cdc-data-shows-lgbtq-youth-are-more-likely-to-be-bullied-than-straight-cisgender-youth
[504] "It would be a mistake, of course, to exaggerate the scale and importance of these emotional dislocations. There are many students of both sexes who don't feel overwhelmed ..."
[505] https://www.focusonthefamily.com/pro-life/abortion-complications/
[506] https://www.mayoclinic.org/drugs-supplements/aspirin-oral-route/side-effects/drg-20152665?p=1#:~:text=This%20medicine%20may%20increase%20risk,including%20stomach%20ulcers%20or%20bleeding.
[507] https://www.mayoclinic.org/diseases-conditions/gender-dysphoria/in-depth/pubertal-blockers/art-20459075
[508] https://www.ncbi.nlm.nih.gov/pmc/articles/PMC6626312/
[509] https://academic.oup.com/jsm/article/20/Supplement_4/qdad062.090/7220244
[510] https://twitter.com/ZJemptv/status/1772650516947894426/photo/2
[511] https://www.transgendermap.com/issues/topics/media/emily-bazelon/replies/
[512] https://www.frontiersin.org/articles/10.3389/fped.2023.1170025/full
[513] https://www.mayoclinic.org/diseases-conditions/precocious-puberty/diagnosis-treatment/drc-20351817
[514] https://www.cedars-sinai.org/blog/puberty-blockers-for-precocious-puberty.html#:~:text=Providers%20can%20treat%20precocious%20puberty,development%20until%20they're%20ready.
[515] https://www.childrens.com/specialties-services/conditions/contrasexual-pubertal-development
[516] https://www.mayoclinic.org/diseases-conditions/precocious-puberty/symptoms-causes/syc-20351811#:~:text=With%20this%20type%20of%20precocious,gland%20causes%20the%20hormone%20release.
[517] https://www.nytimes.com/2023/05/16/us/politics/transgender-care-detransitioners.html

[518] The eight DSM-V criteria for childhood diagnosis of gender dysphoria are a strong desire or preference for: 1) being of the other gender; 2) wearing clothes typical of the gender; 3) cross-gender roles in play or fantasy; 4) toys, games or activities typical of the other gender; 5) playmates of the other gender; and a strong rejection of 6) toys, games and activities typical of their assigned gender; 7) their sexual anatomy; 8) physical sex characteristics that match their experienced gender.

[519] Gender Dysphoria Questionnaire for Adolescents and the Utrecht Gender Dysphoria Scale);

[520] The most common surveys used are Gender Dysphoria Questionnaire for Adolescents and the Utrecht Gender Dysphoria Scale.

[521] https://pubmed.ncbi.nlm.nih.gov/33794108/

[522] https://www.washingtonpost.com/dc-md-va/2023/03/23/takeaways-post-kff-survey/

[523] There are also some in the community who are trying to move away from "trans woman" (which implies a particular kind of individual) to using "trans woman" or "transgender woman" (which implies that all in the category *are* women, but these are a particular *kind of* woman). However, I have tended to use all such terms interchangeably. The same goes for "trans man," "trans man," and "transgender man."

[524] What I've called Real Regret Rates (teens who detransition for reasons other than social or familial hostility or because they have simply changed their identification to nonbinary) is probably are even less than the 1% or so usually quoted—perhaps half that at about 0.5%. That's equal to 1-in-every-200. If our new test is right 95% of the time, when we give it to a group of 200 teens at our gender clinic, it will identify 10 of them—or 5% of the 200—as not-trans. But we already know that only 1 of these 200 teens is actually not-trans. This means that our accurate test just produced 9 *false negatives*—that is, 9 kids who will have their care delayed or denied but who are really transgender. And, on average, it will continue to do this every time we use it.

[525] https://www.nytimes.com/1966/11/27/archives/medicine-surgery-to-change-gender-the-transsexual-a-case-study.html?searchResultPosition=2 1

[526] https://www.nytimes.com/1976/07/24/archives/a-former-male-tennis-player-seeks-to-join-womens-tour.html?searchResultPosition=65

[527] https://www.nytimes.com/1976/08/21/archives/renee-richards-angry-resolute-renee-richards-angered-determined-to.html?searchResultPosition=69

[528] Richards has since reversed herself and decided trans women and girls should not be allowed to compete as females.

[529] Chloe Hadjimatheou, "Christine Jorgensen: 60 Years of Sex Change Ops." *BBC News*, November 30, 2012. https://www.bbc.com/news/magazine-20544095.

[530] https://www.nytimes.com/1976/09/05/archives/renee-richards-controversy-what-is-a-woman.html?searchResultPosition=1

[531] https://www.nytimes.com/1973/10/23/archives/a-transsexual-and-her-family-an-attempt-at-life-as-usual-never.html?searchResultPosition=25
[532] https://www.nytimes.com/1977/04/07/archives/2-missouri-u-surgeons-report-a-medical-first-in-transsexual.html?searchResultPosition=11
[533] The first known transmale phalloplasty was actually performed by U.K. surgeon Harold Gillies on physician Matthew Dhillon in1946. SEE: https://www.ncbi.nlm.nih.gov/pmc/articles/PMC3901910/
[534] https://www.nytimes.com/1972/11/20/archives/new-jersey-pages-500-in-the-us-change-sex-in-six-years-with-surgery.html
[535] https://www.nytimes.com/1973/04/21/archives/doctors-report-transsexual-cure-more-experiments-urged-effect-of.html?searchResultPosition=21
[536] http://ai.eecs.umich.edu/people/conway/TS/Rogue%20Theories/Exorcism/Exorcism%20of%20Transsexualism.html
[537] In 2016, in one of her last valedictory columns for decades later titled, "Being Transgender as a Fact of Nature," Brody would declare, "[T]he controversy now raging over the rights of transgender students to use bathroom and locker-room facilities that match their gender identity rather than their birth sex reflects the persistence of widespread prejudice and misinformation about the nature and behavior of people who identify as transgender."
[538] https://www.nytimes.com/1980/07/25/archives/dressed-to-kill-depalma-mystery.html
[539] https://www.nytimes.com/1984/02/14/us/dismissed-transsexual-pilot-wins-158590-in-back-pay.html?searchResultPosition=137
[540] https://en.wikipedia.org/wiki/Bostock_v._Clayton_County#Introduction
[541] She received 160k, or about $460k in today's dollars.
[542] https://www.nytimes.com/1989/05/24/obituaries/karen-ulane-48-pilot-who-had-sex-change.html
[543] Her lawyer would late say that the Airlines settled out of court for much more than the original lawsuit had asked for. *Times* would also run an obituary for Ulane, when she crashed while piloting a charter plane in 1989. See: https://www.nytimes.com/1989/05/24/obituaries/karen-ulane-48-pilot-who-had-sex-change.html
[544] https://www.nytimes.com/1986/05/11/arts/vanessa-redgrave-s-new-role-makes-a-man-of-her.html?searchResultPosition=156
[545] https://www.nytimes.com/1986/05/13/books/cbs-s-second-serve.html?searchResultPosition=157
[546] https://www.nytimes.com/1986/05/13/books/cbs-s-second-serve.html?searchResultPosition=157
[547] https://www.nytimes.com/1986/02/11/nyregion/suburbs-are-a-magnet-to-many-homosexuals.html?searchResultPosition=1
[548] https://www.nytimes.com/1987/01/04/nyregion/theater-rocky-horror-in-bridgeport-makes-the-best-of-the-bad.html?searchResultPosition=171
[549] https://www.nytimes.com/1989/10/22/books/goodnight-mrs-madrigal.html?searchResultPosition=211

---

[550] https://www.nytimes.com/1989/01/30/us/lesbian-partners-find-the-means-to-be-parents.html#:~:text=Other%20gay%20men%20and%20women,gay%20and%20lesbian%20groups%20said.
[551] https://www.nytimes.com/1991/02/19/movies/how-to-film-a-gory-story-with-restraint.html?searchResultPosition=14
[552] https://www.nytimes.com/1991/03/13/movies/review-film-aching-to-be-a-prima-donna-when-you-re-a-man.html?searchResultPosition=16
[553] https://www.nytimes.com/1993/04/18/style/paris-has-burned.html
[554] A Letter to the Editor would take Green to task for the piece, asserting that "It is unfortunate that Jesse Green's article perpetuates the negative stereotype of 'drag queens' without trying to understand our hearts and souls. It is perverse and judgmental to portray us as the pitiful underbelly of society… There is no doubt there are sad and bad 'queens,' but so are there sad and bad bankers, plumbers and military officers.." See: https://www.nytimes.com/1993/05/02/style/l-macho-hypocrites-flock-to-bars-619393.html?searchResultPosition=52
[555] https://www.nytimes.com/1995/07/16/nyregion/hidden-new-york-the-shantytown-of-the-heshes.html
[556] Lisa Lambert and Philip DeVine; only Lamberts infant in a crib was spared by the killers.
[557] https://www.nytimes.com/1998/09/23/movies/film-review-a-rape-and-beating-later-3-murders-and-then-the-twist.html?searchResultPosition=4
[558] https://www.nytimes.com/1999/10/01/movies/film-festival-reviews-sometimes-accepting-an-identity-means-accepting-a-fate-too.html?searchResultPosition=8
[559] https://www.nytimes.com/1999/10/03/movies/film-a-role-within-a-role-a-girl-who-became-a-boy.html?searchResultPosition=10
[560] https://www.nytimes.com/1996/04/14/nyregion/neighborhood-report-midtown-transsexuals-dual-risk-of-aids.html?searchResultPosition=1
[561] https://www.nytimes.com/1995/06/18/nyregion/neighborhood-report-midtown-the-perilous-times-of-transgender-youth.html?searchResultPosition=1
[562] https://www.nytimes.com/1995/11/02/us/study-links-brain-to-transsexuality.html?searchResultPosition=4
[563] https://www.nytimes.com/1996/02/04/weekinreview/ideas-trends-intersexual-healing-an-anomaly-finds-a-group.html?searchResultPosition=8
[564] The piece also quotes Johns Hopkins dismissing the new intersex movement as "zealots," and physicians defending the indefensible: cutting healthy infant genitals for no reason other than cosmetics, and asserting with absolutely no data that most were happy with their surgeries.
[565] https://www.nytimes.com/1999/03/30/nyregion/new-clinics-let-lesbian-patients-be-themselves-effort-help-group-that-often.html?searchResultPosition=13
[566] https://www.nytimes.com/1996/09/08/us/shunning-he-and-she-they-fight-for-respect.html
[567] Nonbinary had not emerged yet.

[568] https://en.wikipedia.org/wiki/Robert_H._Knight
[569] https://www.nytimes.com/1999/06/11/nyregion/public-lives-issues-of-gender-from-pronouns-to-murder.html?searchResultPosition=14
[570] https://www.mediamatters.org/new-york-times/seen-not-heard-new-york-times-failed-quote-trans-people-over-60-2023-stories-anti
[571] The use of phrases like "hermaphroditic traits" and "indeterminate sex organs" to refer to intersex youth is especially uncalled for, because it ignored the *Times* own coverage, including Anne Fausto-Sterling's widely-cited op-ed, "How Many Sexes Are There" back in 1993, and science writer Natalie Angier's detailed "intersexual Healing: An Anomaly Finds a Group" in 1996.
[572] https://www.nytimes.com/2004/05/20/sports/sports-of-the-times-ioc-enters-a-new-world-and-stumbles.html?searchResultPosition=30
[573] https://www.nytimes.com/2008/08/22/opinion/22iht-edboylan.1.15546353.html
[574] https://www.nytimes.com/2009/10/25/sports/25intersex.html?searchResultPosition=115
[575] https://www.nytimes.com/2002/01/19/nyregion/tolerance-village-wears-thin-residents-up-arms-over-drug-deals-prostitution.html
[576] I had a similar experience with a *Times* journo who was creating a timeline of transgender activism but somehow omitted both GenderPAC the first national trans political group and the Transexual [[sic] Menace, the first national trans protest group. even though her piece showed someone wearing a Menace tee-shirt. When I suggested she could have done a bit more …you know, research, she got very defensive and complaining that the piece wasn't that important and I had hurt her feelings.
[577] https://www.nytimes.com/2006/09/07/garden/07trann.html
[578] https://www.nytimes.com/2000/07/24/nyregion/watershed-of-mourning-at-the-border-of-gender.html
[579] https://www.nytimes.com/2008/08/02/us/02murder.html?searchResultPosition=95
[580] https://www.nytimes.com/2009/04/17/us/17transgen.html?searchResultPosition=107
[581] https://www.nytimes.com/2008/11/18/us/18memphis.html?searchResultPosition=102
[582] https://www.nytimes.com/2001/02/21/movies/film-review-genders-that-shift-but-friends-firm-as-bedrock.html?searchResultPosition=21
[583] https://www.nytimes.com/2002/06/16/magazine/l-about-a-boy-who-isn-t-486990.html
[584] Today it is also one of the few beats that have to outstanding trans reporters on it, J. Wortham and Jamie Lauren Keiles, both of whom would bravely sign the open letter to the *Times* management. See: https://xtramagazine.com/power/what-went-wrong-at-the-new-york-times-246409
[585] https://archive.nytimes.com/atwar.blogs.nytimes.com/2010/07/18/pakistan-hires-transgender-workers-to-shame-tax-delinquents/?searchResultPosition=1

[586] https://archive.nytimes.com/india.blogs.nytimes.com/2012/05/01/indias-largest-transgender-festival-opens-in-koovagam/?searchResultPosition=1
[587] https://archive.nytimes.com/india.blogs.nytimes.com/2012/05/03/koova gams-non-stop-party-comes-with-chaos/?searchResultPosition=2
[588] https://www.nytimes.com/2012/10/06/world/asia/seeking-the-right-to-be-female-in-malaysia.html?searchResultPosition=1
[589] https://www.nytimes.com/2014/11/08/world/asia/malaysian-court-overturns-islamic-law-banning-cross-dressing.html?searchResultPosition=1
[590] https://www.nytimes.com/video/world/americas/100000002768903/thats-not-my-daughter.html?searchResultPosition=91
[591] https://www.nytimes.com/video/world/americas/100000002770175/more-acceptance-for-transgender-models.html?searchResultPosition=92
[592] https://www.nytimes.com/2014/03/16/world/americas/transgender-models-prosper-in-brazil-where-carnival-and-faith-reign.html?searchResultPosition=93
[593] https://www.nytimes.com/2012/05/25/world/americas/transgender-advocates-hail-argentina-law.html?searchResultPosition=2
[594] https://www.nytimes.com/2012/07/24/world/europe/serbia-becomes-a-hub-for-sex-change-surgery.html?searchResultPosition=1
[595] https://www.nytimes.com/2014/12/21/opinion/sunday/cubas-gay-rights-evolution.html?utm_source=affiliate&utm_medium=Linkbux&utm_campaign=wizKxmN8no4&utm_content=486358&utm_term=15819104244&siteID=wiz KxmN8no4-_byJMaY.EdSVJ.YAWp7YBw&ranMID=39812&ranEAID =wizKxmN8no4&ranSiteID=wizKxmN8no4-_byJMaY.EdSVJ.YAWp7YBw
[596] https://www.nytimes.com/2014/04/26/opinion/transgender-rights-in-india.html
[597] https://archive.nytimes.com/cityroom.blogs.nytimes.com/2010/04/19/ask-about-transgender-issues/?searchResultPosition=1
[598] https://archive.nytimes.com/cityroom.blogs.nytimes.com/2010/04/21/answers-about-transgender-issues/?searchResultPosition=4
[599] https://archive.nytimes.com/cityroom.blogs.nytimes.com/2010/04/22/answers-about-transgender-issues-part-2/?searchResultPosition=3
[600] https://archive.nytimes.com/cityroom.blogs.nytimes.com/2010/04/23/answers-about-transgender-issues-part-3/?searchResultPosition=2
[601] https://www.nytimes.com/2010/03/27/movies/27arts-TRANSGENDERC_BRF.html?searchResultPosition=30
[602] https://www.nytimes.com/2010/10/15/movies/15ticked.html?searchResult Position=2
[603] https://www.nytimes.com/2010/03/31/movies/31arts-TRAILERTOCHA_BRF.html?searchResultPosition=34
[604] https://www.nytimes.com/2010/03/31/movies/31arts-TRAILERTOCHA_BRF.html?searchResultPosition=34
[605] https://www.nytimes.com/2010/03/31/movies/31arts-TRAILERTOCHA_BRF.html?searchResultPosition=6

[606] https://archive.nytimes.com/artsbeat.blogs.nytimes.com/2010/03/26/protests-and-defense-of-a-transgender-comedy-at-tribeca-festival/?searchResultPosition=5
[607] https://archive.nytimes.com/artsbeat.blogs.nytimes.com/2010/11/02/mtv-apologizes-to-glaad-for-jersey-shore-segment/?searchResultPosition=143
[608] https://www.nytimes.com/2010/12/09/fashion/09TRANS.html?searchResultPosition=22
[609] https://www.out.com/entertainment/popnography/2010/11/obamas-tranny-nanny.html
[610] https://archive.nytimes.com/well.blogs.nytimes.com/2010/11/05/when-boys-dress-like-girls-for-halloween/?searchResultPosition=145
[611] https://www.nytimes.com/2011/05/08/fashion/08CHAZ.html?searchResultPosition=62
[612] https://www.nytimes.com/2011/08/21/nyregion/some-transgender-women-pay-a-high-price-to-look-more-feminine.html?searchResultPosition=161
[613] https://archive.nytimes.com/cityroom.blogs.nytimes.com/2012/12/02/for-transgender-latinas-a-refuge-in-queens-away-from-streets/?searchResultPosition=194
[614] https://archive.nytimes.com/parenting.blogs.nytimes.com/2011/06/10/navigating-gender-in-pre-k/?searchResultPosition=89
[615] https://archive.nytimes.com/parenting.blogs.nytimes.com/2009/10/28/when-a-boy-wants-a-tutu/
[616] https://archive.nytimes.com/parenting.blogs.nytimes.com/2011/04/14/in-praise-of-pink-polish/
[617] https://www.nytimes.com/2011/06/12/fashion/new-challenge-for-parents-childrens-gender-roles.html
[618] http://www.thedailyshow.com/watch/wed-april-13-2011/toemageddon-2011---this-little-piggy-went-to-hell
[619] https://www.today.com/parents/j-crew-ad-stirs-controversy-pink-nail-polish-1c7399231
[620] In 2014 The Opionator would finally address the issue in, "Parenting the Non-Girlie Girl." See: https://archive.nytimes.com/opinionator.blogs.nytimes.com/2014/04/09/parenting-the-non-girlie-girl/?searchResultPosition=110
[621] https://archive.nytimes.com/parenting.blogs.nytimes.com/2012/05/14/my-son-looks-like-a-girl-so-what/
[622] https://www.nytimes.com/2012/08/12/magazine/whats-so-bad-about-a-boy-who-wants-to-wear-a-dress.html?searchResultPosition=125
[623] https://www.theguardian.com/world/2016/apr/24/now-or-never-says-student-who-came-out-as-non-binary-to-obama
[624] https://www.nytimes.com/2012/01/20/opinion/the-meaning-of-scouting.html?searchResultPosition=4
[625] https://www.nytimes.com/2012/07/26/fashion/a-lively-house-of-xtravaganza-ball-scene-city.html

[626] https://www.nytimes.com/slideshow/2012/07/24/fashion/20120724-SCENE.html
[627] https://www.nytimes.com/2012/07/25/nyregion/in-west-village-living-out-loud-on-a-transgender-runway.html?searchResultPosition=115
[628] https://www.nytimes.com/2012/05/13/nyregion/woman-in-group-of-transgender-performers-dies-in-brooklyn-fire.html
[629] https://xtramagazine.com/power/what-went-wrong-at-the-new-york-times-246409
[630] https://www.nlgja.org/blog/2012/05/reaction-to-the-nyt-coverage-of-the-death-of-lorena-escalera/
[631] Mock would continue tracking and protesting Metro's continued condescending treatment of trans women of color See: https://janetmock.com/2012/07/25/new-york-times-dehumanizes-trans-women/
[632] https://www.vanityfair.com/news/2023/02/new-york-times-trans-coverage-debate
[633] https://www.nytimes.com/2013/05/13/sports/for-transgender-fighter-fallon-fox-there-is-solace-in-the-cage.html?searchResultPosition=81
[634] https://archive.nytimes.com/publiceditor.blogs.nytimes.com/2013/08/22/the-soldier-formerly-known-as-bradley-manning/?searchResultPosition=174
[635] https://www.politico.com/story/2017/05/31/new-york-times-public-editor-239000
[636] It read in total: **"transgender** (adj.) is an overall term for people whose current identity differs from their sex at birth, whether or not they have changed their biological characteristics…". Cite a person's transgender status only when it is pertinent and its pertinence is clear to the reader. Unless a former name is newsworthy or pertinent, use the name and pronouns (he, his, she, her, hers) preferred by the transgender person. If no preference is known, use the pronouns consistent with the way the subject lives publicly."
[637] https://www.nytimes.com/2013/10/27/movies/jared-leto-stayed-in-character-on-dallas-buyers-club-set.html?searchResultPosition=228
[638] https://www.theguardian.com/film/2014/feb/01/jared-leto-dallas-buyers-club
[639] https://www.nytimes.com/2014/08/31/magazine/can-jill-soloway-do-justice-to-the-trans-movement.html?searchResultPosition=103
[640] https://www.nytimes.com/2014/08/31/magazine/can-jill-soloway-do-justice-to-the-trans-movement.html?searchResultPosition=103
[641] https://www.nytimes.com/2014/10/19/magazine/when-women-become-men-at-wellesley-college.html
[642] https://www.nytimes.com/2014/11/25/nyregion/leslie-feinberg-writer-and-transgender-activist-dies-at-65.html?searchResultPosition=189
[643] As it would under Sulzberger of MAGA extremism. As I write, Press Watch's Froomkin has just destroyed the new *Times* On Politics writer, Jess Bidgood, who burbled that among her favorite things in new role is "covering the change people want and what kind of country we're going to be. I love that. And what an adventure it is!" This, at a juncture when (as Froomkin notes) "we

are one election away from becoming a Christian nationalist state." See: https://presswatchers.org/2024/04/the-washington-press-corps-doesnt-have-a-freaking-clue/
And what an adventure it is!
644 https://en.wikipedia.org/wiki/A._G._Sulzberger#cite_note-23
645 https://nymag.com/intelligencer/article/trans-rights-biological-sex-gender-judith-butler.html
646 Years later her would later reverse himself, but declare that he still believed that global warming—which literally threatened the entire planet—had to be someone solved only by private corporations.
647 https://twitter.com/GBBranstetter/status/1532690051527806978?lang=en
648 https://www.youtube.com/watch?v=ahS0VjJNaew
649 The *Times* claimed Paul was not involved, but this beggars credibility.
650 https://xtramagazine.com/power/what-went-wrong-at-the-new-york-times-246409
651 https://www.nytco.com/press/pamela-pauls-next-chapter-times-opinion-columnist/
652 https://www.nytimes.com/2022/03/18/opinion/cancel-culture-free-speech-poll.html
653 https://www.nbcnews.com/nbc-out/out-politics-and-policy/missouri-republican-candidate-torches-lgbtq-inclusive-books-viral-vide-rcna137715
654 https://www.desmoinesregister.com/story/news/crime-and-courts/2019/08/06/book-burning-iowa-man-who-burned-lgbtq-books-trial-paul-dorr-david-levithan-orange-city-library/1936961001/
655 https://mynews4.com/news/local/man-with-gun-turned-childrens-reading-book-event-to-chaos-in-sparks-library-drag-queen-storytime-sparks-library-nevada-washoe-county-lgbtq
656 https://www.nbcnews.com/tech/internet/libs-tiktok-x-chaya-raichik-bomb-threat-twitter-of-libsoftiktok-rcna102784
657 https://www.nbcnews.com/news/us-news/holi-drag-storytime-children-canceled-right-wing-protesters-rcna59990
658 https://www.latimes.com/entertainment-arts/books/story/2022-07-07/pamela-paul-criticized-for-anti-trans-opinion-about-the-word-woman
659 https://www.gawkerarchives.com/media/pamela-paul-is-the-new-worst-columnist-at-the-new-york-times
660 https://www.nytimes.com/by/anemona-hartocollis
661 https://www.nytimes.com/2022/06/12/opinion/sandra-newman-men.html
662 https://www.nytimes.com/2023/10/24/books/review/julia-sandra-newman.html#:~:text=A%20New%2C%20Feminist%20Retelling%20of,by%20Winston%20Smith's%20love%20interest.
663 https://www.nytimes.com/2022/07/24/opinion/book-banning-censorship.html
664 https://www.psychologytoday.com/us/blog/political-minds/202012/new-book-irreversible-damage-is-full-misinformation

[665] https://www.thebookseller.com/news/aba-conducts-internal-review-after-sending-out-book-against-transgender-craze-1274982
[666] https://www.nytimes.com/2022/10/23/opinion/queer-gay-identity.html
[667] https://www.nytimes.com/2022/12/04/opinion/free-to-be-you-and-me-anni.html
[668] https://www.nytimes.com/2022/11/14/health/puberty-blockers-transgender.html
[669] https://fair.org/home/nyts-anti-trans-bias-by-the-numbers/
[670] https://www.nytimes.com/2022/06/15/magazine/gender-therapy.html
[671] https://www.nytimes.com/interactive/2022/11/13/health/puberty-blockers-transgender-youth.html
[672] https://www.reuters.com/investigates/special-report/usa-transyouth-data/
[673] https://www.ncbi.nlm.nih.gov/pmc/articles/PMC9150228/#:~:text=In%20various%20studies%2C%20transwomen%20showed,39%2C40%20and%20eating%20disorders.&text=Transwomen%20participate%20less%20in%20sport,related%20control%20men%20and%20women.
[674] https://academic.oup.com/jes/article/4/9/bvaa065/5866143?login=false
[675] https://sciencebasedmedicine.org/what-the-new-york-times-gets-wrong-about-puberty-blockers-for-transgender-youth/
[676] https://www.persuasion.community/p/keira-bell-my-story
[677] https://apnews.com/article/transgender-treatment-regret-detransition-371e927ec6e7a24cd9c77b5371c6ba2b#:~:text=In%20a%20review%20of%2027,1%25%20on%20average%20expressed%20regret.
[678] Some are quoted on both sides of the issue.
[679] https://www.tampabay.com/opinion/2022/04/27/we-300-florida-health-care-professionals-say-the-state-gets-transgender-guidance-wrong-open-letter/
[680] "The analysis commissioned by the *Times* examined seven studies from the Netherlands, Canada and England involving about 500 transgender teens from 1998 through 2021. Researchers observed that while on blockers, the teens did not gain any bone density, on average—and lost significant ground compared to their peers…[but] change in bone density while adolescents were on blockers was observed to be zero." [*Emphasis added.*]
[681] https://sciencebasedmedicine.org/what-the-new-york-times-gets-wrong-about-puberty-blockers-for-transgender-youth/
[682] https://youth.gov/youth-topics/adolescent-health/federal-data#:~:text=There%20are%2042%20million%20adolescents,percent%20of%20the%20U.S.%20population.
[683] https://www.cbsnews.com/news/florida-surgeon-general-covid-vaccines-fda-claims-misleading/
[684] https://www.bmj.com/content/377/bmj.o1395
[685] https://acpeds.org/press/induced-abortion-increases-risk-for-breast-cancer
[686] https://www.nytimes.com/2022/05/19/science/early-puberty-medical-reason.html

[687] https://www.nytimes.com/2023/01/22/us/gender-identity-students-parents.html
[688] https://www.washingtonpost.com/education/2022/07/18/gender-transition-school-parent-notification/
[689] https://galop.org.uk/wp-content/uploads/2022/04/Galop-LGBT-Experiences-of-Abuse-from-Family-Members.pdf
[690] https://www.americanprogress.org/article/gay-and-transgender-youth-homelessness-by-the-numbers/
[691] https://www.thetrevorproject.org/wp-content/uploads/2022/02/Trevor-Project-Homelessness-Report.pdf
[692] https://youth.gov/youth-topics/lgbtq-youth/homelessness
[693] https://www.rollingstone.com/culture/culture-news/trans-teen-and-homeless-americas-most-vulnerable-population-205769/
[694] https://olympiamanagement.net/2018/05/what-does-it-mean-to-be-housing-insecure/
[695] https://publications.aap.org/pediatrics/article-abstract/123/1/346/71912/Family-Rejection-as-a-Predictor-of-Negative-Health?redirectedFrom=fulltextf
[696] https://pubmed.ncbi.nlm.nih.gov/32345113/
[697] Reading these kinds of outrageous claims has become so routine today, that it's useful to recall that less than 10 years ago, before WCN groups discovered trans was political dynamite, groups like ADF didn't see themselves as having anything to do with trans kids.
[698] It's never explained whether this is for pedophilia or medical transition, but the slur is almost always used on the right for the former.
[699] https://www.nytimes.com/2023/01/23/opinion/trans-kids-privacy-gender-identity.html
[700] https://www.leftvoice.org/the-new-york-times-is-wrong-trans-kids-need-support-not-gender-skepticism/
[701] https://xtramagazine.com/power/what-went-wrong-at-the-new-york-times-246409l
[702] https://www.assignedmedia.org/breaking-news/nyt-parents-rights-nonsense
[703] Komodo health found that 121,882 kids age 6-17 were diagnosed as trans over five years, or about 24,376 per year. See: https://www.reuters.com/investigates/special-report/usa-transyouth-data/
[704] https://www.theguardian.com/us-news/2023/feb/17/new-york-times-contributors-open-letter-protest-anti-trans-coverage
[705] https://www.nbcnews.com/news/asian-america/tom-cotton-backlash-tiktok-ceo-shou-chew-rcna136673
[706] https://twitter.com/kathyvsinternet/status/1268914329140822017
[707] https://www.politico.com/news/magazine/2023/12/14/james-bennet-nyt-firing-00131826
[708] https://xtramagazine.com/power/what-went-wrong-at-the-new-york-times-246409

[709] https://www.semafor.com/article/05/14/2024/new-york-times-staff-complain-of-unwillingness-to-tolerate-dissent
[710] https://www.thenation.com/article/culture/new-york-times-kahn/
[711] https://www.thenation.com/article/society/new-york-times-trans-coverage-gay-rights-history/
[712] https://translash.org/transcript-capturing-the-new-york-times/
[713] https://presswatchers.org/2024/03/why-is-new-york-times-campaign-coverage-so-bad-because-thats-what-the-publisher-wants/
[714] Froomkin was commenting on the *Times* refusal to warn readers that democracy was at stake in the 2024 election while it obsessed over Biden's age, but his observation works equally well for what he would terms its "unremittingly hostile coverage of gender-affirming care for young people…"
[715] https://www.vanityfair.com/news/2023/02/new-york-times-trans-coverage-debate
[716] https://presswatchers.org/2024/05/new-york-times-editor-joe-kahn-says-defending-democracy-is-a-partisan-act-and-he-wont-do-it/
[717] https://www.thedailybeast.com/ny-times-fires-off-warning-to-staffers-after-trans-coverage-brouhaha?source=twitter&via=desktop
[718] https://twitter.com/GrahamStarr/status/1628237220049035266
[719] https://www.nlgja.org/blog/2012/05/reaction-to-the-nyt-coverage-of-the-death-of-lorena-escalera/
[720] The following is drawn from a timeline released on April 6, 2023 by the *Times*' contributors signatories, and available online as a Google Doc at: https://docs.google.com/document/d/1ZQzMqy3H1JDwffnoUw1LaZ66DvBFeVziyWolNCWvk84/edit
[721] https://nytletter.com
[722] https://www.npr.org/2023/02/25/1159565358/the-new-york-times-coverage-of-transgender-people-sparks-newsroom-divide
[723] https://twitter.com/GrahamStarr/status/1628237220049035266
[724] https://twitter.com/jk_rowling/status/1580639051774054404?lang=en
[725] https://www.thepinknews.com/2019/12/19/jk-rowing-maya-forstater-tweets-transphobia-accusations/
[726] https://www.vox.com/culture/21449215/troubled-blood-review-jk-rowling-transphobia-controversy
[727] https://twitter.com/KatyMontgomerie/status/1763171214950842620
[728] https://www.vox.com/culture/23622610/jk-rowling-transphobic-statements-timeline-history-controversy?utm_content=voxdotcom&utm_campaign=vox.social&utm_medium=social&utm_source=twitter
[729] https://www.theguardian.com/books/booksblog/2020/sep/15/rowling-troubled-blood-thriller-robert-galbraith-review
[730] https://www.telegraph.co.uk/books/what-to-read/troubled-blood-robert-galbraith-review-jk-rowling-fails-strike/

[731] https://www.vox.com/culture/21449215/troubled-blood-review-jk-rowling-transphobia-controversy
[732] https://www.theonion.com/it-is-journalism-s-sacred-duty-to-endanger-the-lives-of-1850126997?utm_medium=sharefromsite&utm_source=_twitter
[733] https://www.mediaite.com/news/top-new-york-times-journalists-sign-on-to-letter-slamming-their-own-union-for-defending-paper-amid-trans-coverage-row/
[734] https://www.vanityfair.com/news/2023/02/new-york-times-trans-coverage-debate
[735] https://xtramagazine.com/power/what-went-wrong-at-the-new-york-times-246409
[736] https://www.theguardian.com/us-news/2023/feb/17/new-york-times-contributors-open-letter-protest-anti-trans-coverage
[737] https://www.nbcnews.com/nbc-out/out-politics-and-policy/mississippi-governor-signs-bill-banning-transgender-health-care-minors-rcna72765
[738] https://docs.google.com/document/d/1QjOWf6DBdqTMtCnLM0l6n8s HPv2BuvUiwsvaMR8pruM/edit
[739] https://www.cbsnews.com/news/tennessee-ban-gender-affirming-care-trans-youth-drag-shows/
[740] https://www.thedailybeast.com/how-the-new-york-times-trans-coverage-debacle-was-years-in-the-making?utm_medium=socialflow&utm_source=twitter_owned_tdb&via=twitter_page&utm_campaign=owned_social
[741] https://www.nytimes.com/2023/03/29/us/kentucky-anti-transgender-bill.html?searchResultPosition=1
[742] https://www.wyomingpublicmedia.org/news/2023-03-20/gov-gordon-lets-draconian-anti-trans-sports-bill-pass-into-law
[743] https://nytletter.com
[744] https://twitter.com/ErikWemple/status/1628797461614526469
[745] https://www.vanityfair.com/news/2023/02/new-york-times-trans-coverage-debate
[746] https://glaad.org/no-nyt-pulitzers-gma-ny-2023/
[747] https://glaad.org/no-nyt-pulitzers-gma-ny-2023/
[748] https://www.thenation.com/article/society/new-york-times-trans-coverage-gay-rights-history/
[749] https://www.nytimes.com/2023/08/23/health/transgender-youth-st-louis-jamie-reed.html
[750] https://www.documentcloud.org/documents/24088042-project-2025s-mandate-for-leadership-the-conservative-promise
[751] https://www.statista.com/statistics/192894/number-of-employees-at-the-new-york-times-company/#:~:text=In%202023%2C%20The%20New%20York,in%20the%20company's%20journalism%20operations.
[752] https://www.assignedmedia.org/breaking-news/jamie-reeds-allegations-are-not-even-partially-confirmed

---

753 https://www.stltoday.com/news/local/metro/parents-push-back-on-allegations-against-st-louis-transgender-center-i-m-baffled/article_a94bc4d2-e68b-535f-b0c7-9fefb9e8e9f4.html

754 https://missouriindependent.com/2023/03/01/transgender-st-louis-whistleblower/

755 https://apnews.com/article/missouri-transgender-youth-health-care-attorney-general-84da1c977c44bba9907f13b2d3a7141f

756 https://www.cbsnews.com/news/inquiry-into-the-transgender-center-at-st-louis-childrens-hospital-finds-allegations-of-misconduct-unsubstantiated/

757 https://www.erininthemorning.com/p/missouri-anti-trans-whistleblower

758 https://www.adfchurchalliance.org/post/should-schools-notify-parents-if-their-child-claims-to-be-transgender

759 Reed's attorney, Vernadette Broyles, had also been President of the anti-trans group Child & Parental Rights Campaign which was the recipient of an $85,000 grant from ADF. See: https://accountable.us/alliance-defending-freedom-used-funding-boost-to-push-anti-democratic-anti-lgbtq-agenda/

760 https://www.nytimes.com/2024/02/02/opinion/transgender-care.html?bgrp=c&smid=em-share

761 Paul says that "94% still identified as transgender" but Ghorayshi correctly reported it was 97.5%.

762 https://www.assignedmedia.org/breaking-news/erin-reed-evan-urquhart-pamela-paul-response

763 https://www.splcenter.org/captain/defining-pseudoscience-network

764 https://twitter.com/CamomileOgden/status/1787223543568048528

765 https://transsafety.network/posts/segm-uncovered/

766 https://www.erininthemorning.com/p/splc-designates-genspect-segm-as

767 https://www.aclu.org/cases/poe-v-labrador?document=Appellants-Opening-Brief

768 https://www.motherjones.com/media/2024/02/new-york-times-pamela-paul-anti-trans-bills/

769 https://pubmed.ncbi.nlm.nih.gov/38436975/

770 https://truthout.org/articles/wv-saw-a-flurry-of-anti-trans-bills-in-2024-now-most-of-those-bills-are-dead/

771 https://prospect.org/education/23-11-17-right-wing-school-board-groups-losses/

772 https://www.hrc.org/press-releases/icymi-how-did-anti-trans-attacks-fare-with-voters-last-night-that-strategy-failed-again

773 https://www.politico.com/news/magazine/2024/04/25/new-york-times-biden-white-house-00154219

774 https://www.assignedmedia.org/breaking-news/biden-politico-new-york-times-drama?ss_source=sscampaigns&ss_campaign_id=662b97de7b9a3b03ebefe326&ss_campaign_name=Behind+the+NYT+Curtain%2C+Chloe+Cole%E2%80%99s+Lawsuit%2C+and+more%E2%80%A6&ss_campaign_sent_date=2024-04-26T13%3A02%3A06Z

About the Author

Riki Wilchins regular columns about trans issues and politics can be found on her blog at:

www.medium.com/@rikiwilchins.

Other Riverdale Avenue Books by Riki Wilchins

Read My Lips:
Sexual Subversion & the End of Gender

GenderQueer:
Voices from Beyond the Sexual Binary

Queer Theory/Gender Theory: An Instant Primer

Burn the Binary! Selected Writings on the Politics of Trans, Genderqueer and Nonbinary

TRANS/gressive:
How Transgender Activists Took on Gay Rights, Feminism, the Media & Congress… and Won!

When Loving Your Kid Is a Crime:
Parents of Transgender Children Speak Out

When Texas Came for Our Kids;
How Evangelical Extremists Launched a War on Transgender Teens

From Rowman & Littlefield

Gender Norms & Intersectionality: Connecting Race, Class & Gender

From Amazon Books

The Broken Places: Transgender People Speak Out about Addiction & Recovery

www.ingramcontent.com/pod-product-compliance
Lightning Source LLC
Chambersburg PA
CBHW031424270326
41930CB00007B/571
* 9 7 8 1 6 2 6 0 1 6 8 2 8 *